Workshop on Language Resources, Technology and Services in the Sharing Paradigm 2011

Held at the 5th International Joint Conference on Natural Language Processing 2011 (IJCNLP 2011)

Chiang Mai, Thailand
12 November 2011

ISBN: 978-1-62276-454-9

Printed from e-media with permission by:

Curran Associates, Inc.
57 Morehouse Lane
Red Hook, NY 12571

Some format issues inherent in the e-media version may also appear in this print version.

Printed by Curran Associates, Inc. (2012)

For permission requests, please contact the Association for Computational Linguistics at the address below.

Association for Computational Linguistics
209 N. Eighth Street
Stroudsburg, Pennsylvania 18360

Phone: 1-570-476-8006
Fax: 1-570-476-0860

acl@aclweb.org

Additional copies of this publication are available from:

Curran Associates, Inc.
57 Morehouse Lane
Red Hook, NY 12571 USA
Phone: 845-758-0400
Fax: 845-758-2634
Email: curran@proceedings.com
Web: www.proceedings.com

Table of Contents

Conference Program

Saturday, November 12, 2011

8:30–8:40 Introduction

Language Services, Resources, Applications

8:40–9:00 *Prospects for an Ontology-Grounded Language Service Infrastructure*
Yoshihiko Hayashi

9:00–9:20 *A Method Towards the Fully Automatic Merging of Lexical Resources*
Núria Bel, Muntsa Padró and Silvia Necsulescu

9:20–9:40 *Service Quality Improvement in Web Service Based Machine Translation*
Sapa Chanyachatchawan, Virach Sornlertlamvanich and Thatsanee Charoenporn

9:40–10:00 *The Semantically-enriched Translation Interoperability Protocol*
Sven Christian Andrä and Jörg Schütz

10:00–10:30 Coffee/Tea Break

Interoperability

10:30–10:50 *Interoperability and Technology for a Language Resources Factory*
Marc Poch and Núria Bel

10:50–11:10 *Interoperability Framework: The FLaReNet Action Plan Proposal*
Nicoletta Calzolari, Monica Monachini and Valeria Quochi

11:10–11:30 *Promoting Interoperability of Resources in META-SHARE*
Paul Thompson, Yoshinobu Kano, John McNaught, Steve Pettifer, Teresa Attwood, John Keane and Sophia Ananiadou

11:30–11:50 *Federated Operation Model for the Language Grid*
Toru Ishida, Yohei Murakami, Yoko Kubota and Rieko Inaba

11:50–12:00 Short Discussion

Saturday, November 12, 2011 (continued)

12:00–14:00 Lunch

Services and Functionalities for the Community

14:00–14:20 *Open-Source Platform for Language Service Sharing*
Yohei Murakami, Masahiro Tanaka, Donghui Lin and Toru Ishida

14:20–14:50 *Proposal for the International Standard Language Resource Number*
Khalid Choukri, Jungyeul Park, Olivier Hamon and Victoria Arranz

14:50–15:10 *A Metadata Schema for the Description of Language Resources (LRs)*
Maria Gavrilidou, Penny Labropoulou, Stelios Piperidis, Monica Monachini, Francesca Frontini, Gil Francopoulo, Victoria Arranz and Valérie Mapelli

15:10–15:20 *The Language Library: Many Layers, More Knowledge*
Nicoletta Calzolari, Riccardo Del Gratta, Francesca Frontini and Irene Russo

15:20–15:30 Short Discussion

15:30–16:00 Coffee/Tea Break

Sharing and Infrastructures

16:00–16:20 *Sharing Resources in CLARIN-NL*
Jan Odijk and Arjan van Hessen

16:20–16:40 *META-NORD: Towards Sharing of Language Resources in Nordic and Baltic Countries*
Inguna Skadina, Andrejs Vasiljevs, Lars Borin, Koenraad De Smedt, Krister Lindén and Eiríkur Rögnvaldsson

16:40–17:30 PANEL Language Resources and Technologies Sharing: Priorities and Concrete Steps

We wish to thank our sponsors

Gold Sponsors

www.google.com

www.baidu.com

The Office of Naval Research (ONR)

The Asian Office of Aerospace Research and Development (AOARD)

Department of Systems Engineering and Engineering Managment, The Chinese University of Hong Kong

Silver Sponsors

Microsoft Corporation

Bronze Sponsors

Chinese and Oriental Languages Information Processing Society (COLIPS)

Supporter

Thailand Convention and Exhibition Bureau (TCEB)

We wish to thank our sponsors

Organizers

Asian Federation of Natural Language Processing (AFNLP)

National Electronics and Computer Technology Center (NECTEC), Thailand

Sirindhorn International Institute of Technology (SIIT), Thailand

Rajamangala University of Technology Lanna (RMUTL), Thailand

Maejo University, Thailand

Chiang Mai University (CMU), Thailand

Introduction

The Context

Some of the current major initiatives in the area of language resources – FLaReNet (http://www.flarenet.eu/), Language Grid (http://langrid.nict.go.jp/en/index.html) and META-SHARE (www.meta-share.org, www.meta-net.eu) – have agreed to organise a joint workshop on infrastructural issues that are critical in the age of data sharing and open data, to discuss the state of the art, international cooperation, future strategies and priorities, as well as the road-map of the area.
It is an achievement, and an opportunity for our field, that recently a number of strategic-infrastructural initiatives have started all over the world. It is also a sign that funding agencies recognise the strategic value of our field and the importance of helping a coherent growth also through a number of coordinated actions. Some of these initiatives, two European and one Asian, have agreed to join forces to foster a debate that may lead to future coordinated actions all over the world.

- FLaReNet aims at providing recommendations for future initiatives in the field of Language Resources and Technologies: we are aware that it is important to discuss future policy and priorities not only on the European scene, but also in a worldwide context. This is true both when we try to highlight future directions of research, and – even more – when we analyse which infrastructural initiatives are needed. The growth of the field should be complemented by common efforts that try to look for synergies and to overcome fragmentation. FLaReNet is now ready to deliver its final recommendations and priorities deriving from the various events it organised, summarised in the FLaReNet Blueprint of actions and infrastructures.

- The Language Grid aims at constructing a multilingual service infrastructure on the Internet that allows users to share language services such as online dictionaries, bilingual corpora, and machine translations, and create new language services by combining existing services to support intercultural collaboration. The Language Grid service-oriented infrastructure shifts from language resources to language services. The Language Grid is operated by Kyoto and Bangkok operation centers in a federated fashion. More than 110 language services are registered and shared by 140 groups in 18 countries.

- META-SHARE aims to build an open, integrated, secure and interoperable exchange facility for language resources (data and tools) for the Language Technologies domain and other applicative domains (e.g., digital libraries, cognitive systems, robotics, etc) where language plays a critical role. It aims to act as an infrastructure that will enable language resources documentation, cataloguing, uploading and storage, downloading and exchange, aiming to support a resources economy at large. META-SHARE has defined the principles underlying its design and governance model, its proposed architecture for language resources sharing and collaborative building as well as the technical and legal instruments supporting its operation.

Topics and Aims

Cooperation is an issue that needs to be prepared. This joint strategic Workshop intends to continue a discussion, started on several occasions in the last years, on the usefulness and the interest of promoting international cooperation among various initiatives and communities around the world, within and around

the field of Language Resources and Technologies.
The Workshop aims at addressing (some of the) technological, market and policy challenges posed by the "sharing and openness paradigm", the major role that language resources can play and the consequences of this paradigm on language resources themselves.
Examples of topics and issues addressed by the 14 papers accepted are:

- Sharing Language Resources and Language Technologies, as implemented in a number of international initiatives
- Need for global information on Language Resources and Language Technologies: relevant initiatives in the various regions/countries
- Interoperability and Reusability, both in infrastructures and in applied systems (MT)
- Linguistic web services and language applications development
- Metadata and Cataloguing
- Collaborative initiatives for annotated resource creation
- Infrastructures, policies, gaps and critical areas

We hope that the papers will contribute to boosting a constructive and fruitful debate.
The Workshop is also an occasion for the researchers interested in infrastructural initiatives to get together to discuss and promote collaboration actions. It should also lead to discussing the modalities of how to organise the cooperation among various initiatives. In a conclusive Panel these topics will be discussed, with invited panellists from all the continents and with all the Workshop participants, with the aim of delineating:

- Common roadmap and strategies: local, regional, international frameworks
- International cooperation, models for collaboration and agreements on joint initiatives

We hope that by organising this workshop in Thailand we can attract participation of many Asian initiatives and can lead to fruitful collaboration between Asian and other international initiatives.
Finally, we wish to thank very much Irene Russo who has significantly helped in the organisation of the Workshop and in the preparation of the Proceedings.

Nicoletta Calzolari
Toru Ishida
Stelios Piperidis
Virach Sornlertlamvanich

Workshop Chairs:

Nicoletta Calzolari (ILC-CNR, Pisa, Italy)
Toru Ishida (Kyoto University, Japan)
Stelios Piperidis (ILSP, Athens, Greece)
Virach Sornlertlamvanich (NECTEC, Thailand)

Organizational and Editorial Assistant:

Irene Russo (ILC-CNR, Pisa, Italy)

Program Committee:

Sophia Ananiadou
Nuria Bel
Emily Bender
Nicoletta Calzolari
Tommaso Caselli
Khalid Choukri
Yoshihiko Hayashi
Chu-Ren Huang
Nancy Ide
Toru Ishida
Steven Krauwer
Joseph Mariani
Monica Monachini
Yohei Murakami
Stelios Piperidis
Valeria Quochi
Claudia Soria
Virach Sornlertlamvanich
Thepchai Supnithi
Take Tokunaga
Dan Tufis
Kiyotaka Uchimoto

Prospects for an Ontology-Grounded Language Service Infrastructure

Yoshihiko Hayashi
Graduate School of Language and Culture, Osaka University
1-8 Machikaneyama, Toyonaka, 5600043 Japan
hayashi@lang.osaka-u.ac.jp

Abstract

Servicization of language resources (LR) and technologies (LT) on an appropriately designed and adequately operated infrastructure is a promising solution for sharing them effectively and efficiently. Given this rationale, this position paper reviews relevant attempts around the Language Grid, and presents prospects for an ontology-grounded language service infrastructure. As the associated issues may have substantial depth and stretch, collaborations among international and inter-cultural experts are finally called for.

1 Introduction

Servicization of language resources (LR) and technologies (LT) on an appropriately designed and adequately operated infrastructure is a promising solution for effectively and efficiently sharing them. Such an infrastructure would enable: (a) More non-expert users to have accesses to LR/LT without being too much bothered by cumbersome IPR issues; (b) virtual/dynamic language resources to be realized as language services through useful combination of the existing language services. To enjoy the benefit particularly described in (b), however, we need to address the issue of *interoperability* (Calzolari, 2008).

In the rest of this position paper: The notion of an ontology-grounded language service infrastructure is first introduced; An ontological construct for describing language services and the associated linguistic elements, referred to as *language service ontology*, is then sketched out; By reviewing the attempts around the Language Grid (Ishida, 2006; Ishida, 2011), including the language service ontology, issues and the prospects for an ontology-grounded language service infrastructure is then discussed. As the associated issues may have substantial depth and stretch, collaborations among international and inter-cultural experts are finally called for.

2 Language Service Infrastructure

A language service infrastructure is a software platform on which effective and efficient dissemination and utilization of servicized language resources will be possible. As nicely demonstrated by the Language Grid, such an infrastructure can provide a solid foundation for supporting activities of certain types. For example, the primary goal of the Language Grid was to support a range of activities associated with intercultural collaboration. However, such an infrastructure can attract more audiences as originally intended, if it could provide easier access to a reasonable set of language resources; the Language Grid, for instance, has been utilized by researches in the field of information and communication sciences.

Therefore a language service infrastructure should be designed, built, and operated while considering a wide variety of potential users, which include not only activists/end-users (service consumers) but also LR/LT experts (service providers). In addition, further cooperations among language service infrastructures should be considered as probably discussed in this workshop.

Given the potential benefits of language resource servicization, as discussed in the previous section, one of the most important features of a language service infrastructure is to provide a sufficient set of actual services, each classified into a reasonable service type. This is particularly important, as a service interface (or application program interface: API) should be specified according to the type of a service. To enable this, we primarily have to have a reasonable list or taxonomy of language service types.

As of February 2011, the Language Grid accommodates more than 100 Web services, which

Proceedings of Workshop on Language Resources, Technology and Services in the Sharing Paradigm, pages 1–7,
Chiang Mai, Thailand, November 12, 2011.

Figure 1: Language services in the Language Grid

are classified into one of the around 20 service types[1]. A user can utilize the provided language services through accordingly defined APIs. Figure 1 shows a screenshot from the Language Grid Web site, where a user can search for a language service based on the service type and/or supported languages.

To identify possible language service types and to further organize them structurally, we should, at least, consider two aspects: (1) functionality of the service, and (2) the input/output data types. The issue of interoperability arises here: as the underlying language resources are independently developed, they essentially exhibit idiosyncrasies in many aspects. A promising approach to partly address this issue would be to have a comprehensive vocabulary, or an ontological construct, so as to we can define and describe a language service type and the accordingly defined interface.

3 Language Service Ontology

Among the relevant attempts (Klein and Potter, 2004; Villegas et al., 2010), one came out from around the Language Grid is an ontological construct referred to as *language service ontology* (Hayashi et al., 2011). The language service ontology is intended to cover not only language services but their necessary elements including types of linguistic data object.

Figure 2 illustrates the top-level of the proposed language service ontology. The upper half of the diagram depicts our notion of the fundamental structure of a language service: (1) a language service is provided by a language process; (2) a language process operates upon linguistic objects by using language data resources; (3) a language data resource consists of linguistic objects; (4) a language data resource is created by organizing a set of linguistic objects each processed by language processes.

It should be noted here that the linguistic object class includes a range of linguistic annotations as well as linguistic expressions, which are the targets of annotations. These types of abstract objects comprise the data to/from NLP tools/systems, as well as the content of language data resources.

The lower half of the diagram, on the other hand, additionally introduces some important classes. Each box in the diagram denotes a top-level class in the whole ontology; some of these classes further induce corresponding sub-ontologies (Hayashi et al., 2011).

Among these top-level classes, `LanguageService` is functionally the top-most one: a language service is provided by an instance of `LanguageProcessingResource` class. Note that a language data resource does not provide a language service by itself; as it is a static resource, it is always activated through an access mechanism, which is an instance of a language processing resource subclass.

A language processing resource takes `LinguisticObject` as the input/output, and may use `LanguageDataResource`. `LanguageDataResource` consists of `LinguisticObject`, which might have been brought about by the results of `LanguageProcessingResource`. The language processing resources should be further classified according to their functionalities; the functionality is largely characterized by the types of associated objects. More specifically, the types of used language resources and/or the types of input/output language objects induce the taxonomy of language processing resources as displayed in Fig. 3

`LinguisticObject`, according to Saussure tradition, can have linguistic forms (`LinguisticExpression`) and meanings (`LinguisticMeaning`), where the former denotes the latter. Additionally, a linguistic meaning can be described by `TextualDescription`.

[1]`http://langrid.org/service_manager/language-services`

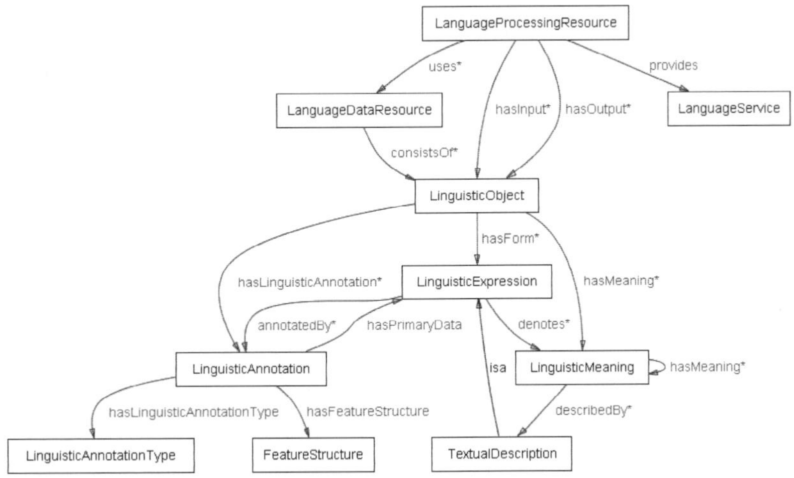

Figure 2: Top-level of the Language Service Ontology

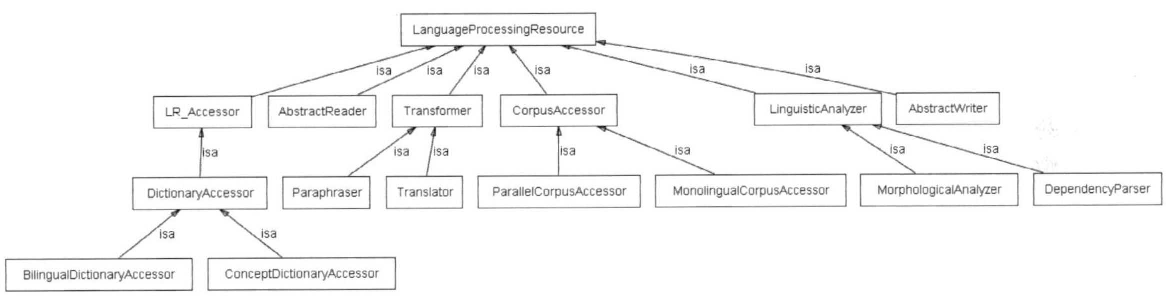

Figure 3: Taxonomy of the Language Processing Resources

Note here that an instance of the linguistic meaning class functions as a place holder for representing a semantic equivalent relation among linguistic objects. On the other hand, a `LinguisticObject` instance can be annotated by instances of `LinguisticAnnotation`, which should have actual annotation content represented with `FeatureStructure`.

4 Prospects for an Ontology-Grounded Language Service Infrastructure

4.1 Two issues uncovered

Each language service in the Language Grid is classified as one of the around twenty service types, including: CONCEPT DICTIONARY, MORPHOLOGICAL ANALYSIS, DEPENDENCY PARSER, and TRANSLATION. Each service type specifies its API, which includes data type specification for the input/output. The input/output data types, as also discussed previously, contributes to forming the taxonomy of language processing resources. Table 1 demonstrates this by listing major Language Grid service types and relating them to classes in the language service ontology. Note here that the ontology classes shown in the table are placed relatively upper in the taxonomy.

Through this review, the following two issues are uncovered.

- Although the language service ontology has been formalized so as to be comprehensive and linguistically-sound, the consensus among the related experts has not yet been reached. Also the current coverage may not be sufficient, insisting that the language service ontology has to be further expanded and revised.

- Although the set of Language Grid service types has been developed so as to be compatible with the language service ontology, there are no direct connections between them, insisting that actual utility of the language

Table 1: Major Language Grid Service Types and the Associated Ontology Classes

Service type	Ontology class	Input type	Output type
TRANSLATION	`Translator`	sentence string	sentence string
PARAPHRASE	`Paraphraser`	sentence string	sentence string
CONCEPT DICTIONARY	`DictionaryAccessor`	query string	lexical entry
BILINGUAL DICTIONARY	`DictionaryAccessor`	query string	lexical entry
PARALLEL CORPUS	`CorpusAccessor`	query string	annotation
MORPHOLOGICAL ANALYSIS	`LinguisticAnalyzer`	sentence string	morphological annotation
DEPENDENCY PARSER	`LinguisticAnalyzer`	sentence string	dependency annotation

service ontology is still not obvious, hence should be attested and demonstrated.

We will look at these issues in more detail.

4.2 Refining the language service ontology

The language service ontology should be considerably expanded and detailed in order for it to be used as an effective vocabulary for describing a wide variety of language services and the elements.

To accomplish this, we first need to identify the current and potential language service types and the elements. An actual language service infrastructure such as the Language Grid provides us with a concrete list of such elements, we however have to go beyond to further enrich the list; this, at least, requires collaborations among LR/LT experts. We however may further need to incorporate user requirements, particularly in a collaborative environment, for example the one offered by the Language Grid. Figure 4 generally illustrates necessary steps toward the goal, where we have to:

- Identify possible language service types. To this end, bottom-up activities, such as "LREC2010 Map of Language Resources, Technologies and Evaluation"[2], are crucially important. In parallel, we need to establish more connections with potential user communities of various kinds to discover novel service functionalities.

- Classify and describe the service types. We first have to clarify the dimensions of classification. Obviously, input/output linguistic data type and language processing functionality are two important things. We then need to organize ontological knowledge that includes a taxonomy of application-oriented use intentions as well as LR/LT domain ontologies: these domain ontologies can partly be organized by basing on the relevant international standards for linguistic data modeling, as further noted below.

- Facilitate the Web-servicization. We will be able to facilitate this by giving a wrapper template for each service type. Ontological knowledge would be further beneficial, as they could be utilized in (semi-)automatic service composition as discussed later.

A note on another role of LR standards: In further detailing some of the important sub-ontologies, on the other hand, we believe it is crucial to incorporate relevant international standards to deal with the issue of interoperability. In this sense, we have been looking at Linguistic Annotation Framework (LAF) (Ide and Romary, 2004) and Lexical Markup Framework (LMF) (Francopoulo et al., 2009) and the associated standards discussed in ISO[3]. LAF has been incorporated into our ontology not only for specifying the input/output data type of NLP tools, but also for defining the content type of corpora; while LMF has been introduced to develop a taxonomy of lexicon classes, which obviously forms a part of the language data resource taxonomy.

Figure 5 depicts how a particular class for syntactic annotation can be defined in the language service ontology by incorporating the Syntactic Annotation Framework (SynAF) (Declerck, 2008) standard, which is a subtype of general LAF in the sense that it focuses on syntactic annotations. Similarly Fig 6 shows that subtypes of lexicon class can be defined in terms of types of lexical entry, and the types of lexical entry should be speci-

[2] http://www.lrec-conf.org/lrec2010/?LREC2010-Map-of-Language-Resources

[3] http://www.tc37sc4.org/

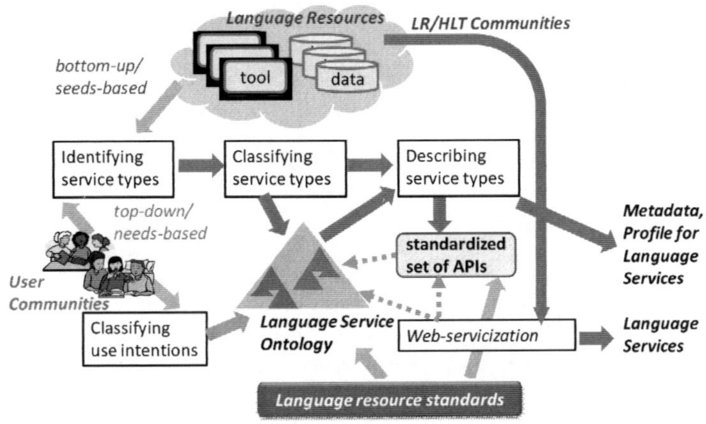

Figure 4: Steps toward standardized service APIs

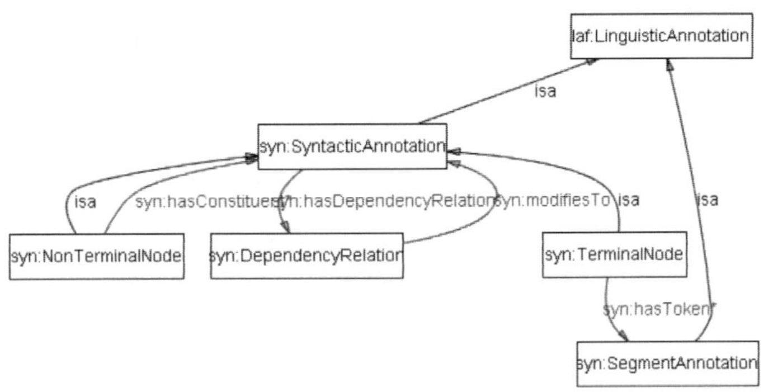

Figure 5: Ontologization of LAF and SynAF

fied by incorporating the *ontologized* LMF specification.

4.3 Linking service specifications with service ontology

The current standard for giving the concrete technical specification to a Web service (type) is to assign a Web Service Description Language (WSDL)[4] document to the Web service. Although a WSDL document defines the service name, functions, and input/output data types, it does not provide any semantic annotation to the elements. For example, the input/output data types defined in a WSDL document do not give us any ideas about which abstract linguistic object type is associated with which concrete data type. Therefore, to ensure the interoperability of a service and its service description, the WSDL document should be associated with the background service ontology in some way.

Among several possible solutions to this issue[5], we see adoption of the W3C recommendation Semantic Annotations for WSDL and XML Schema (SAWSDL)[6] could be a reasonable first step. The most prominent reason for this is its simplicity: as semantic annotations are just added to a WSDL document, the current Web service practices around WSDL can be maintained; SAWSDL does not require any special language for representing semantic models for the annotations, meaning that we could interrelate a WSDL document with the language service ontology. In fact, with the `sawsdl:modelReference` construct provided by SAWSDL, we can semantically annotate a WSDL document by making references to the classes in the language service ontology.

Although this solution could be a reasonable first step toward the full-fledged semantic Web services as discussed in (Yu, 2007), we will

[4] `http://www.w3.org/TR/wsdl`

[5] (Villegas et al., 2010) also discuss this topic and adopt a MyGrid approach (Wolstencroft et al., 2007), where descriptions about service invocation are also separated from the service ontology.

[6] `http://www.w3.org/TR/sawsdl/`

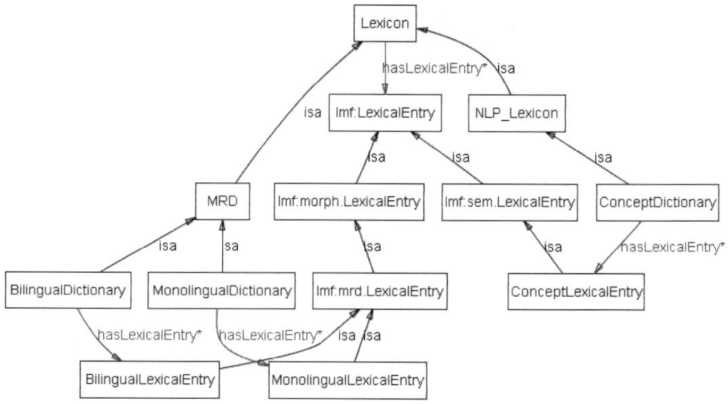

Figure 6: Lexicon Taxonomy as based-on LMF

have to develop an external mechanism for service discovery and compositions on top of the language service ontology and semantically augmented descriptions of the set of language Web service types. Furthermore, if we are stepping forward to the direction of planning-based automatic service composition, we have to device a system for representing goals and statuses. This is an area where almost nothing has been worked out, particularly with respect to the language service ontology.

5 Discussion

In this section, two distinct topics are discussed as below.

The first topic is about the activities for achieving an effective linguistic service infrastructure or software platform. A number of activities can be mentioned; among them, UIMA (Hahn et al., 2008) has gained a prominent position, particularly in text mining applications. U-Compare (Kano et al., 2009) is one of the representative software platforms that utilizes UIMA as the foundation. U-Compare, in particular, has stressed on task-dependent comparison and evaluation of the linguistic processing elements, and provides utilities to accomplish these tasks. A type system for a range of linguistic annotations with the UIMA framework is proposed in (Hahn et al., 2007), sharing common objectives with a part of the language service ontology. Heart of Gold (Schäfer, 2008) is another example of software platform, in which XML together with XSLT play a crucial role. In Heart of Gold, the integration of shallow and deep NLP components is particularly focused on. It should be noted that these platforms, in general, center on the effective creation of a so-called NLP pipeline, and pay little attention to access to lexical resources.

The second topic is just associated with the access to lexical resources. Maybe needless to say, there exist types of resource and/or types of resource access that do not suit well with the query-based access usually provided by language Web services. For example, an access requesting transferring large amount of data would be impossible or prohibited. Moreover, types of access requiring long computational time, for example one that demands complex corpus statistics figures, would be inadequate in a language service infrastructure. Nevertheless, as pointed out at the beginning of this paper, easier access to lexical resources might allow the users to realize a virtual/dynamic resource, that actually does not exist as a whole. One might expect classes of hybrid dictionary, as exemplified in (Hayashi, 2011), to be virtually realized in a language service infrastructure on a query-driven and an on-demand basis.

6 Concluding Remarks

This position paper argued that realizing and maintaining a standardized set of Web APIs is crucially important, and the APIs should be formally classified and described by grounding on a shared ontological foundation. However it is obvious that we have to address a number of issues to achieve the goal. Therefore this paper broke down some of the important issues by reviewing the attempts made around the Language Grid project, and showed general steps and presented some detailed proposals, in hope of making some contribution toward the goal. As the issues however may have substantial depth and stretch, collaborations among international experts, as discussed in (Calzolari and Soria, 2010), are called for. We also argued that user involvements, particularly in a collaborative environment, would be necessary to identify possible language services and resources that are definitely required but remained unaware to the LR/LT experts.

Acknowledgments

The presented work was largely supported by the Strategic Information and Communications R&D Promotion Programme (SCOPE) of the Ministry of Internal Affairs and Communications of Japan. The author would like to thank Toru Ishida, Yohei Murakami, Chiharu Narawa, and other Language Grid members, as well as the international experts in collaboration: Thierry Declerck (DFKI, Germany), Nicoletta Calzolari, Monica Monachini, Claudia Soria (ILC-CNR, Italy), and Paul Buitelaar (DERI, Ireland).

References

Nicoletta Calzolari. 2008. Approaches towards a ' Lexical Web ' : the Role of Interoperability. *Proc. ICGL2008*, pp.34–42.

Nicoletta Calzolari, and Claudia Soria. 2010. Preparing the Field for an Open and Distributed Resource Infrastructure: the Role of the FlaReNet Network. *Proc. LREC2010.*

Thierry Declerck. 2008. A Framework for Standardized Syntactic Annotation. *Proc. LREC2008.*

Gil Francopoulo, Núria Bel, Monte George, Nicoletta Calzolari, Monica Monachini, Mandy Pet, and Claudia Soria. 2009. Multilingual Resources for NLP in the Lexical Markup Framework (LMF). *Language Resources and Evaluation*, Vol.43, No.1, pp.57–70.

Udo Hahn, Ekaterina Buyko, Rico Landefeld, Matthias Muhlhausen, Michael Poprat, Katrin Tomanek , and Joachim Wermter. 2008. An overview of JCoRe, the JULIE lab UIMA component repository, *Proc. LREC'08 Workshop on Towards Enhanced Interoperability for Large HLT Systems: UIMA for NLP*, pp.1–7.

Udo Hahn, Ekaterina Buyko, Katrin Tomanek , Scott Piao, John McNaught, Yoshimasa Tsuruoka, and Sophia Ananiadou. 2007. An annotation type system for a data-driven NLP pipeline. *Proc. the Linguistic Annotation Workshop*, pp.33–40.

Yoshihiko Hayashi, Thierry Declerck, Nicoletta Calzolari, Monica Monachini, Claudia Soria, and Paul Buitelaar. 2011. Language Service Ontology. Toru Ishida (editor). *The Language Grid: Service-Oriented Collective Intelligence for Language Resource Interoperability*, Springer.

Yoshihiko Hayashi. 2011. A Representation Framework for Cross-lingual/Interlingual Lexical Semantic Correspondences. *Proc. IWCS2011*, pp.155–164.

Nancy Ide, and Laurent Romary. 2004. International Standard for a Linguistic Annotation Framework. *Journal of Natural Language Engineering*, Vol.10, No.3–4, pp.211–225.

Toru Ishida. 2006. Language Grid: An Infrastructure for Intercultural Collaboration. *Proc. SAINT-06*, Keynote address, pp.96–100.

Toru Ishida (editor). 2011. *The Language Grid: Service-Oriented Collective Intelligence for Language Resource Interoperability*, Springer.

Kano, Yoshinobu, William A. Baumgartner Jr., Luke McCrohon, Sophia Ananiadou, K. Bretonnel Cohen, Lawrence Hunter and Jun'ichi Tsujii. 2009. U-Compare: share and compare text mining tools with UIMA, *Bioinformatics*, 25(15), pp.1997–1998.

Ewan Klein, and Stephen Potter. 2004. An Ontology for NLP Services. *Proc. LREC2004 Workshop on REgistry of Linguistic Data Categories.*

Urlich Schäfer. 2008. *Integrating Language Processing Components with XML.* VDM Verlag.

Liayng Yu. 2007. Introduction to the Semantic Web and Semantic Web Services. Chapman & Hall/CRC.

Martha Villegas, Núria Bel, Santiago Bel, and Victor Rodríguez. 2010. A Case Study on Interoperability for Language Resources and Applications. *Proc. LREC2010.*

Katy Wolstencroft, Pinar Alper, Duncan Hull, Christopher Wroe, Phillip Lord, Robert Stevens, and Carole Goble. 2007. The myGrid Ontology: Bioinformatics Service Discovery. *International Journal of Bioinformatics Resesearch and Applications*, Vol. 3, No. 3, pp.303–325.

A Method Towards the Fully Automatic Merging of Lexical Resources

Núria Bel
Universitat Pompeu Fabra
Barcelona, Spain
nuria.bel@upf.edu

Muntsa Padró
Universitat Pompeu Fabra
Barcelona, Spain
muntsa.padro@upf.edu

Silvia Necsulescu
Universitat Pompeu Fabra
Barcelona, Spain
silvia.necsulescu@upf.edu

Abstract

Lexical Resources are a critical component for Natural Language Processing applications. However, the high cost of comparing and merging different resources has been a bottleneck to obtain richer resources and a broader range of potential uses for a significant number of languages. With the objective of reducing cost by eliminating human intervention, we present a new method towards the automatic merging of resources. This method includes both, the automatic mapping of resources involved to a common format and merging them, once in this format. This paper presents how we have addressed the merging of two verb subcategorization frame lexica for Spanish, but our method will be extended to cover other types of Lexical Resources. The achieved results, that almost replicate human work, demonstrate the feasibility of the approach.

1 Introduction

The automatic production, updating, tuning and maintenance of Language Resources for Natural Language Processing is currently being considered as one of the most promising areas of advancement for the full deployment of Language Technologies. The reason is that these resources that describe, in one way or another, the characteristics of a particular language are necessary for Language Technologies to work.

Although the re-use of existing resources such as WordNet (Fellbaum, 1998) in different applications has been a well known and successful case, it is not very frequent. The different technology or application requirements, or even the ignorance about the existence of other resources, has provoked the proliferation of different, unrelated resources that, if merged, could constitute a richer repository of information augmenting the number of potential uses. This is especially important for under-resourced languages, which normally suffer from the lack of broad coverage resources. In the research reported in this paper, we wanted to merge two hand-written, large scale Spanish subcategorization lexica to obtain a new one that is larger and validated. Because subcategorization frames contain highly structured information, difficult to compare, it was considered a good scenario for testing new lexical resource merging methods. Other experiments merging resources containing different levels of information are also envisaged.

1.1 Related Work

Several attempts of resource merging have been addressed and reported in the literature. Hughes et al. (1995) report on merging corpora with more than one annotation scheme. Ide and Bunt (2010) also report on the use of a common layer based on a graph representation for the merging of different annotated corpora. Teufel (1995) and Chan & Wu (1999) were concerned with the merging of several source lexica for part-of-speech tagging. The merging of more complex lexica has been addressed by Crouch and King (2005) who produced a Unified Lexicon with lexical entries for verbs based on their syntactic subcategorization in combination with their meaning, as described by WordNet, Cyc (Lenat, 1995) and VerbNet (Kipper et al., 2000).

In this context, a proposal such as the Lexical Markup Framework, LMF (Francopoulo et al. 2008) is understood as an attempt to standardize the format of computational lexica as a way to avoid the complexities of merging lexica with different structures. But it only considers manual comparison of resources and manual mapping from non-standard into the standard.

Despite the undeniable achievements of the research just mentioned, most of it reports the need for a significant amount of human intervention to extract information of existing resources and to map it into a format in which it can be compared with another lexicon, or towards proposed standards, such as the mentioned LMF. Thus, there is still room for improvement in reducing human intervention. This constituted the main challenge of the research reported in this paper: finding a method that can perform, without human intervention, semantic preserving information extraction and format mapping operations to allow for automatically merging two lexical resources, in this

Proceedings of Workshop on Language Resources, Technology and Services in the Sharing Paradigm, pages 8–15,
Chiang Mai, Thailand, November 12, 2011.

particular case two subcategorization frame (SCF) lexica for Spanish. The best results achieve up to 92% in precision and 93% in recall when comparing automatically and manually extracted entries, show the potential of our approach.

1.2 Merging Lexica

Basically, the merging of lexica has two well defined steps (Crouch and King, 2005). In the first, because information about the same phenomenon can be expressed differently, the information in the existing resources has to be extracted and mapped into a common format, making merging possible in a second step, where the extracted information from both lexica is mechanically compared and combined to form the new resource.

While automation of the second step has already proved to be possible, human intervention is still critically needed for the first. In addition to the cost of manual work, note that the exercise is completely adhoc for particular resources to be merged. The cost is what explains the lack of interest in merging existing resources, even though it is critically needed, especially for under-resourced languages. Any cost reduction will have a high impact in the actual re-use of resources.

Thus, our objectives were: first, to carry out a more traditional merging exercise achieving some improvements for step two by using graph unification as the only, basic mechanism. Second, to investigate to what extent we could reduce human intervention in the first step, we devised a semantic preserving mapping algorithm that covers the extraction of the information of any particular lexicon and its mapping onto another format that allows, later, the merging with another resource.

In the next section we introduce the two SCF lexica that we used to validate our proposal. Section 3 reports on the work done in manually extracting the information of our lexica and their mapping onto a common format in order to merge them and thus getting a gold-standard to evaluate the results of the automation exercise. Section 4 presents our proposal to use unification for the merging phase of both the manual and the automatically extracted resources. Section 5 explains how we addressed the problem of automatically mapping the contents of two lexica onto a common format in order to avoid manual extraction. Finally, section 6 states conclusions drawn and further research directions.

2 Information encoded in SCF lexica

Subcategorization frames (SCF) are meant to explicitly demonstrate the number and role of the complements that a predicate, most typically a verb, needs for forming a correct sentence and, more importantly, being correctly interpreted. Note that the most usual case is that one lemma has more than one SCF.

In the experiment we report here, we merged two subcategorization lexica, developed for rule-based grammars, with the goal of creating a SCF gold-standard for Spanish. The two lexica are the Spanish working lexicon of the Incyta Machine Translation system (Alonso, 2005) and the lexicon of the Spanish Resource Grammar, SRG, (Marimon, 2010) developed for LKB framework (Copestake, 2002). Note that different senses under the same lemma were not distinguished in these lexica, and thus, are not addressed in the research reported here. In the case of one lexicon enriched with different senses for one lemma, the merging mechanism would be the same. The difference would stay in the lexicon indexation. Instead of grouping the SCFs with respect to a lemma, they will be grouped under each pair's lemma-sense.

SRG and Incyta lexica encode phenomena related to verbal complements, their role and categorical characteristics expressed as restrictions. SCFs in the SRG lexicon are formulated in terms of feature-attribute value pairs, so they have a graph structure. In the Incyta lexicon, SCFs are represented as a list of parenthesis-marked components, each with a list-based, non structured information[1] declaration. In next sections we briefly introduce the format of both lexica.

2.1 The encoding of SCF in the Incyta lexicon

In the Incyta lexicon, the subcategorization information for each verb is encoded as a parenthesized list of all the possible subcategorization patterns that a given verb can have, even if the different patterns imply a change in the meaning of the verb.

The information contained in each SCF includes a list of the possible complements, indicating for each of them the grammatical function ($SUBJ, $DOBJ, $IOBJ, $POBJ, $SCOMP, $OCOMP, $ADV), the phrase type that can fulfill each grammatical function ('N1' for noun phrase, 'N0' for clausal complement, 'ADJ' for adjective phrase) and the preposition required in case of prepositional objects ($POBJ). In the case of clausal complements, the information is further specified, indicating the type of clause (finite, 'FCP', or non-finite, 'ICP') in the interrogative ('INT') or non-interrogative ('0') forms, and the mode ('SUB' or 'IND' in the case of a finite clause) or the control structure ('PIV $SUBJ', 'PIV $DOBJ', etc.), in the case of non-finite clauses. Incyta further specifies if one of

[1] Decorated lists, parenthetical or otherwise marked, have been a quite common way of representing SCF information, i.e. COMLEX, VERBNET among others.

the complements can be fulfilled by a reflexive and/or reflexive pronoun ('$DOBJ APT RFX'). Apart from the number and type of the complements, the subcategorization pattern includes other subcategorization requirements, represented by the GFT tag (General Frame Test), such as whether the verb is impersonal for weather like verbs (LEX-IMPS T), can take the "se" clitic (RFX), that is, pronominal verbs, or can occur in the form of an absolute past participle construction.

2.2 The encoding of SCF in SRG lexicon

The SRG is grounded in the theoretical framework of Head-driven Phrase Structure Grammar, HPSG, (Pollard and Sag, 1994), a constraint-based, lexicalist approach to grammatical theory where all linguistic objects (i.e. words and phrases) are represented as typed feature structures. In the SRG, each lexical entry consists of a unique identifier and a lexical type (one among about 500 types, defined by a multiple inheritance type hierarchy).

Verbs are encoded by assigning a type and adding specific information of the lexical entries. Verbal types are first distinguished by the value for the SUBJ-list. Thus, we have subtypes for impersonal verbs taking an empty SUBJ-list, verbs taking a verbal subject and verbs taking a nominal subject.

The feature COMPS has as value a list of the complements which specifies the phrase structure type of each complement; i.e. NP, PP, AP, ADV, and SCOMP. Verbal complements are specified for their form (finite or infinitive), mode (indicative or subjunctive), and control or raising relation of verbal complements. Marking prepositions are given as specific information in the lexicon and included as variables in the types. Alternations of complements, as well as other valence changing processes that verb frames may undergo are dealt with lexical rules, which are triggered by lexical feature-value attributes that encode whether a verb can enter, for instance, a passive or a pronominal construction.

2.3 The encoding of SCF in the common lexicon

As we have said, in order to execute the merging of these two lexica, we first needed to convert them into a common format. In order to approach current proposals for standard formats (Francopoulo et al. 2008; Ide & Bunt, 2010) that recommend graph-based and attribute-value formalisms, we chose to map Incyta information towards the SRG format. Since this format already had a graph structure, it was compliant to the standard recommendations. Furthermore, the use of feature structures has several strong points for our work:

- It allowed us to easily combine the information contained in two lexica by graph unification, as we will see in section 4.
- Since graphs are structured representations, they can easily be transformed, after merging, to other standard formats for further reuse, so we consider them a good representation for our final SCF gold-standard.

Although SRG lexicon had already a graph structure, we still needed to perform some preprocessing, related to how we wanted to encode different subcategorization phenomena in our final SCF lexicon[2].

In both lexica, there were some phenomena to be treated by lexical rules which we decided to encode according to the following rules:

- The SCFs that contain an optional complement are split into two SCFs, one with the optional complement and one without it.
- SRG handles some phenomena, such as systematic complement alternations, by lexical rules. These rules are applied in order to create one SCF for each possible complement type. For example, a verb that has a complement that may be fulfilled by both a finite and an infinitive clause is represented with just a type that triggers a lexical rule that will produce the alternation in processing time. Thus, in this example one SRG frame would be converted into two: one with finite and one with an infinite clause complement.

We applied these preprocessing rules to SRG lexica, and converted Incyta lexicon into the graph-based format of SRG, ensuring that SCF patterns and the above mentioned phenomena are encoded in the same way.

3 Manual Extraction Phase

As previously said, the first step of the unification process was to convert Incyta lexicon into the chosen standard graph format, in this case, the feature-value structures of SRG lexicon.

This exercise of converting information contained in a lexicon is referred to by Crouch and King (2005) as the extraction phase. As a first exercise, we performed this conversion with several rules that were manually written according to the intended interpretation of the encoding found in the lexica. These extraction rules mapped the information of Incyta lexicon into a graph represented as an attribute-value matrix. This is what we called the manual extraction phase.

[2] The ultimate goal of the merging was to produce a complete lexicon that could be used as gold-standard in a SCF automatic acquisition experiment.

The manual extraction phase revealed major differences between the two lexica in the following cases:

- Different information granularity. For example, this was the case of the Incyta tag "N0" for referring to the verbal category of the phrase that can fulfill a particular complement. The SRG encoding had a different tag for the finite clause case than for the infinitive case.
- Different grammatical coverage. For instance, the Incyta lexicon lists bound prepositions, while the SRG lexicon sometimes refers to the type of the bound prepositions (i.e. locative or manner).

This exercise was very time consuming, since it was necessary to study the codification of Incyta lexicon and to develop several rules to map them into SRG feature structures.

4 Unification Step

After the manual effort of conversion into a ready to unify format, the second step was the unification of the two lexica represented with the same structure and features. The objective of merging two SCF lexica is to have a new, richer lexicon with information coming from both. The resulting lexicon was richer in SCFs for each lemma, on average, as shown in Table 1.

Once the SCFs were converted into comparable graphs (in the sense that they have the same structure and possible feature-value pairs), we used the basic unification mechanism for merging the list of entries, i.e. lemmas, and the SCFs under the same lemma, from the two lexica. We used the implementation of feature structure representation and unification available in NLTK (Bird et al., 2009). The unification process tries to match many-to-many SCFs under the same lemma. This means that for every verb, each SCF from one lexicon tries to unify with each SCF from the other lexicon.

Thus, the resulting lexicon contains lemmas from both dictionaries and for each lemma, the unification of the SCFs from the Incyta lexicon with those from the SRG lexicon. The unified SCFs can be split in three classes:

- SCFs of verbs that were present in both dictionaries, i.e. A_{SCF} is contained under one lemma in both lexica, thus the resulting lexicon, contains A_{SCF} under this lemma.
- SCFs that, though not identical in both lexica, unify into a third SCF, so they are compatible. This is due to SCF components that were present in one of the lexica but not in the other. For example, assume one SCF in the Incyta lexicon is equal to one SCF in SRG lexicon except that in the Incyta lexicon it contains information about the bound preposition (e.g. has the component "prep=in") while in SRG lexicon it contains only information about the preposition type (e.g. "prep_type=location"). The result of unifying these two SCFs is a richer SCF that contains both, the information of preposition and of preposition type.
- SCFs that were present in one of the lexicon but not in the other: the Incyta lexicon contains SCF_1, while the SRG lexicon contains SCF_2 under the same lemma. SCF_1 and SCF_2 cannot unify, thus the resulting lexicon contains for this lemma both frames, SCF_1 and SCF_2.

Group (3) can signal the presence of inconsistent information in one or the two lexica, like a lack of information in one lexicon (e.g. SCF_1 appears in Incyta but it does not have a corresponding SCF in SRG) or an error in the lexica (at least one of SCF implicated into the unification is an incorrect frame for its lemma). Thus, we can detect conflicting information searching the lemmas with SCFs that do not unify at all, or SCFs in one or the other lexicon that never unify with any other SCF. In a further step, with a human specialist, this information can be manually analyzed and eventually eliminated from the final lexicon. Nevertheless, in our work we do not approach this analysis step, so our final lexicon, contained all SCF obtained by unification and also those that did not unify with another SCF.

Lexicon	Unique SCF	Total SCF	Lemmas	Avg.
SRG	326	13.864	4303	3.2
Incyta	660	10.422	4070	2.5
Merged	919	17.376	4324	4

Table 1: Results of merging exercise of manually extracted lexica

Table 1 shows the results of the manual merging exercise in terms of number of SCFs and lemmas in each lexicon. It can be seen from the number of unique SCFs that the Incyta lexicon has many more SCFs than the SRG lexicon. This is due to different granularity of information. For example, the Incyta lexicon always gives information about the concrete preposition accompanying a PP while, in some cases, the SRG gives only the type of preposition, as explained before.

The number of unique SCFs of the resulting lexicon, which is close to the sum between the numbers of the unique SCFs in the lexica, may seem surprising. Nevertheless, a closer study showed that for 50% of the lemmas we have a complete unification; thus, the high number of SCF's in the merged lexicon comes from the many-to-many unification, that is, from the fact that one SCF in one lexicon unified with several SCFs in the other lexicon, so all SCFs resulting from these unifications will be added to the final lexicon. This is the case for cases of different granularity, as explained before.

The final lexicon contains a total of 4,324 lemmas. From those, 94% appeared in both lexica, which means the resulting lexicon contained 274 lemmas that appear just in one lexicon. Those lemmas are added directly to the final lexicon. They are good proof that the new lexicon is richer in information.

Regarding lemmas that are in both lexica, 50% of them unified all their SCFs, signifying a total accord between both lexica. This is not surprising given that both are describing the same phenomena. On the other hand, 37% of lemmas contained some SCFs that unified and some that did not, which revealed differences between both lexica, as explained in section 3.

Only 274 lemmas (6,3%) did not unify any SCFs because of conflicting information, which we consider a very good result. These verbs may require further manual analysis in order to detect inconsistencies. An example of complete unification failure comes from the inconsistent encoding of pronominal and reflexive verbs in the lexica.

To summarize, the resulting lexicon is richer than the two it is composed of since it has gained information in the number of SCFs per lemma, as well as in the information contained in each SCF. Furthermore, note that the unification method allowed us to automatically detect inconsistent cases to be studied if necessary. For more information about these results and a more accurate discussion, see (*autocite*, 2011).

5 Automatic Mapping

Thus far, we have introduced our proposal to perform automatic merging of two lexica once they are represented as graph-based feature structures. Nevertheless, the most consuming part of the previous task was the extraction and mapping from the original format of a lexicon to a common graph structure. In this section, we present our proposal to automatically perform this mapping, which is the main contribution of this paper. In section 5.2 we will compare the results of the manual and the automatic extraction and mapping phase to assess the usability of our approach.

Our experiment to avoid manual intervention when converting the two lexica into a common format with a blind, semantic preserving method departs from the idea of Chan and Wu (1999) to compare information contained in the same entries of different lexica, looking for consistent, significant equivalences validated by a significant number of cases in the whole lexica. However, they were only mapping part-of-speech tags, while we needed to handle complex, structured information. Thus, our main goal was to reduce human intervention especially including the need to know the internal structure and semantics of the lexica to be merged. The basic idea behind the devised method is to let the system find semantically equivalent pieces of information coming from different resources and to substitute one with the other, in our case to substitute the parenthetical list of Incyta lexicon with the attribute-value equivalent matrix in the SRG lexicon.

5.1 Methodology

The only requirement of the following proposal for automatic mapping is to have a number of lemmas encoded in both lexica. With the same lemmas in both lexica, it is possible to assess that a piece of code in lexicon A corresponds to a piece of code in lexicon B, and to validate this hypothesis if a significant number of other lemmas hold the same correspondence. Thus, when a correspondence is found, the relevant piece in A can be substituted by the piece in B, performing the conversion into a common format to allow for the real merging. This is the basis of our method for carrying out the extraction phase automatically.

In order to maximize comparisons, each SCF was split into pieces in both lexica. Thus, the system had to search for parts of Incyta SCFs that correspond to parts of SRG graphs, i.e. single attribute-values or groups of them. Nevertheless, this search for relevant pieces had to be done automatically and only formal characteristics would be used. Since we did not want our method to be informed by human knowledge of the particular lexica to be merged, and in order to make it applicable to more than one lexicon, the first point to solve was how to compare two different SCFs code with no available previous information about their internal semantics. The only information used was that SCFs in the SRG lexicon were formulated in terms of feature-attribute value pairs and in the Incyta lexicon in terms of a list of parenthesis with less structured internal information.

An example of the code of one SCF in Incyta lexicon is (1):

(1) (($SUBJ N1 N0 (FCP 0 INT) (MD-0 IND) (MD-INT SUB)) ($DOBJ N1))

Therefore, the information that had to be discovered was the following:

- The Incyta lexicon marks each SCF as a list of parenthesis, where the first level of parenthesis indicates the list of complements. In example (1) there are two main parentheses, one representing the subject structure ($SUBJ ...) and the other with direct object structure ($DOBJ ...).
- Each component of the list begins with an identifier ($SUBJ or $DOBJ in (1)) followed, without necessarily any formal marker, by additional information about properties of the component in the form of

tags. For example, in (1) above, direct object ($DOBJ) is fulfilled by a noun phrase (N1).

- Incyta marks disjunction as a simple sequence of tags. In (1), subject ($SUBJ) may be fulfilled by N1 (noun phrase) or N0 (clause phrase). Furthermore, properties of one of the elements in the disjunction are specified in one or more parenthesis following the tag, as it is the case of N0 in (1). The 3 parenthesis after N0 are in fact properties of its realization: it is a sentential complement (FCP) whose verb should appear in indicative (MD-0 IND) unless it is an interrogative clause (MD-INT SUB). Note that this information is not structured so it was necessary to look for a way to detect that these parentheses refer to N0 and not to N1.

We devised an algorithm to discover and extract this internal structure from scratch. Our algorithm first splits every SCF in all possible ways according to only formal characteristics (minimal but complete parenthetical components for Incyta and minimal but complete attribute-value matrices for SRG) and looks, independently in each lexicon, for the most frequently repeated pieces along the whole lexicon, in order to assess that a particular piece is a meaningful unit in a particular lexicon. Note that we wanted to discover minimal units in order to handle different information encoding granularity. If we would have mapped entire SCFs or large pieces of them, the system could substitute information in A with information in B although possibly missing a difference.

Note that when performing the extraction, we aimed to ensure that as much information as possible from the original lexicon is preserved by splitting the lexicon into small pieces. However, in some cases, this created incomplete SCFs. Nevertheless, as our ultimate goal is to merge the two lexica, it is in the merging step that the partial elements will get the missing parts.

To sum up, our algorithm does the following with the Incyta SCF code:

- It splits SCF into each parentheses that conforms the list (this is, to find $SUBJ and $DOBJ in example (1)).
- For each of these pieces, it considers the first element as its key, and recursively splits the following elements.
- It detects the relationship among the different elements found inside the parentheses by assessing those that always occur together. For instance, in (1), it detects that FCP appears only when there is a N0, and that MD-0 appears only when (FCP 0) appears. In this way, the constituents of the parentheses grouped according to their dependency are automatically identified. The elements that always occur together are treated as minimal units.

On the other hand, it is also necessary to look for minimal units of the SRG lexicon. In this case, these minimal units are the values or features structures obtained when taking the values of the attributes at the first level of embedding. In this way, in the target format the minimal units are guaranteed to be semantically justified.

Once the minimal units of each Incyta and SRG SCFs are extracted, our algorithm does the following mapping:

- For each element extracted from the Incyta SCF, it creates a list of verbs that contain it. This list is represented as a binary vector whose element i is 1 if the verb in position i is in the list.
- For each minimal unit obtained from the SRG lexicon, it also builds a binary vector with the verbs that contain each element.
- For each Incyta SCF minimal unit, it assesses the similarity with each SRG unit comparing the two binary vectors using the Jaccard distance measure, especially suited for calculating distances between binary vectors and also used by Chan and Wu (1999).
- It chooses as mapping elements those that maximize similarity.

Once we had the mapping elements, new feature structures substituting Incyta units with SRG mapping elements are produced. Thus, a new version of the Incyta lexicon represented with feature-value structures is produced. The new feature structure-based entries could then be merged with the ones in SRG using unification, as we did with the manually extracted feature structures in section 4. Eventually, we obtained a new lexicon by merging the two lexica in a completely automatic way.

5.2 Evaluation and Results

To evaluate the results, we compared the two resulting lexica: the one resulting from the manual extraction and later unification and the lexicon resulting from the automatic extraction by mapping and again unification. Specifically, we use the manually built lexicon as a gold-standard. The evaluation is done using traditional precision, recall and F1 measures for each verb entry because most of them have more than one SCF and then we compute the mean of these measures over all the verbs.

We first counted only identical SCFs in the entries of every verb entry. However, we also took into account what we call the "compatible" entries. Note that in some cases the results of the automatic mapping are parts of SCFs instead of complete SCFs, because of the piece splitting process. As said, merging by unification automatically adds the information as to complete them in numerous cases, but the Incyta SCFs that did not find any of the SGR SCFs to unify with can result in an additional but incomplete SCF in the final lexicon. They may be considered correct, although incomplete, when they are compatible with the information in the gold-standard, that is, when the automatically created entry subsumes the SCF in the gold-standard. Thus, in a second measurement, we also count these pieces that are compatible with SCFs in the gold-standard as a positive result. We keep figures separated, though, in table 2.

The results, shown in table 2, are near 88% of F1 in the strict case of identical SCFs. If we compare compatible SCFs, the results are even more satisfactory.

	P	R	F1
A-identical	87,35%	88,02%	87,69%
B-compatible	92,35%	93,08%	92,72%

Table 2: Average results of the mapping exercise

For a more detailed analysis of the results, we plot in Figure 1 the system performance in terms of number of SCFs under a lemma that are either identical or compatible in the gold-standard and in the merged lexicon. We also plot the ratio of verbs that have a particular number of SCFs or less (cumulative). The verbs that have one or two SCFs (about 50% of the verbs) obtain high values both in the exact matching and compatible SCFs, as it may be expected. Nevertheless, 95% of verbs (those with 11 or less SCFs per lemma) obtain at least F1=80% when counting only identical resulting SCFs and F1 over 90% when counting compatible resulting SCFs. Note that these figures are the lower threshold, since verbs with less SCFs have better results, as it can be seen in Figure 1. To summarize, the obtained precision and recall of all verbs, even those with more than two SCFs, are very satisfactory and constitute a proof of the feasibility of the approach.

As for the error analysis, the results revealed that some SCFs in the gold-standard are not in the automatically built lexicon. One case is SCFs with adverbial complements. Our algorithm maps adverbials onto prepositional phrases and the resulting SCF misses part of the original information. Nevertheless, our algorithm correctly adds information when there are gaps in one of the dictionaries. It is able to learn correspondences such as "INT" (Incyta for interrogative clause) to "q" in SRG and to add this information when it is missed in a particular entry of the SRG lexicon but available in the Incyta entry.

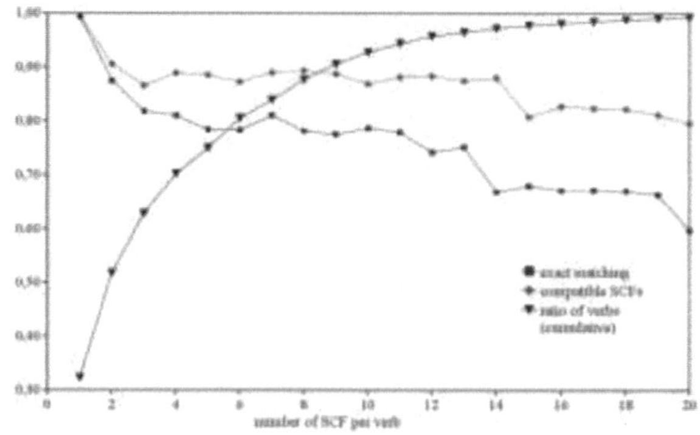

Figure 1: Average F1 and cumulative number of verbs with respect to the number of SCFs

6 Conclusions and Future Work

We have studied a method to reduce human intervention in the merging of lexical resources, and we have proved the concept with two SCF lexica. In order to merge different lexica by means of an automatic operation like unification, the resources need to be mapped into a common format. To reduce the cost of extracting and comparing the lexica contents, we proposed a method to make the mapping automatically. We consider the results obtained, above 80%, very satisfactory. Our method can indicate the possibility of avoiding the manual information extraction phase, which is a big bottleneck for the re-use and merging of language resources.

Furthermore, we can see the advantages of representing the lexica as feature structures because it enables the use of graph unification as an automatic mechanism for actual merging.

The strongest point of our method for automatically mapping the lexica into a common format is that it can be applied without the need of knowing the semantics of the lexica to be merged because it finds significant common code in existing lexica as to draw correspondences. This allows us to think our method can be extended to other types of Lexical Resources. The only requirement is that all resources to be mapped contain some common data. Although further work is needed for assessing how much common data guarantees the same results, the current work is indicative of the feasibility of our approach.

It is important to note that the results presented here are obtained without using what Crouch and King (2005) call patch files. Automatic merging produces consistent errors that can be object of further refinement. Thus, it is possible to devise specific patches that correct or add information in particular cases where either wrong or incomplete information is produced. It is future work to study the use of patch files to improve our method.

Acknowledgments

This work has been funded by the PANACEA project (EU-7FP-ITC-248064) and the CLARA project (EU-7FP-ITN-238405).

References

Juan Alberto Alonso, András Bocsák. 2005. Machine Translation for Catalan-Spanish. The Real Case for Productive MT; In Proceedings of the tenth Conference on European Association of Machine Translation (EAMT 2005), Budapest, Hungary.

Steven Bird. 2006. NLTK: the natural language toolkit. In Proceedings of the COLING/ACL on Interactive presentation sessions. Association for Computational Linguistics, Morristown, NJ, USA.

Daniel K. Chan and Dekai Wu. 1999. Automatically Merging Lexicons that have Incompatible Part-of-Speech Categories. Joint SIGDAT Conference on Empirical Methods in Natural Language Processing and Very Large Corpora (EMNLP/VLC-99). Maryland.

Ann Copestake. 2002. Implementing Typed Feature Structure Grammars. CSLI Publications, CSLI lecture notes, number 110, Chicago.

Dick Crouch and Tracy H. King. 2005. Unifying lexical resources. Proceedings of Interdisciplinary Workshop on the Identification and Representation of Verb Features and Verb Classes. Saarbruecken; Germany.

Christiane Fellbaum. 1998. WordNet: An Electronic Lexical Database. MIT Press.

Gil Francopoulo, Núria Bel, Monte George, Nicoletta Calzolari, Mandy Pet, and Claudia Soria. 2008. Multilingual resources for NLP in the lexical markup framework (LMF). Journal of Language Resources and Evaluation, 43 (1).

John Hughes, Clive Souter, and E. Atwell. 1995. Automatic Extraction of Tagset Mappings from Parallel-Annotated Corpora. Computation and Language.

Nancy Ide and Harry Bunt. 2010. Anatomy of Annotation Schemes: Mapping to GrAF. Proceedings of the Fourth Linguistic Annotation Workshop, ACL 2010

Karin Kipper, Hoa Trang Dang, and Martha Palmer. 2000. Class-based construction of a verb lexicon. In Proceedings of AAAI/IAAI.

Anna Korhonen. 2002. Subcategorization Acquisition. PhD thesis published as Technical Report UCAM-CL-TR-530. Computer Laboratory, University of Cambridge

Doug Lenat. 1995. Cyc: a large-scale investment in knowledge infrastructure. In CACM 38, n.11.

Montserrat Marimon. 2010. The Spanish Resource Grammar. Proceedings of the Seventh Conference on International Language Resources and Evaluation (LREC'10). Paris, France: European Language Resources Association (ELRA).

Monica Monachini, Nicoletta Calzolari, Khalid Choukri, Jochen Friedrich, Giulio Maltese, Michele Mammini, Jan Odijk & Marisa Ulivieri. 2006. Unified Lexicon and Unified Morphosyntactic Specifications for Written and Spoken Italian. In Calzolari et al. (eds.), LREC2006: 5th International Conference on Language Resources and Evaluation: Proceedings, pp. 1852-1857, Genoa, Italy.C.J.

Silvia Necsulescu, Núria Bel, Muntsa Padró, Montserrat Marimon and Eva Revilla: Towards the Automatic Merging of Language Resources. In Proceedings of WoLeR 2011. Ljubljana, Slovenia.

Carl Pollard and Ivan A. Sag. 1994. Head-driven Phrase Structure Grammar. The University of Chicago Press, Chicago.

Simone Teufel. 1995. A Support Tool for Tagset Mapping. In EACL-Sigdat 95.

Service Quality Improvement in Web Service Based Machine Transaltion

Sapa Chanyachatchawan and **Virach Sornlertlamvanich** and **Thatsanee Charoenporn**
National Electronics and Computer Technology Center (NECTEC)
112 Phahon Yothin Rd., Klong 1, Klong Luang, Pathumthani 12120,Thailand
{sapa.cha,virach.sor,thatsanee.cha}@nectec.or.th

Abstract

There are many approaches to increase web service based machine translation result. However, perfect result alone does not guarantee the quality of translation service or user satisfaction. This paper proposes framework to improve translation service by using non functional attributes information. In this paper, we present methodology to measure quality of composite translation service using existing services information and also the guideline for selecting the composition web service which has highest quality of service.

1 Introduction

The advantage of web service based machine translation is the ability to create new language pairs from existing language pairs. This process is based on web service composition in SOA (Service Oriented Architecture). Langrid Project (NICT, 2011) is an example of machine translate service based on web service composition technique. Langrid user can create multihop translation from existing language pairs. The automatic composition process increases accessibility for end users transparently. The most challenging task among the automatic composition processes is the discovery process. Based on W3C, web service description standard (WSDL1.1) defines only input and output name and basic data type for web service with a few descriptions. OWL-S is used to embed semantic into service input and output which enable software agent to discover service. However, translation accuracy does not relate to quality of composite service or user satisfaction. By embedding QoS (Quality of Service) attributes as nonfunctional attributes into web service description, we can improve quality of composite service result. This paper proposes machine translation service framework that can automatically create new language pair from existing resources. The objective of this paper is to provide framework with model to managed nonfunctional attributes and semantic of service. Framework is presented in section 2, where component and overall process are explained in brief. In section 3 discovery process is presented in general idea along with model for evaluate quality of web service and selection method.

2 Framework

In this section, we describe framework for managing web service composition process. The framework is illustrated in Figure 1. From user aspect, our framework is service provider. Users do not need to search and compose web service by themselves. In this paper, existing translation service and composite translation service are called service and composite service respectively.

Component of the framework consists of

- *Proxy Agent* is responsible to interact with users and manage user session.
- *Discovery Agent* is responsible to search and interact with external web service registies.
- *Service Agent* is responsible to invoke external web services.
- *Repository* is responsible for record composite web services and non functional attributes information that do not included in the original WSDL.
- *Compose Agent* is responsible for 1) interact with other component in framework 2) compose web service 3) evaluate web service quality.

The process flow of framework is describe as follow:

Proceedings of Workshop on Language Resources, Technology and Services in the Sharing Paradigm, pages 16–23,
Chiang Mai, Thailand, November 12, 2011.

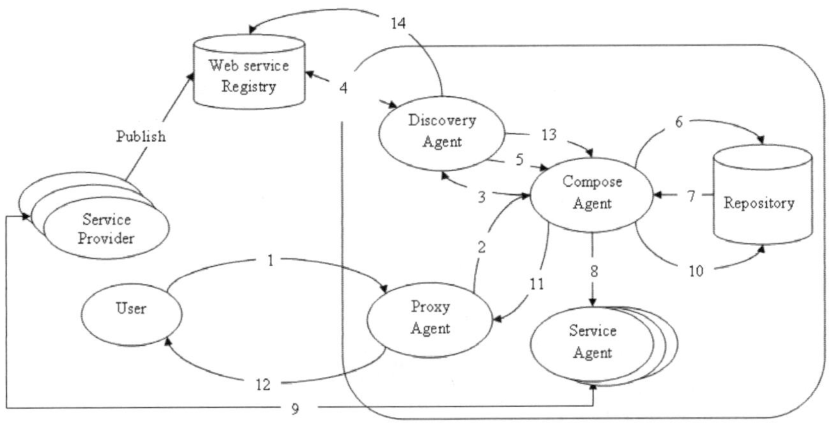

Figure 1: Framework

1. User send request to *Proxy Agent*. User request consists of input, output, and also semantic information.

2. User send request to *Proxy Agent*. User request consists of input, output, and semantic information.

3. *Proxy Agent* forwards request to *Compose Agent*.

4. *Compose Agent* forwards request parameters to *Discovery Agent*.

5. *Discovery Agent* searches services from web service registry.

6. *Discovery Agent* returns candidate results to *Compose Agent*

7. *Compose Agent* consults *Repository* if there is additional information about candidate results.

8. *Repository* returns related information to *Composer Agent*.

9. *Compose Agent* evaluates, selects web service, creates workflow, creates instances of *Service Agent*.

10. *Service Agents* binds web service.

11. After finish execution, *Service Agents* returns result to *Compose Agent*.

12. *Compose Agent* updates service information in *Repository*

13. *Compose Agent* forwards result to *Proxy Agent*.

14. *Proxy Agent* returns output to user

15. *Compose Agent* creates WDSL for composite service and forward to *Discovery Agent* and stores in *Repository*

16. *Discovery Agent* publishes composite service to web service registry

3 Evaluate quality of sevices

After discovery process, there are many composite services that satisfy user request. In order to select the highest quality service, quality of service is calculated using non functional attributes of service.

3.1 Non functional attributes of web services

Non function attributes can represent QoS(Quality of Service) which use to differentiate good service from others. QoS values in interval or ratio scale can be concerned as criterias for selecting optimal services. QoS values in nominal scale value use to reduce number of services. Some fundamental attributes will be used in this paper as an example

For any web service S, the QoS attributes list below:

Cost of service: denotes as $QoS_{Cost}(S)$, this is the cost to pay for service provider in order to run service. The attributes consist of two parts; first part is taken directly from service provider called *direct cost*. Second part is cost for set up and maintenance services called *indirect cost* which assume that the value is constant for every process throughout the whole system.

Time of service: denotes as $QoS_{Time}(S)$, this is the time measure from invoke service to receive respond from service in case of service process successfully. Time of service consists of *process time* and *delay time. process time* is time needed to run instance of service, *delay time* is overhead time. This value is kept in *Repository* and be updated every time that process finish as following equation

$$QoS_{Time}(S) =$$

$$\frac{((QoS_{Time}(S)_{N-1})*(N-1))+Time_N(S)}{N}$$

whereas $QoS_{Time}(S)_N$ is the average time of process after be invoked for N time. This information is kept in *Repository*.

Failure ratio: denotes as $QoS_{Failure}(S)$, is ratio between number of failure and total number of execution. *Failure ratio* initial value is set to 0 and be updated by following formula

In case of service terminate normally;

$$QoS_{Failure}(S) = \frac{((QoS_{Failure}(S)_N)*(N-1))}{N}$$

In case of service terminate abnormally;

$$QoS_{Failure}(S) =$$

$$\frac{((QoS_{Failure}(S)_N)*(N-1))+1}{N}$$

whereas $QoS_{Failure}(S)_N$ is the failure ratio of process after be invoked for N time.This information is kept in *Repository*.

Unavailability: denotes as $QoS_{Unavl}(S)$, is value to represent the unavailability of services. $QoS_{Unavl}(S)$ is obtained using this formula:

$$QoS_{Unavl}(S) = \frac{T(S)}{C}$$

Whereas, $T(S)$ is total amount of time (seconds) which service S is not available in last C seconds, C is set by framework.

User satisfaction: denotes as QoS_{Sat}, is cardinal scale value represent satisfaction level of user, this value is variance depend on each users. This information is kept in *Repository*.

Security level: denotes as QoS_{Sec}, is cardinal scale value represent security level, this value is taken directly from service or trusted third party providers. This value is taken directly from service providers.

Bandwidth: denotes as QoS_{Band}, is bandwidth required for running process. This value is taken directly from service providers.

There are number of basic attributes used for measure QoS in streaming application which allow some errors and lossy information.

Error: denotes as QoS_{Error}, is represent total number of noise and error (in bytes) occur while execute services.

Delay: denotes as QoS_{Delay}, is total delay and jitter time (in seconds) while execute services.

Some nominal scale non functional attributes that can not be convert to ratio scale, such as user context. These attributes are used to prune web services. Examples of these attributes are:

Context: denotes as $QoS_{Context}$, is set of context attributes represent context of users and their environment, such as location, demography information, or user browser environment.

Summarization of non functional attributes is presented in Table 1

3.2 Normalize QoS value

In order to compare or measure different attributes, QoS need to be normalized. Each attributes is assigned preference of its value (minimum, maximum). Each attributes are normalized as following:

Cost of service: is normalized by using transform table because of cost of service should not be linear function. Table 2 shows the example of normalization of $QoS_{Cost}(S)$.

Time of service: is normalized using formula:

$$\frac{QoS_{Time}(S)}{C_{MaxTime}}$$

Table 1: Non functional attributes summarization

Attribute	Scale	Source	Description
$QoS_{Cost}(S)$	Ratio	Service Provider	Service cost
$QoS_{Time}(S)$	Ratio	*Repository*	Average execute time
$QoS_{Failure}(S)$	Ratio	*Repository*	Failure ratio
$QoS_{Unavl}(S)$	Ratio	*Repository*	Unavailability ratio
$QoS_{Sat}(S)$	Cardinal	*Repository*	User satisfaction
$QoS_{Sec}(S)$	Cardinal	Service Provider	Security level
$QoS_{Band}(S)$	Ratio	Service Provider	Reqiured Bandwidth
$QoS_{Error}(S)$	Ratio	*Repository*	Number of error information
$QoS_{Delay}(S)$	Ratio	*Repository*	Service delay time
$QoS_{Context}(S)$	Nominal	User	User context

Table 2: Cost of service transform table example

Cost(Dollars)	Value
0-0.5	0.0
0.5-1	0.3
1-5	0.5
5-10	0.8
≥ 5	1.0

Whereas $C_{MaxTime}$ is the maximum execute time assigned by framework.

Failure ratio: does not need to be normalized, because $QoS_{Failure}(S) \in [0, 1]$

Unavailability: does not need to be normalized, because $QoS_{Unavl}(S) \in [0, 1]$

User satisfaction: is not normalized and will be used as constraint.

Security level: is not normalized and will be used as constraint.

Bandwidth: is normalized using formula:

$$\frac{QoS_{Band}(S)}{C_{MaxBand}}$$

Whereas $C_{MaxBand}$ is the maximum bandwidth of framework.

Error: is normalized using formula:

$$\frac{QoS_{Error} - C_{MinError}}{C_{MaxError} - C_{MinError}}$$

Whereas $C_{MinError}$ and $C_{MaxError}$ are minimum and maximum error that framework allow to happen.

Delay: is normalized using formula:

$$\frac{QoS_{Delay} - C_{MinDelay}}{C_{MaxDelay} - C_{MinDelay}}$$

Whereas $C_{MinDelay}$ and $C_{MaxDelay}$ are minimum and maximum error that framework allow to happen.

Context: can not be normalized and will be used as constraint.

Table 3 is the summarization of normalized attributes.

3.3 Quality of composite service

Once the service has been composed, the QoS of composite service will be calculated. Workflow of composite service determines how QoS be computed. Workflow of composite service is divided into four types 1)sequential, 2)parallel, 3)conditional, 4)loop, and 5)complex. Parallel, conditional, loop and complex workflow are reduced into one atomic task.As the result of reduction, new workflow will consist of sequential workflow only, and then sequential workflow is reduced to one atomic workflow. Only ratio scale and interval scale attributes will computed here. Hence, QoS of composite service is calculated.

3.3.1 Sequential workflow

Sequential workflow CS (Figure 2)consists of n sequential process denote as $S_i; 1 \leq i \leq n$. The work flow start at service S_1 and finish at service S_n. Process S_i must finish before process S_{i+1} can start.

The QoS of CS can be obtained as follows:

$$QoS_{Time}(CS) = \sum_{i=1}^{n} QoS_{Time}(S_i)$$

Table 3: Normalized functional attributes

Attribute	Range	Preferred value	Description
$QoS_{Cost}(S)$	$[0,1]$	Minimum	Service cost
$QoS_{Time}(S)$	$[0,1]$	Minimum	Average execute time
$QoS_{Failure}(S)$	$[0,1]$	Minimum	Failure ratio
$QoS_{Unavl}(S)$	$[0,1]$	Minimum	Unavailability ratio
$QoS_{Sat}(S)$	-	-	User satisfaction
$QoS_{Sec}(S)$	-	-	Security level
$QoS_{Band}(S)$	$[0,1]$	Minimum	Required Bandwidth
$QoS_{Error}(S)$	$[0,1]$	Minimum	Number of error information
$QoS_{Delay}(S)$	$[0,1]$	Minimum	Service delay time
$QoS_{Context}(S)$	-	-	User context

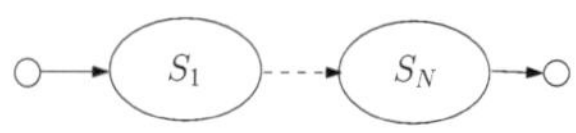

Figure 2: Linear workflow

$$QoS_{Cost}(CS) = \sum_{i=1}^{n} QoS_{Cost}(S_i)$$
$$QoS_{Failure}(CS) = 1 - \prod_{i=1}^{n}(1 - QoS_{Failure}(S_i))$$
$$QoS_{Unavl}(CS) = 1 - \prod_{i=1}^{n}(1 - QoS_{Unavl}(S_i))$$
$$QoS_{Band}(CS) = MAX_{1\leq i\leq n}(QoS_{Band}(S_i))$$
$$QoS_{Error}(CS) = \sum_{i=1}^{n} QoS_{Error}(S_i)$$
$$QoS_{Delay}(CS) = \sum_{i=1}^{n} QoS_{Delay}(S_i)$$

3.3.2 Parallel workflow

Parallel workflow (Figure 3) CS consists of n parallel process denote as $S_i; 1 \leq i \leq n$, each process work independently and can start at same time.

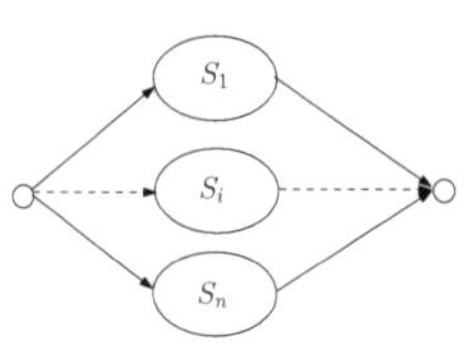

Figure 3: Parallel workflow

The QoS of CS can be obtained as follows:

$$QoS_{Time}(CS) = MAX_{1\leq i\leq n}(QoS_{Time}(S_i))$$
$$QoS_{Cost}(CS) = \sum_{i=1}^{n} QoS_{Cost}(S_i)$$
$$QoS_{Failure}(CS) = 1 - \prod_{i=1}^{n}(1 - QoS_{Failure}(S_i))$$
$$QoS_{Unavl}(CS) = 1 - \prod_{i=1}^{n}(1 - QoS_{Unavl}(S_i))$$
$$QoS_{Band}(CS) = \sum_{i=1}^{n} QoS_{Band}(S_i)$$
$$QoS_{Error}(CS) = \sum_{i=1}^{n} QoS_{Error}(S_i)$$
$$QoS_{Delay}(CS) = MAX_{1\leq i\leq n}(QoS_{Delay}(S_i))$$

3.3.3 Conditional workflow

Conditional workflow CS (Figure 4)consists of n process denote as $S_i; 1 \leq i \leq n$, only one process will be execute. p_i is the probability of process S_i to be execute and $\sum_i^n p_i = 1$, these value store from $Repository$.

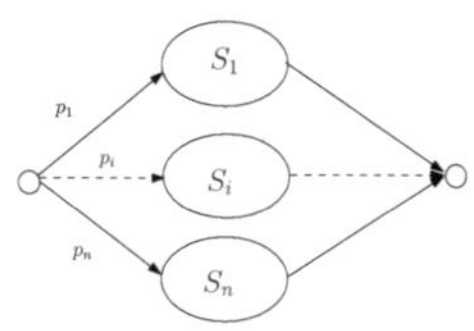

Figure 4: Conditional workflow

The QoS of CS can be obtained as follows:

$$QoS_{Time}(CS) = \sum_{i=1}^{n}(p_i * QoS_{Time}(S_i))$$
$$QoS_{Cost}(CS) = \sum_{i=1}^{n}(p_i * QoS_{Cost}(S_i))$$
$$QoS_{Failure}(CS) = \sum_{i=1}^{n}(p_i * QoS_{Failure}(S_i))$$
$$QoS_{Unavl}(CS) = \sum_{i=1}^{n}(p_i * QoS_{Unavl}(S_i))$$
$$QoS_{Band}(CS) = \sum_{i=1}^{n}(p_i * QoS_{Band}(S_i))$$
$$QoS_{Error}(CS) = \sum_{i=1}^{n}(p_i * QoS_{Error}(S_i))$$
$$QoS_{Delay}(CS) = \sum_{i=1}^{n}(p_i * QoS_{Delay}(S_i))$$

3.3.4 Loop workflow

For loop workflow (Figure 5), there is condition of loop to simplify the calculation. Give CS is composite service that created by repeat execution of service S with p is the chance that service will be repeat and loop must be execute service S at least one time.

The QoS of CS can be obtained as follows:

$$QoS_{Cost}(CS) = \frac{QoS_{Cost}(S)}{(1-p)}$$
$$QoS_{Time}(CS) = \frac{QoS_{Time}(S)}{(1-p)}$$

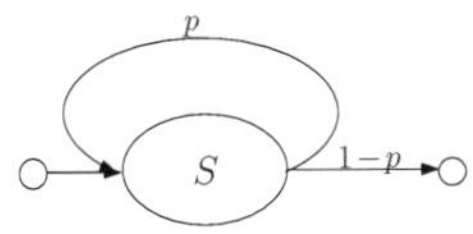

Figure 5: Loop workflow

$$QoS_{Failure}(CS) = 1 - \frac{(1-p)*(1-QoS_{Failure}(S))}{(1-p*(1-QoS_{Failure}))}$$

$$QoS_{Unavl}(CS) = 1 - \frac{(1-p)*(1-QoS_{Unavl}(S))}{(1-p*(1-QoS_{Unavl}))}$$

$$QoS_{Band}(CS) = QoS_{Band}(S_i)$$

$$QoS_{Error}(CS) = \frac{QoS_{Error}(S)}{(1-p)}$$

$$QoS_{Delay}(CS) = \frac{QoS_{Delay}(S)}{(1-p)}$$

3.3.5 Complex workflow

Complex workflow CS (Figure 6)consists of N process denote as $S_i; 1 \leq i \leq n$, it is acyclic directed graph.

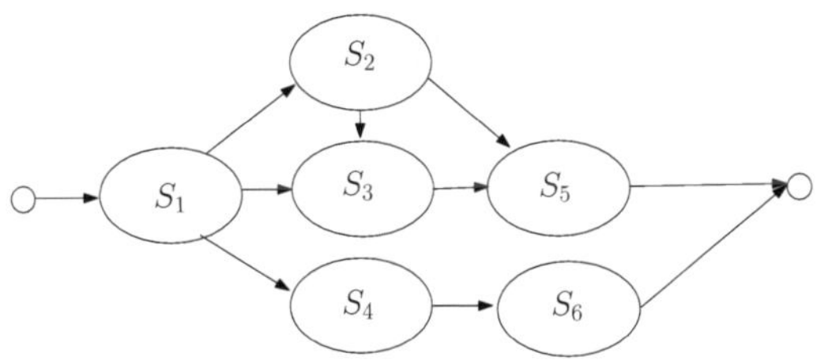

Figure 6: Complex workflow

The QoS of CS can be obtained as follows:

$$QoS_{Cost}(CS) = \sum_{i=1}^{n} QoS_{Cost}(S_i)$$

$$QoS_{Failure}(CS) = 1 - \prod_{i=1}^{n}(1 - QoS_{Failure}(S_i))$$

$$QoS_{Unavl}(CS) = 1 - \prod_{i=1}^{n}(1 - QoS_{Unavl}(S_i))$$

$$QoS_{Error}(CS) = \sum_{i=1}^{n} QoS_{Error}(S_i)$$

For the calculation of QoS_{Time} and QoS_{Delay}, concept of finding critical path in work flow is applied, method such as *Finding the critical path in a time-constrained workflow*(Son and Kim, 2000) , *Finding Multiple Possible Critical Paths Using Fuzzy PERT* (Chen and Chang, 2001) or *Critical Path Method (CPM)*(Samuel, 2004) can be used to critical path. Given set A that member of service A are services in critical path. QoS_{Time} and QoS_{Delay} will be:

$$QoS_{Time}(CS) = \sum_{S_i \in A} QoS_{Time}(S_i)$$

$$QoS_{Delay}(CS) = \sum_{S_i \in A} QoS_{Delay}(S_i)$$

Due to complexity of workflow, the composite bandwidth will be use the maximum bandwidth required by services.

$$QoS_{Band}(CS) = MAX_{1 \leq i \leq n}(QoS_{Band}(S_i))$$

3.4 Objective function

Objective function is used to evaluate the fitness of composite service. As many attributes are considered, the single unique value is needed for comparison between each possible combination. In framework, QoS of composite service is defined by formula:

$$QoS(X) = \sum_{i=1}^{N} (w_i * QoS_i(X))$$

whereas N=number of attributes; w_i=weight of attribute i^{th}

Our objective is to find composite service that have minimum QoS value, thus objective function will be

$$\min QoS(X) = \min (\sum_{i=1}^{N} (w_i * QoS_i(X)))$$

some constraints are defined for composite service to represent real life constraints.

$$QoS_i(CS) \leq C_i \text{ for each } i \in 1, ..., N$$

whereas N=number of attributes; C_i=constraint of attribute i^{th}

3.5 Selecting web service

QoS function from previous section consists of non linear parameter which make calculation complex. To simplify problem, some assumptions are given 1) suppose that only one possible workflow returned from discovery process 2) composite service is not streaming application. 3) user context is irrelevant. 4) workflow consist only sequential processes. Figure 7 show an example of such a workflow.

Cardinal and nominal scale QoS and non-linear composite QoS ($QoS_{Failure}$, QoS_{Unavl}, QoS_{Band}, QoS_{Sat} and $QoSSec$) are excluded from objective function and used to prune to discovered services. Hence, workflow objective function and constraints are solely linear function, and then 0-1 linear programming model is applied.

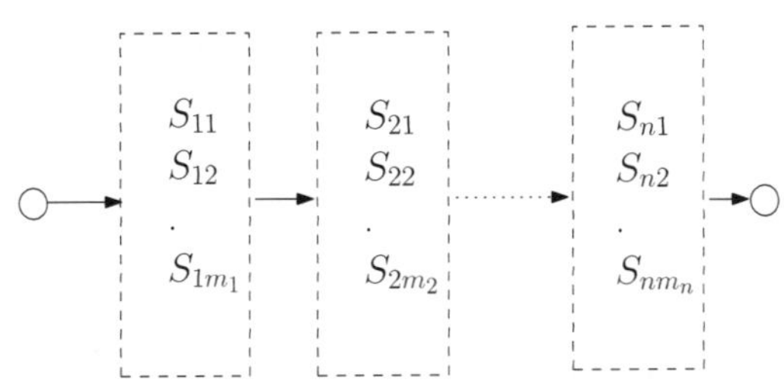

Figure 7: Output from discovery process

After discovery process, set of discovered service is pruned with set of constraints

$\{QoS_{Failure}, QoS_{Unavl}, QoS_{Band}, QoS_{Sat}, QoS_{Sec}\}$.

The workflow consists of n process, each processes there is set or service with size $m_i; 1 \leq i \leq n$ that can fulfill process requirements.

Then we introduce set of variable x_{ij} to represent decision variable.

$$\begin{pmatrix} x_{11} & & x_{n1} \\ \vdots & \ddots & \vdots \\ x_{1k} & & x_{nm_i} \end{pmatrix}$$

The variable x_{ij} is correspond to $S_{ij}; 1 \leq i \leq n$ and $1 \leq j \leq m_i$. Whereas n is number of process. $x_{ij} = 1$ iff service x_{ij} has been selected, otherwise $x_{ij} = 0$

Hence, problem is transformed to linear programming problem:

minimize: $\sum_{i=1}^{n} \sum_{j=1}^{m_i} QoS(S_{ij}) * x_{ij}$

whereas $QoS(S_{ij}) = (w_{Time} * QoS_{Time}(S_{ij})) + (w_{Cost} * QoS_{Cost}(S_{ij}))$

subject to

$$\sum_{j=1}^{m_i} x_{ij} = 1$$

$$x_{ij} \in \{0, 1\}$$

$$QoS_{Time}(S_{ij}) \leq C_{Time}$$

$$QoS_{Cost}(S_{ij}) \leq C_{Cost}$$

4 Update repository information

After composite that have the best *QoS* has been selected and executed, there are processes after finish. There are two cases 1) composite service terminate normally 2) composite service terminate abnormally. In later case, we update service information ($QoS_{Failure}$) in *Repository*. Process will not repeat because of services that makes composite service fail tends to have better *QoS* value than others. As the result, other combination of this service must be excluded and rediscover web services again. In case of composite service terminate normally, service information ($QoS_{Failure}$, and QoS_{Time}) is updated in to *Repository*, and publish composite service to *Web service Registry* with *QoS* information. *QoS* information can be added to WSDL as extension (*Unreaveling the web services: an introduction to SOAP, WSDL, and UDDI*)(Curbera, 2002),using *Semantic Annotations for WSDL* ,or using OWL-S.

5 Related works

There are many related studies about quality of machine translation notably ones include *Automatic Evaluation of Machine Translation Quality Using Longest Common Subsequence and Skip-Bigram Statistics* (Lin and Och, 2004) and *METEOR: An Automatic Metric for MT Evaluation with Improved Correlation with Human Judgments* (Banerjee and Lavie, 2005). There are researches about quality of service in service composition process such as *QoS-Aware Middleware for Web Services Composition - A Qualitative Approach* (Yeom, Yun and Min, 2006). There are two important processes that we do not focus in our framework. The first process is discovery process which are managed by *Discovery Agent* in our framework. Algorithms for discovery services are not included in this paper. There are many related studies in searching non perfect match web service such as *Automate Composition and Reliable Execution of Ad-hoc Processes* (Binder, Constatinescu, Faltings, Haller, and Turker, 2004) and *A software Framework For Matchmaking Based on Semantic Web Technology* (Li and Horrocks, 2003). Other research work as in *Ontology assisted Web services discover* (Zhang and Li, 2005) and *Web Service Discovery via Semantic Association Ranking and Hyperclique Pattern Discovery* (Paliwal, Adam, Xiong and Bornhovd, 2006) use semantic information to discover web services.

The second process is how to search for the optimal quality composite service from all possible combination of services. We can apply linear programming technique as described cutting method in *A lift-and-project cutting plane algorithm for mixed 01 programs* (Balas, Ceria and Cornuejols, 1993) to perform this search task.

6 Conclusion and future work

The main contribution of this paper is to propose a web service based machine translation framework that enhances quality of translation. We present the concept of embedding quality of service information, method to measurement QoS, and calculation of composite translation QoS.

For future work, we plan to work on simplifing the search space, discovery techniques using semantic, mathemetic model for solving integer programming problem, fault tolerance, and implementation of ontology to describe QoS attributes in services.

References

Language Grid. 2011. *Language Grid* http://http://langrid.nict.go.jp/en/index.html

Samuel L. Baker. 2004 *Critical Path Method (CPM)* http://hadm.sph.sc.edu/COURSES/J716/CPM/CPM.html

Jin Hyun Son and Myoung Ho Kim. 2000. *Finding the critical path in a time-constrained workflow* Seventh International Conference on Real-Time Computing Systems and Applications (RTCSA'00) 2000 p. 102

Shyi-Ming Chen and Tao-Hsing Chang. 2001. *Finding Multiple Possible Critical Paths Using Fuzzy PERT* IEEE Transactions on Systems, Man and Cybernetics, Part B,2001

Walter Binder, Ion Constatinescu, Boi Faltings, Klaus Haller, and Can Turker. Barcelona, 2004 2004. *Automate Composition and Reliable Execution of Ad-hoc Processes* Second European Workshop on Multi-Agent Systems (EUMAS)

I. Li and Horrocks. 2003 *A software Framework For Matchmaking Based on Semantic Web Technology* In Proc, 12th Int Conf on the World Wide Web, 2003

Curbera F. 2002. *Unreaveling the web services: an introduction to SOAP, WSDL, and UDDI* IEEE Internet Computing, Vol. 6. No.2,pp. 86-93,2002.

Egon Balas ,Sebastian Ceria and Gerard Cornuejols. 1993 *A lift-and-project cutting plane algorithm for mixed 01 programs* Mathematical Programming, Volume 58, Numbers 1-3 / January, 1993,pp. 295-324

Po Zhang, Juanzi Li. *Ontology assisted Web services discover.* Service-Oriented System Engineering, 2005. IEEE International Workshop, 20-21 October 2005 Page(s):45 - 50

Paliwal, A.V.; Adam, N.R.; Hui Xiong; Bornhovd, C. 2006 *Web Service Discovery via Semantic Association Ranking and Hyperclique Pattern Discovery* Web Intelligence, 2006. WI 2006. IEEE/WIC/ACM International Conference on 18-22 Dec. 2006 Page(s):649 - 652

Issa, H.; Assi, C.; Debbabi, M.; 2006. *QoS-Aware Middleware for Web Services Composition - A Qualitative Approach* Computers and Communications, 2006. ISCC '06. Proceedings. 11th IEEE Symposium on 26-29 June 2006 Page(s):359 - 364

Chin-Yew Lin and Franz Josef Och 2004. *Automatic Evaluation of Machine Translation Quality Using Longest Common Subsequence and Skip-Bigram Statistics.* 42nd Annual Meeting of the Association for Computational Linguistics, Barcelona, Spain, July 21- 26, 2004.

Banerjee, S. and Lavie, A. 2005. *METEOR: An Automatic Metric for MT Evaluation with Improved Correlation with Human Judgments* Workshop on Intrinsic and Extrinsic Evaluation Measures for MT and/or Summarization at the 43rd Annual Meeting of the Association of Computational Linguistics (ACL-2005), Ann Arbor, Michigan, June 2005

The Semantically-enriched Translation Interoperability Protocol

Sven Christian Andrä
ONTRAM Inc.
10 South Third Street
San José, CA 95113, USA
sca@ontram.com

Jörg Schütz
bioloom group
Bahnhofstraße 12
66424 Homburg, Germany
joerg@bioloom.de

Abstract

In this paper, we present the semantically enriched (SE) version of the Translation Interoperability Protocol (TIP). TIP is designed to foster and enable the seamless sharing of data and information between different TMS based on open standards for data representations by means of the TIP Package (TIPP) as transport container. SE-TIP is a research sideline that employs Semantic Web technologies to support modeling identification and interaction of sharing tasks, and uses the Web architecture to ensure extensibility and scalability of the SE approach.

1 Introduction

1.1 User Story

Imagine a small young bio-pharmaceutical organization, say nanopharm, that recently has developed a new nano scale therapy for drug targeting. Their technology has been approved by national and European health administration authorities, and now the company wants to expand their market to several European countries as well as the entire world market. To accomplish this challenge, the company is faced with a huge amount of administrative business tasks, processes and workflows which have to be fulfilled in several languages and adapted to multiple cultures according to local rules and regulations.

Initial tests with freely available machine translation services on the Web have shown promising and even partly acceptable results. However, these results come with a serious lack of an appropriate vocabulary coverage of the bio-pharmaceutical field, and particularly the company's own terminology and style. In addition, general globalization, internationalization, localization and translation (GILT) project management capabilities are missing with these services as well as severe security and trust problems including appropriate and convenient configuration and customization facilities.

Buying and maintaining their own translation automation solution is currently too expensive for the small company, and so they are looking for a Web based solution for their translingual communications needs. The envisioned solution should also support the effective communication with language service providers (LSPs), individual translators, and possible social network services for crowdsourced translation.

In summary, the actual needs and requirements of the nanopharm example enterprise are those of a fully fledged secure Web-scale translation service management framework (TSMF) that requires no software installation, can be personalized easily to suit individual habits and preferences, is secure and extensible, and works fast, reliable and effective in solving multilingual global business challenges, extending the company's value, and helping to decide what translation process size fits their needs in changing environments.

1.2 Ultimate Solution

The envisioned Web-scale TSMF can be seen as an innovative cloud computing application within the broad field of GILT process modeling, automation and intelligence. This framework combines, controls and manages a number of services that are accessible through the Web by intuitive webbrowser interfaces. The services are dedicated particularly to quality, competence and performance in terms of their result delivery, and they enable users to optimize and maximize their trans-

Proceedings of Workshop on Language Resources, Technology and Services in the Sharing Paradigm, pages 24–31,
Chiang Mai, Thailand, November 12, 2011.

lingual communications processes and workflows, and to gain new revenues in existing and new customer relationship operations.

This service scenario might also include the checking and automated streamlining of information content for machine translation readiness, various terminology related operations such as term mining, the deployment of fully automated translation workflows and post-editing tasks to gain optimized quality, as well as the static and dynamic configuration and the management of complete internationalization and localization project life-cycles. Since multiple services are involved within such a framework of services, interoperability between the service connectors and components is key, particularly the sharing of data and metadata, is a necessary and challenging requirement.

1.3 Good Practice Solution

In this paper, we will solely focus on the interoperability of translation related data and metadata between translation management systems (TMS) because this is one of the essential needs and requirements within the broader application scenario of the nanopharm example company. Firstly, the already existing solution of the Translation Interoperability Protocol[1] (TIP) ensures the freedom of tool choice for GILT service buyers, vendors, and individuals within GILT workflows. Secondly, TIP is based on existing standards and best practices for data exchange formats employed in the TIP Package (TIPP) as transport container. Thirdly, the semantically-enriched TIP extension SE-TIP employs Semantic Web technologies for different modeling purposes, and is grounded in the Web architecture to allow for a thorough extensibility and scalability.

2 TIP Package

2.1 Basics

Exchanging and interchanging various types of data between different TMS gains more and more attention in the field of product and media localization and translation. It comprises multiple workflows with various activities and tasks of humans and machines on different data types and formats in tandem with several actors, technologies and tools.

The need interoperability issue arises because a translation buyer, remember the example company, might use other systems and tools for handling and managing language data than the translation vendor LSP, or uses even multiple systems within their enterprise infrastructure. Additionally, there might be different freelance individuals involved in these processes who again employ yet another computational infrastructure, say, mainly based on free or open source software. In either case, lossless data and information sharing is considered a valuable asset in many natural language related processes that deal with terminological data, translation memory content, machine translation systems, etc.

Today, many proprietary solutions of LSPs exist, however, with the ultimate danger of entering into a vendor lock-in. Therefore, over the last two decades several initiatives – public and private – have been working on standardized data representation formats, frameworks and best practices to support the interchange of natural language vocabulary material and translation memory content. But even if we rely on these open standards, they mostly deal with the content part only, and not with associated processing information and general metadata.

2.2 Open Standards and Best Practices

Over the last two decades, a set of open standards related to localization and translation has been developed to support the various data and processing needs in technical communications and documentation of the software and manufacturing industry in close collaboration with internal and external translation services. Today, the most widely accepted open standards in the GILT industry are:

ITS: The Internationalization Tag Set (ITS) is a markup language for the identification of internationalization related aspects in XML documents including terminological and glossary information. The work on ITS is with W3C.

TBX: The Term Base Exchange (TBX) is a means to describe terminological data either as concept-oriented data or flat glossary data in an XML style. After the demise of LISA in February 2011, the continuation of TBX and other localization related standards maintained by LISA is still an open issue. Recently, the GALA localization

[1] TIP is the result of the Interoperability Now! (IN!) initiative of several independent enterprises, which started in the second quarter of 2010.

organization has started a standards initiative in this context.

TMX: The Translation Memory Exchange (TMX) is a collection of translation memory data in possibly multiple languages. The formal means are based on XML; LISA was also responsible for this exchange format.

OLIF: The Open Lexicon Interchange Format (OLIF) is a highly complex description format for lexical material. It has been created to support the needs of NLP tools that operate with linguistic rules for morphological, syntactic and semantic processing, including machine translation (mainly RBMT). OLIF has been pursued by industrial and research organizations and partners such as SAP, SDL/Trados, Systran, DFKI, IAI, etc.

XLIFF: The XML Localization Interchange File Format (XLIFF) is a transport container that stores and carries extracted text through the various steps of a localization process. As such it is the only format that was designed with a process oriented view on the represented data. An XLIFF file is bilingual, i.e. only one source language and one target language are permitted. The work on XLIFF is under the supervision of the OASIS group, and several tools are available for handling the different aspects of XLIFF including editing.

Related Other Standards: Other standards comprise, for example, formats for describing segmentation rules (SRX – Segmentation Rules Exchange, LISA) of natural language expressions, quantitative measures of documents (GMX – Global Information Management Metrics Exchange, LISA), authoring memories (xml:tm – XML-based text memory, OASIS), and the GNU gettext for Portable Objects (PO) in software engineering. Complete frameworks for metamodel markup languages for lexical data and terminology data are LMF (Lexical Markup Framework) and TMF (Terminological Markup Framework) that have been designed and developed within ISO/TC37 (ISO 16642) contexts and the EU project SALT which also initiated the work on TBX.

2.3 Existing Gaps and TIP

The introduced standards for GILT data have all in common that they are markup languages for content data with only a limited support of metadata, mainly for administrative purposes. XLIFF is an exception because it also allows for the specification of process related data and metadata through its support of XML namespaces for non-XLIFF elements and attributes. This approach opens a multitude of possibilities and thus interpretations across applications which also discourages interoperability.

What is needed is a framework that combines content, resource information and workflow information in a coherent and agreed upon or even standardized way with one single interpretation across applications. For each of these types of data we need to provide specifications for identification, representation and interaction to ensure effective interoperability. The aim of TIP is therefore to integrate the description models of the various disruptive GILT technologies and their associated data, and to allow for optimizing their deployment in even disruptive GILT workflows. The main challenging areas in GILT workflows across different industries are:

- coordination and distribution of data and information within and across organization department boundaries in multiple languages
- harmonization and monitoring of translation business processes
- language and cultural specific, i.e. locale specific, challenges with time-to-market delivery issue

TIP and especially SE-TIP combine these technologies through a dynamic object view that links data, resources and possible functions and processes with metadata models. In addition, TIP consuming applications may modify the TIP Package content in an automated way.

2.4 TIP Package Layout

The TIP Package (TIPP) is a container that consists of a TIP *Manifest File* (MF) encoded in XML which includes references to and administrative information about the different TIP objects, and a series of either object files or object folders with object files. The latter structure applies if more than one object file of a given object type is part of the TIPP distribution. As of this writing, we distinguish the following object types with their possible representation formats including the extensions of SE-TIP[2]:

[2] Currently, the TIP, TIPP and XLIFF:doc specifications are under beta review, and they will be presented to the general public at TM Europe 2011 with implementations that also demonstrate the round-trip capabilities of TIP.

- *Translation Object* contains in one file the source language input, and after translation the target language output, both represented in XLIFF:doc[3] as described in (Bly, 2011).
- *Translation Memory Object* is a partial or a complete database extract of already translated and aligned natural language segments in source and target language, and encoded either in TMX or XLIFF. SE-TIP uses an RDF serialization format for TM content.
- *Terminology Object* is either a partial, i.e. relevant for the translation task, or a complete extract of a term database represented in either OLIF or TBX. SE-TIP is experimenting with SKOS and OWL .
- *Reference Object* contains general reference material. TIPP does not specify any data format yet, and in SE-TIP references are modeled in RDF.
- *Workflow Object* encodes process information in RDF (SE-TIP only).
- *Metrics Object* delivers accompanying administrative information such as word counts, pricing, quality, etc. in RDF (SE-TIP only).
- *Style Object* describes translation, editing and general governance rules in RDF (SE-TIP only).

All these object ingredients constitute the entire TIP Package in both flavors. In SE-TIP, the MF information is also encoded in RDF, and maintains direct links to the TIP objects.

2.5 TIP Supported Formats

When building distributed applications the employed formats of the resources matter mostly. The meaning, or semantics, behind the data and information in a resource must be understood by all parties involved in an interaction in order to successfully achieve a business goal. In this section, we explore and discuss in detail the formats that are supported in TIP with a particular emphasis on SE-TIP. In the following sections, the term *data* means the raw and uninterpreted streams of bits, *information* refers to the interpretation of the data within the context of a particular application domain or a specific task, and *knowledge* represents the understanding of a domain after collecting, analyzing, and reasoning over the available data and information.

The XML Case and XLIFF:doc

Now consider, for example, a text translation task of our example company nanopharm with a particular set of vocabulary and a certain style of localization, which has to be executed in a specific sequence of steps and in compliance with already existing translations stored in TMX format to ensure natural language consistency on different levels.

The description of each step of this translation task and the sequential ordering of the steps can be encoded in several ways. Nowadays an XML based representation is favored because it explicitly expresses hierarchical structures, and is often self-describing due to its textual nature. This allows us to separate the structured data and the represented information in terms of the data's interpretation.

This idea has been the general guidance for the design of XLIFF which in real-life applications, however, turned out as being too broadly specified in some cases, and too narrowly in others. On the one hand, because some XLIFF definitions are unclear and provide no orthogonality, or different mechanisms apply for the same concept, it is often impossible to support the specifications adequately across XLIFF tool implementations and interchanging applications. On the other hand, flexibility in storing, for example, translation project information, terminological data, or particular software contexts of user interfaces is missing or is too narrowly specified in order to being effectively applied in real-life translation projects.

Therefore, in the context of TIP the streamlining of XLIFF was a major task because it appeared easier to fully specify a usable and workable core subset of XLIFF than to invent the wheel anew. The XLIFF:doc (Bly, 2011) of the TIP approach takes care of the mentioned shortcomings, and directly supports interoperability between TMS.

Within SE-TIP we aim at an even tighter integration of the TIPP objects through link relations in order to provide a semantic context for

[3] XLIFF:doc is a robust, fully documented subset of XLIFF 1.2 with the namespace extension "dx:" designed within the IN! initiative to ensure interoperability between TMS.

better controlling and monitoring workflows and resources. The use of links and their relation to objects is similar to (software) contracts, which also ensure the fulfillment of the interoperability requirement. In TIP, we still have the unsatisfactorily need to employ some level of human involvement. In order to accomplish full machine automation, we have to enrich such contracts for machines particularly on the level of choice of information representation to ensure the ability to share that information in an interoperable manner.

Semantic Web Case of TIP Package Objects

The main challenge in our interoperability scenario is to interpret information consistently across TMS applications. In this context, we use the term *semantics* to refer to the shared understanding that is defined by the TIPP objects in a contract-like way, and by which the meaning of, for example, a sequence of request-response exchanges, or the way in which a resource representation should be interpreted and used is modeled unambiguously.

In the following, we distinguish between the general approach of computing based on semantic technologies, such as machine learning, ontologies, inferencing, etc., and the Semantic Web (SW), which is the term used to refer to a specific ecosystem of technologies, such as RDF, RDFS, RDFa, OWL, etc. maintained by W3C. We only provide some brief insights on how we utilize RDF and OWL as well as SPARQL for SE-TIPP object representations and access because a fully fledged introduction to the SW technologies is beyond the scope of this paper – see (Schütz, 2010) for their employment within the business process and business performance field.

One could ask why should we use SW technologies because they are apparently very similar to a pure XML representation? The strength of RDF with its model of representing data as a directed, labeled graph lies in its processing model and the use of Uniform Resource Identifiers (URIs) to build statements, i.e. all aspects related to any TMS application and the associated processes can be dynamically described by using RDF statements about resources and their interrelationships.

Statements in RDF are of the form [subject, predicate, object], also known as triples, and they are quite near to a natural language expression which makes them evenly consumable by humans and machines. Subject and predicate of an RDF statement are always URIs, and an object can be either a URI or a literal. RDF also permits the specification of complex expressions based on the simple s-p-o schema. Within the SE-TIPP object scenario, additional statements can be either embedded directly in an already existing TIPP object representation or delivered to consumers through yet another object incarnation. In addition, RDF makes it easy to combine information from different graphs, as long as matching URIs are used to ensure the identity relationship. This allows software libraries to bring together the known statements about a resource in a variety of levels and complexity.

In Figure 1 the following simple natural language statements, which describe two qualities of a fictional task of our example company, are represented in the graph notation of RDF:

- *task 1* has *taskname term-harvest* (s-p-o statement with URIs only)
- *task 1* has *costbase 2.0* (s-p-o statement with a literal in object position)

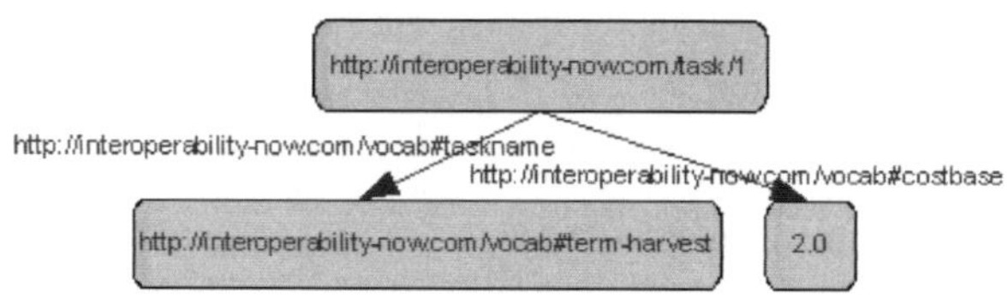

Figure 1: RDF Graph - Part of Task Description

The complete task description of task 1 with the additional information slot "costitem" that accounts for "wordcount," "maxsize," and "reference" in RDF/XML notation is depicted in Figure 2.

```
<?xml version="1.0"?>
<!DOCTYPE rdf:RDF [<!ENTITY xsd "http://www.w3.org/2001/XMLSchema#">]>
<rdf:RDF xmlns:rdf="http://www.w3.org/1999/02/22-rdf-syntax-ns#"
      xmlns:interop="http://interoperability-now.org/vocab#">

   <rdf:Comment>This graph represents a simple Interoperability-Now task</rdf:Comment>
   <rdf:Description rdf:about="http://interoperability-now.org/task/1">
      <interop:taskname rdf:resource="http://interoperability-now.org/vocab#term-harvest"/>
      <interop:costbase rdf:datatype="&xsd;decimal">2.0</interop:costbase>
      <interop:costitem rdf:resource="_:item1" />
   </rdf:Description>

   <rdf:Description rdf:about="_:item1">
      <interop:wordcount rdf:resource="http://interoperability-now.org/vocab#all" />
      <interop:maxsize rdf:resource="http://interoperability-now.org/vocab#full" />
      <interop:reference rdf:resource="http://interoperability-now.org/vocab#harvesting />
   </rdf:Description>
</rdf:RDF>
```

Figure 2: RDF Statements for Task Description

Additional information can be integrated easily in such an RDF representation. For example, the representation of the task might also state that the URI representing the domain choice "biopharm" is associated with the corresponding label "biopharmaceutical" in English and the appropriate label "biopharmazeutisch" in German by using a link to a vocabulary specification; that the company's origin is a small town in Germany by using a geographical name service; and that its application domain is "drug targeting" by using a proprietary and shareable biotechnology vocabulary.

The processing model of RDF defines a set of basic rules and constructs that software applications can use as the building blocks for constructing the objects they might exchange. Because these constructs can also be used as the basis for developing vocabularies of concepts, such as "order," "cost," "metric," "wordcount," etc., which we employ to describe particular task qualities within our TMS application, they might evenly describe the meaning of certain XLIFF constructs which are beyond the XLIFF:doc specifications.

As such, the RDF approach allows us to define task-specific information by means of employing vocabularies for different purposes and specified in the Web Ontology Language (OWL) of W3C. For example, similar to the case that due to the absence of a widely used bio-pharmaceutical industry terminology, nanopharm can define a vocabulary that only applies within its own specific localization tasks. Such a vocabulary can be extended to provide a shared knowledge base that ensures effective interoperability and assures a common understanding of the employed SE-TIPP objects[4]. In both cases, an application-specific ontology[5] is defined.

2.6 SE-TIP Information Processing

In this section, we introduce the processing of SE-TIPP objects, and how applications can access the information encoded in these object data elements, i.e. s-p-o triples. We distinguish two main TMS application scenarios with each having its own SE-TIPP processing style:

- An application that becomes aware of SE-TIPP and starts to consume, understand and interpret the package content in the intended way.
- An application that accepts SE-TIPP and just routes it through a particular workflow.

The former application scenario represents an active and dynamic processing style that accomplishes changes the originally delivered SE-TIPP objects in a controlled manner, whereas the latter scenario is a passive processing style with only a delivery and routing functionality.

A particular SE-TIPP within a given workflow always contains an information record of the applications in the form of additional s-p-o statements in the workflow objects, which are obligatory to ensure full traceability, control and monitoring, and possibly in the other objects, which extend or amend the represented data and information with, for example, revised and new translation memory and terminological content.

As we have seen, RDF and OWL can be combined into a single information graph of s-p-o triples. To access and to query these statements by matching a graph or subgraph, the W3C language SPARQL was designed to support the RDF data model with a query language for graphs. The result of a SPARQL query may consist of a set of resources and the interrelationships that satisfy the given conditions, answers to true and false questions based on the encoded knowledge, or entirely new graphs that are generated by inferring new triples from the existing set of statements – inference is the only mechanism at work in the SW context. Figure 3 shows an example SPARQL query which makes use of the publicly available vocabulary "FoaF" (Friend-of-a-Friend) to describe attributes of persons such as "person" and "age."

```
PREFIX foaf: <http://xmlns.com/foaf/0.1/>
PREFIX nanopharm: <http://nanopharm.com/vocab#>
PREFIX xsd: <http://www.w3.org/2001/XMLSchema#>

SELECT ?name
FROM <http://internal.nanopharm.com/translators.rdf>
WHERE { ?x foaf:name ?name;
      foaf:age ?age.
    FILTER (xsd:positiveInteger(?age) > 30) }
```

Figure 3: Example SPARQL Query

2.7 SE-TIP Security and Trust

In this section, we discuss the aspects of SE-TIP that are related to:

[4] The Semantic Web community refers to such vocabularies as ontologies.

[5] A less complex formal means for terminology data is SKOS (Simple Knowledge Organizing System) of W3C. The difference between SKOS and OWL is their intention for different purposes: OWL allows the explicit modeling of a domain, whereas SKOS provides vocabulary and navigational structure.

- Confidentiality which keeps SE-TIP information private while in transit or storage.
- Integrity which prevents SE-TIP information from being changed undetectably.
- Identity which authenticates the parties involved in interactions.
- Trust which authorizes a party to interact with a package in a prescribed manner.

For these areas, the Web community has developed a number of higher-order protocols that address the issues of identity and trust which sit atop of HTTP, and allow systems to interoperate securely. HTTP natively supports authentication to establish identity, and authorization to basically help to establish trust. In a SE-TIP application, we can secure access to the SE-TIP resources with these capabilities. For instance, we may allow only authorized "consumers" to access a terminology resources. Privileged resources are accessed by providing certain credentials in an authorization header.

The integrity of SE-TIP Package objects is maintained through the built-in control and monitoring capabilities which allow for a dynamic "supervision" of the involved processes without influencing the actual processing of the shared data and information. As such, even the transitivity of application or process sequences is guaranteed as long as the information records maintained by consuming applications are not exposed to being attacked or harmed (vulnerability).

Additionally, package objects might be encrypted for privacy reasons; for example, to fully secure a company's terminology and translation memory content, and to grant access to these resources only to trusted "consumers".

2.8 Related Work

Currently, we are not aware of any directly related work to SE-TIP. Most approaches in GILT environments are still dealing with the syntactic level. There are also other container based approach emerging but none of these envisiones to employ explicit semantic descriptions. In the field of cloud computing, the community discusses similar aspects for modeling and representation purposes including aspects of security and trust.

Because SE-TIP maintains workflow information as one essential resource, there is also an indirect relationship to business process management (BPM) and business process intelligence (BPI) as well as to SOA, and particularly to the area of governance which is reflected in SE-TIP through the objects that deal with references and style rules.

2.9 SE-TIP Next Steps and Future

One of the advantages of SW technologies is that we can build graphs of information facts without having to decide on a predefined and fixed data schema as it is the case when designing information structure schemes. Sometimes we might not even have a schema for our information model at all, see, for example, the ongoing discussions on how to effectively organize terminologies and translation memories in a sharable manner. Unlike relational database technologies, RDF allows us to combine information in arbitrary ways, without having to adhere to a data layout that is defined and fixed in advance of an application's deployment.

To fully employ the power of RDF, OWL, etc. in interoperability scenarios, RDF in attributes (RDFa) might fill an initially existing technology gap by bringing RDF to pure XML based approaches. While RDFa is targeted primarily at the human use of the Web, we believe it is also useful as a first step for understanding and building distributed Web-scale applications in combination with our SE-TIP approach.

The premise of RDFa is that Web documents can convey both presentation and semantic information. Through the use of XML attributes, presentation constructs are annotated with semantic information. This allows software applications other than webbrowsers to process and reason over the embedded information. As an example, Figure 4 exemplifies how an XHTML nanopharm translation ticket – here an offer for a translation task – could be presented in a way that allows both the person Joanna Da Rui and a software application to process the ticket appropriately. In the example, the relevant data elements are highlighted with a bold font.

A webbrowser can render this information for a human to read, while a software application that is part of a machine-to-machine interaction can extract the necessary information for making forward progress in a business process involving a translation offer for an individual.

```
<?xml version="1.0" encoding="UTF-8"?>
<!DOCTYPE html PUBLIC "-//W3C//DTD XHTML+RDFa 1.0//EN"
               "http://www.w3.org/MarkUp/DTD/xhtml-rdfa-1.dtd">
<html xmlns="http://www.w3.org/1999/xhtml"
    xmlns:nanopharm="http://nanopharm.com/vocab#"
    xmlns:foaf="http://xmlns.com/foaf/0.1/"
    version="XHTML+RDFa 1.0" xml:lang="en">
  <head>
    <title>Glocalization Task Request</title>
    <!-- Digitally signed thumbprint of a ticket number -->
    <meta property="nanopharm:ticketnumber" content="1234-56" />
  </head>
  <body>
    <h1>Receipt for Translation Delivery 1234</h1>
    <p about="nanopharm:ticket-recipient">Dear
      <span property="foaf:name" typeof="foaf:Person">Joanne Da Rui</span>,
    </p>
    <p about="nanopharm:translation-product">Thank you for your recent translation
      service. Since you have been always an excellent foreign language expert,
      we would like to offer you an additional <span property="nanopharm:taskname">
      Glocaltask</span>.
    </p>
  </body>
</html>
```

Figure 4: RDFa Translation Ticket Example

For example, we might leverage RDFa statements in nanopharm's XML documents in order to avoid the initially expensive transition – in terms of costs and time – to fully fledged RDF, OWL, etc. for translation related interactions. Such a step-by-step move to SW technologies might be appropriate to introduce initial TIP based applications. In such a scenario the TIPP objects would be represented in RDFa instead of a RDF, OWL, etc.

Last but not least, the introduced approaches to interoperability between TMS obviously allow for a seamless integration into the Web architecture (Fielding, 2000, and Richardson, 2008).

3 Conclusions and Perspective

In this paper, we have presented a semantically enriched version of TIP which further extends this solution to overcome the interoperability shortcomings of todays GILT industry. Based on the needs and requirements of the example company nanopharm, we have outlined the capabilities and potentials of the SE-TIP solution, and also shown that it is very important that a shared understanding of exchanged data and information does not get translated into a shared way of processing that data and information. Participants in loosely coupled distributed applications, as it is the use case with different TMS, shall remain free to deal with the data and information they receive in any way and by any tool they wish, but with the ability of a shared understanding.

Natural language specifications provide a mechanism for designers and developers to agree on the meaning of the data they exchange and share. However, as the volume, complexity and scale of distributed data and applications grow exponentially, it is important to consider a representation of information that employs machine-processable formats. Today, SW technologies are ready and mature to support the definition of data formats, protocols, and contracts.

SE-TIPP contains the data, information and knowledge that is necessary to fulfill the GILT tasks of nanopharm in an effective and efficient way encoded in SW formalisms and processable by machines. This encoding model provides the representation basis to ensure full interoperability based on a shared understanding of the resource descriptions. In addition, SE-TIP can also be seen as an enabler of forthcoming cloud-based services and sustainable language resources ecosystems (see Andrä and Schütz, 2009; and Andrä and Schütz, 2010).

Acknowledgments

Thanks for support in various ways, and valuable comments on the formal and representational aspects are due the members of the »Interoperability-Now!« initiative as well as the discussions with other community efforts in similar directions. Thanks are also due to the anonymous reviewers of this paper.

References

Sven C. Andrä and Jörg Schütz. 2009. MT Bazaar: Translation Ecosystems in the Cloud. In *Proceedings of the 12th Machine Translation Summit*, pp. 395-402, Ottawa, Ontario, Canada, August 26-30.

Sven C. Andrä and Jörg Schütz. 2010. Effectual MT within a Translation Workflow Panopticon. In *Proceedings of the 9th Conference of the Association for Machine Translation in the Americas (AMTA),* Denver, Colorado, USA, October 31-November 5.

Micah Bly. 2011. XLIFF Representation Guide for Documents. Internal Working Paper of the Interoperability-Now! Initiative. Draft v0.9.0, August.

Roy Thomas Fielding. 2000. Architectural Styles and the Design of Network-based Software Architectures. PhD Dissertation, University of California, Irvine, USA.

Leonard Richardson. 2008. Introducing Real-World REST. Presentation at Qcon (particularly: Act 3), San Francisco, California, USA, November 19-21.

Jörg Schütz. 2010. Semantic Technologies in Multilingual Business Intelligence. Invited Talk at the 1st Multilingual Web W3C Workshop, Madrid, Spain, October 26-27.

Interoperability and technology for a language resources factory

Marc Poch
UPF / Barcelona, Spain
marc.pochriera@upf.edu

Núria Bel
UPF / Barcelona, Spain
nuria.bel@upf.edu

Abstract

This document describes some of the technological aspects of a project devoted to the creation of a factory for language resources. The project's objectives are explained, as well as the idea to create a distributed infrastructure of web services. This document focuses on two main topics of the factory: (1) the technological approaches chosen to develop the factory, i.e. software, protocols, servers, etc. (2) and Interoperability as the main challenge is to permit different NLP tools work together in the factory. This document explains why XCES and GrAF are chosen as the main formats used for the linguistic data exchange.

1 A factory for language resources

1.1 Introduction

A strategic challenge for today's globalised economy is to overcome language barriers through technological means. In particular, Machine Translation (MT) systems are expected to have a significant impact on the management of multilingualism. This project addresses the most critical aspect of MT: the so-called language-resource bottleneck. Although MT technologies may consist of language independent engines, they depend on the availability of language-dependent knowledge for their real-life implementation, i.e., they require Language Resources. In order to supply MT for every pair of languages, every domain, and every text genre, appropriate language resources covering all of these aspects must be found, processed and supplied to MT developers. At present, this is mostly done by hand.

The objective of the project is to build a factory of Language Resources that automates the stages involved in the acquisition, production, updating and maintenance of language resources required by MT systems, and by other applications based on Language Technologies, and within the time required. This automation will cut down cost, time and human effort significantly. These reductions of costs and time are the only way to guarantee the continuous supply of Language Resources that Machine Translation and other Language Technologies will be demanding in the multilingual world.

1.2 Web services and workflows

The idea behind the factory is to help users to create complex chains of components which accomplish concrete tasks, i.e. "crawl the web and align text" or "extract text from PDF files and get the Part of Speech (PoS) tagging". These complex chains are called workflows.

Every component is in charge of a concrete task, i.e. "tokenization", "pdf to text conversion", "PoS tagging", etc. and will be deployed as a web service.

Web services (sometimes called application services) are services (usually including some combination of programming and data, but may possibly include human interaction as well) made available from a web server for users or other connected programs.

The technology behind web services is based on different protocols, servers and programming languages. It's continuously growing and evolving due to its massive use. This growth and immense amount of users has "forced" the technology to be open and very interoperable.

Before web services, every researcher or laboratory needed installation and maintenance of the tools. Now, with web services, only the service provider needs to have deep knowledge of the software installation and maintenance, allowing many users to benefit from this work. Researchers can focus on their tasks on a high level without the effort to work with the tools, they only need a web service client or workflow editor to call different services and get the results.

Proceedings of Workshop on Language Resources, Technology and Services in the Sharing Paradigm, pages 32–40, Chiang Mai, Thailand, November 12, 2011.

1.3 Technologies state of the art

Before the first development began in our project, an analysis of existing technologies was conducted. Some technologies were tested and studied to verify their features, ease-of use, installation and maintenance issues. The idea was to find the tools, protocols, programming languages, etc. which could provide more features with user-friendly interfaces at a low cost while also considering ease of installation, maintenance, computer science knowledge required and the learning curve involved working with such tools.

Finally a concrete option from the Bioinformatics field was chosen to be used and adapted to work with NLP because of its numerous advantages.

2 Bioinformatics: myGrid approach

The myGrid [1] team, led by Professor Carole Goble[2] of the School of Computer Science at the University of Manchester [3] UK, is a research group focusing on e-Science. The team is formed with different institutions and people from different disciplines together in an international environment.

The myGrid team works to develop a suite of tools designed to help scientists with the creation of e-laboratories and have been used in domains as diverse as systems biology, social science, music, astronomy, multimedia and chemistry. These tools have been adopted by a large number of institutions.

The most relevant tools developed by the myGrid team are explained in the following sections.

2.1 Web Services (Soaplab)

MyGrid makes use of Soaplab (and its new version Soaplab2) to deploy already existing command line tools as web services. Soaplab is a free software package under an Apache License, Version 2.0 based on metadata.

A web service provider can deploy a command line tool as a web service using Soaplab without any software programming. Soaplab only requires a metadata file used to describe the inputs, outputs, and parameters of the tool.

[1] http://www.mygrid.org.uk/

[2] http://www.mygrid.org.uk/about-us/people/core-mygrid-team/carole-goble/

[3] http://www.manchester.ac.uk/

2.2 Workflow editor (Taverna)

Taverna[4] is an open source application that allows the user to create high-level workflows that integrate different resources into a single analysis. Such analyses can be seen in the bioinformatics field as simulation experiments which can be reproduced, tuned and easily shared with other researchers.

An advantage of using workflows is that the researcher doesn't need to have background knowledge of the technical aspects involved in the experiment. The researcher creates the workflow based on "functionalities" (every web service provides a function) instead of dealing with tools, software, etc.

2.3 The Registry (Biocatalogue)

BioCatalogue[5] is a registry of curated biological Web Services where users, researchers and curators can register, annotate and monitor Web Services.

BioCatalogue is used as a single registration point for web service providers and is used by researchers to annotate and search services. The objective is to join the entire community together to obtain high quality services, annotations, monitoring data, etc.

BioCatalogue features service filtering by tags on services, operations, inputs, and outputs, as well as by providers, submitters, and locations. It supports annotation of services by tags, user comments and text description. These annotations can take the form of free text, tags, terms from selected ontology and example values.

Users can perform all of these tasks in a specially designed user-friendly web 2.0 interface.

2.4 Sharing experiments (myExperiment)

MyExperiment is a social network where researchers and professionals can share their workflows. Moreover, they can share complete experiments: a workflow, input data, parameters, comments, etc. Users can find, share and annotate workflows and files in a virtual environment especially designed to share expertise and avoid reinvention. MyExperiment also allows users to create closed groups to work on specific topics while publishing their work on a save environment.

[4] http://www.taverna.org.uk

[5] http://www.biocatalogue.org

3 Using myGrid tools to work NLP

MyGrid tools have been adopted by many projects, researchers, etc. and have been used in very different domains with success. Our project aims to use and adapt these bioinformatics' tools to work with NLP. These tools have been chosen among others because of their successful histories, flexibility, and ease of use (from the point of view of the web service provider, user and researcher).

The project is in the second phase of its factory development. In the first phase, several NLP tools were deployed as web services and a Biocatalogue instance was prepared to be used as the Registry. When the users were able to find and test the web services it was time to combine them to create complex workflows. Some guidelines have been developed to assist users on the best way to design workflows for the project.

For the second phase of the project, workflows are developed in a more robust way and they can handle larger amounts of data using some special techniques from Soaplab and Taverna. It was then deemed necessary to share workflows. To this aim, a myExperiment instance has been deployed and is being used to present the workflows designed inside the project, as well as its improvements or newer versions.

In the second phase of the project larger experiments are being used challenging the tools and protocol robustness to long lasting tasks and large data files. Some tools have been modified to better suit these tasks, for example: Soaplab, which had a technical problem regarding a concrete scenario of web service technology. The following sections are devoted to describe this adaptation of the Bioinformatics tools to the NLP tasks.

3.1 Creating NLP web services with Soaplab

There are many existing tools for NLP; most of them are command line applications and scripts. Some of them require good computer skills to be installed and maintained. The idea behind web services is to offer these tools to users who will then be able to use them without dealing with installation issues, maintenance, etc.

However, the service provider will have to deal with installation and maintenance of the tools while also needing the necessary computer skills to deploy web services: server installation and configuration, programming language knowledge to develop the web service, etc.

Typical web service technologies (SOAP) require some Java programming and other good programming skills to deploy a web service in a production environment: multiple users, synchronous and asynchronous calls, provenance data handling, error handling, etc. The aim of Soaplab[6] is to easily deploy command line applications as a web service. Soaplab can be used without programming skills; it requires only server installation and maintenance (Apache Tomcat for example) and Soaplab configuration know-how.

Since interoperability is a crucial issue for the project, the first adaptation of Soaplab was basically to develop some concrete rules which must be followed by all partners. A common interface was designed for most of the tools (it will be explained later) to guarantee that all web services share the same naming convention and same kind of parameters (URL or a stream of characters).

3.2 Improving Soaplab for large data

Soaplab has proven to be a very useful tool, not only to easily deploy command line tools as a web service but to handle large data too. When client software makes a request to a web service, Soaplab or any other one, waits for its response. All clients have a timeout to stop waiting in case there's an error. This timeout can be a problem for long lasting workflows, which can be avoided with polling[7] techniques.

All of the polling techniques are already programmed in Soaplab and can be easily used from Taverna (with the "Soaplab plug-in"). However, a problem was found during the first tests with large files. When output data files were bigger than 2 MB soaplab web services failed to give their response to Taverna. This only happened when using the plug-in so it could be avoided by calling web services without it. However, most of our workflows were designed to be used with the plug-in because of its advantages: smaller workflows to do the same tasks and polling parameters are easily tuned.

Therefore, it was decided to realize a deeper study of the problem. All of the Soaplab outputs were configured to be sent inside the message between the client and the web service in two ways: as a stream of characters and a URL. This

[6] http://soaplab.sourceforge.net/soaplab2

[7] Iterative method used to make continuous requests to a server to check whether a task has finished avoiding timeouts.

was causing messages to be too big. To avoid this, Soaplab source code has been modified to add a size limit parameter to only use URLs (and not the character stream) as outputs when the data size is bigger than this limit. This solution has proven to be useful and it has increased network use efficiency because a lot less data is being transmitted.

3.3 The Registry

BioCatalogue is a Ruby on Rails web application and it's free under the BSD License[8]. An instance of BioCatalogue has been installed on a server to be used as the Registry for the project and it has been modified and adapted to suit NLP requirements: The web interface has been changed to include color changes, logos, etc. For example, the BioCatalogue instance is tailored to the bioinformatics field with "service categories" such as "Genomics" or "Biostatistics" which are used to classify web services. In the PANACEA registry "service categories" have been changed to NLP relevant categories including "Morphosyntactic Tagging" or "Tokenization".

3.4 Taverna

Taverna is the workflow editor and manager in myGrid environment. It hasn't been adapted or modified to be used in our project. However, it has been tested in numerous situations to guarantee ease of use and interoperability between our web services.

There are many different ways to chain components in Taverna and many parameters to be set. Users can connect Soaplab web services using character streams or URL and there are several parameters used for "polling" which should be taken into account. When dealing with large data it's important to design workflows with some correctly set error handling parameters and with some parallelization option to increase total workflow throughput. As a result of these tests, some guidelines and tutorials have been developed to assist workflow designers. For instance, it is recommended to use URLs to transfer data between components.

3.5 MyExperiment

The MyExpermient instance has recently been deployed and it is still under testing. Thus, no major changes or adaptations have been done. However, it is proving to be very useful and it is fulfilling the project expectation for a portal designed to share workflows.

4 Interoperability

This new architecture based on web services introduced a new paradigm in NLP tools: users don't need to install and perform the maintenance of the tools. As soon as the first web services were ready to be used and were easily discovered using the Registry, users wanted to try them. The web interfaces facilitate the first contact with new tools and help users get used to them.

The next step was soon required by users: chain web services to create complex workflows. Interoperability became a fundamental necessity for the factory. Workflows cannot be made if the designer doesn't know how to connect inputs and outputs or the tools don't "understand" each other.

This interoperability need was foreseen on the design phase of the project. There are two levels of interoperability that need to be addressed in a factory based on web services: (1) the data being transferred between components must follow a concrete format. Tools must be able to process this format which is being transferred across the factory. This data object was called Travelling Object (TO) because of the distributed nature of the factory (web services are deployed in different locations across Europe). (2) The other aspect is the parameters of the web services. All web services must use the same naming convention for parameters, not only to help developers but for automatic processes to check compatibility, etc. However, some technical aspects of these parameters also needed to be established. For example if the parameter is optional or mandatory. To this aim, it was decided to create a Common Interface (CI) for all web services deployed to work in the factory.

4.1 Common Interface

Tools are very different depending on the functionality they try to fulfill and so are their parameters. A general web service CI has been designed for different functionalities like PoS tagging, tokenization, lemmatization, alignment, etc. The idea is to have a common parameters definition for all web services providing a specific functionality i.e. two different PoS taggers will be deployed as web services using the same mandatory parameters.

On the other hand, tools have particular and very concrete idiosyncrasies, even when they are

[8] Terms of use: http://beta.biocatalogue.org/termsofuse

used for the same functionality. The use of a CI should not make the tool lose some of its particular parameters. To this aim, the designed CI establishes that all particular parameters of a tool must be configured as optional parameters.

The final idea is that all web services, for a given functionality, use the same mandatory parameters so they can be easily replaced. For example, all "Pos Tagging" web services must have two mandatory parameters: "input" and "language". The CI is even more concrete, "language" parameter must use ISO-639 and "input" parameter must have two options two send data: as a character stream or URL.

All of these specifications and designs are presented in a XML schema and online documentation for easy access to all the information. Web service providers can use the XML schema to deploy their web services even if they don't use Soaplab and all of them will be CI compliant.

4.2 Travelling Object

Two web services can be chained making use of the CI. Output parameters of the first component can be easily connected to the second component inputs following the CI naming convention and data type (stream or URL). However, this is not enough. To guarantee interoperability web services must be able to work with the received data format.

There have been relevant proposals made by the Language Resources (LR) community to reach a consensus about a format to represent annotated corpora. The Linguistic Annotation Framework (LAF) (Ide and Romary, 2004) is an ISO standard proposal which can be used as the starting point for a standard data model in the project. After LAF, standardization efforts have been focused on concrete annotation types and they are at different stages of development: for morphosyntactic annotations there is the Morphosyntactic Annotation Framework (MAF) (Clément and Villemonte de la Clergerie, 2005), for syntactic annotations the Syntactic Annotation Framework (SynAF) (Declerck, 2006) and for semantic annotations the Semantic Annotation Framework (SemAF) (Lee et al. 2007). However it has been observed that these proposals have not been widely used. Other relevant projects have adapted some of these proposals to its concrete needs. KYOTO project (ICT-211423) needed particular aspects found on LAF, MAF and SynAF which are really difficult to combine. Thus, a new annotation framework was designed to be compatible with LAF and with some benefits from MAF and SynAF. The KYOTO Annotation Framework (KAF) (Agirre et al. 2009) is a layered stand-off format for concrete annotations. Another project which was facing a similar situation was D-SPIN (Heid, 2008). The approach was much more practical and a new XML format was proposed and designed from scratch which is compatible with LAF as well.

All these options, even those concrete adaptations from other projects, required considerable resources before they could be implemented on the factory. As it was mentioned before, for the first phase of the project only PoS tagging annotations were needed as well as the bilingual data processing capabilities. Nevertheless, the interoperability requirement of the factory made it mandatory to find a common format for the data representation soon. Thus, for the first phase of development, it was agreed upon to find an already existing format to be used as the TO, which represented the minimum change or conversion process from the in-house formats used by our tools. More complex representations and stand-off annotation were left for the next phase of the factory development.

Most of the deployed tools were using the usual vertical in-line formats with no header or metadata at all. The Corpus Encoding Standard for XML (XCES[9]) was chosen to be the first version of the Travelling Object (TO1) because of its simplicity and fulfillment of the aforementioned requirements.

4.2.1 Travelling Object 1: XCES

Although most of the deployed tools don't use an XML format, it was considered to be the best option due to its numerous advantages, such as XML schemas, transformations, complex path queries, etc.

XCES is the XML version of CES (Ide et al., 2000) which is a part of EAGLES guidelines for corpus representation to work in natural language processing applications. XCES documents used in the factory make use of the "header" and the "text" tags proposed. Thanks to the header, TO1 can store metadata to annotate the origin of the document, its title, the date, some key words, the language and some annotations to keep track of the web services which have processed the document. The "text" part of the XML contains the data itself. Depending of the level of data annota-

[9] www.xces.org

tion, this part has different versions. The basic and PoS versions are presented here.

The basic representation follows the idea that text is basically divided in paragraphs. Thus, a "p" tag is used for every paragraph on the source data. This representation is very straightforward considering that most of the data being used in the project is crawled from the web and cleaned afterwards.

For the first phase of the project, only annotations up to PoS tagging were considered so there was no need for stand-off annotations. Since the idea was to make the easiest move from the in-house formats of the tools to the TO1 tags "s" for sentences and "t" for tokens were used. Information of the "word", "tag" and "lemma" is stored in the attributes of the token tag.

There are several tools deployed as web services, which are used to process bilingual corpora. CesAlign is a concrete XCES file which has been used to create the links between two different XCES documents. It can be used to align documents, paragraphs, sentences, tokens, etc. Thus sentence and word aligners can use it to represent their respective results using the TO1 format.

At the end of the first phase of the project converters had been deployed as web services to transform in-house formats to the TO1 and backward. Those converters were used to build workflows for sentence and word alignment, PoS tagging annotation and other complex functionalities working with crawled data or plain text.

4.2.2 Travelling Object 2: GrAF

For the second version of the factory the idea is to include more complex annotations according to the new web services. "Chunking" and "dependency parsing" annotations for example make the TO1 deprecated for these concrete tasks. The idea was to find an already existing standard format representation. This format needed to use stand-off annotation and be as flexible as possible due to the multiple in-house formats used by the tools.

As mentioned before, there is still an open discussion in the community about how to represent annotated corpora. The idea was to find a standard format compatible with already existing ISO standards which was flexible enough to be used to encode various in-house formats like a data container.

The Graph Annotation Format (Ide and Sudermam, 2007) is the XML serialization of LAF (ISO 24612, 2009). GrAF can be used as a container for different annotation types with variable complexity. Its flexibility makes it suitable for most tools already deployed on the factory and the more complex annotations that will be deployed soon. This is due to the fact that GrAF specifies how to make annotations but not which are their names or content. It is focused on the syntactic consistency of annotations rather than their semantic consistency. There are other standardization efforts focused on providing sets of data categories and their definitions to finally obtain the desired semantic consistency but this is not the aim of GrAF. This means that a certain level of annotation can be encoded or extracted from GrAF documents regardless the annotations content. However, it must be taken into account, that this doesn't signify the annotations are comparable.

One clear advantage of using GrAF container capabilities is that there no need to make any modification or adaptation to the format. Other projects and format proposals required schema adaptation and some modifications from the original while our project is going to use GrAF as it is: with no modifications at all. Another advantage of using GrAF is that cesAlign still can be used for bilingual corpora. Thus, all tools developed to work with cesAlign documents need no updates and will be used together with GrAF for bilingual workflows.

The project is now under the second phase of development and the necessary converters to work with GrAF are being developed. Some GrAF examples have been created to be used as models using some in-house format example data of some of the already deployed web services. These examples have been developed with PoS tagging, dependency parsing and other annotation types. To illustrate how GrAF can be used as a pivot format, capable to contain different annotations and tool idiosyncrasies, three GrAF examples can be found in the Appendix. The same sentence has been processed by three PoS tagging web services already deployed (Berkeley tagger does not contain Spanish capabilities; thus the sentence was entered in English) and the respective outputs are represented in GrAF.

5 Conclusion

This document presents the tools which are being used to create a factory for LR integrating NLP tools to work together. Some modifications and improvements to these tools are explained and a global vision of the whole infrastructure is presented. One of the main challenges for a factory with these characteristics is interoperability; other relevant problems were also presented. To make it possible to chain components, a Common Interface is presented and data formats were studied. For the first stage of the platform XCES format was chosen as a low-cost approach which perfectly fulfilled the requirements for data exchange. For the second stage the stand-off and more complex annotations are needed and GrAF was chosen to be used as a pivot format.

Taverna, Biocatalogue, Soaplab, etc. have proven to be very useful and user-friendly tools for the first phase of factory development. Now the requirements of the project are higher and large data processing capabilities are a challenge for these technologies and developers. We expect to continue learning more about these tools, which can still provide more features and elicit more satisfactory results

On the other hand, we are in the middle of the GrAF adoption. We expect it to be a very useful and flexible data format for the factory. The standard will be used with no adaptation or modification at all, in order to facilitate interoperability with other projects using GrAF. We expect to have complex workflows using GrAF soon.

Deploying new web services is easy and has low cost thanks to the used tools. This is a big advantage to facilitate interoperability between this factory and other relevant projects like the Heart of Gold, U-Compare and the Language Grid. If data converters are developed, they could easily be integrated in the factory to work together with these other projects. Deploying data converters as web services can push cooperation forward.

Acknowledgments

This research has been funded by the PANACEA project (EU-7FP-ITC-248064).

References

Eneko Agirre, Xabier Artola, Arantza Diaz de Ilarraza, German Rigau, Aitor Soroa, and Wauter Bosma. 2009. *KAF: Kyoto Annotation Framework.* Technical Report TR 1-2009, Dept. Computer Science and Artificial Intelligence, University of the Basque Country.

K. Belhajjame, C. Goble, F. Tanoh, J. Bhagat, K. Wolstencroft, R. Stevens, E. Nzuobontane, H. McWilliam, T. Laurent, and R. Lopez. 2008. "*BioCatalogue: A Curated Web Service Registry for the Life Science Community,*" in Microsoft eScience conference.

Lionel Clément and Eric Villemonte de la Clergerie. 2005. *Maf: a morphosyntactic annotation framework.* In Proceedings of the 2nd Language & Technology Conference, page 90–94, April 2005.

Thierry Declerck.2006. *Synaf: Towards a standard for syntactic annotation.* Proceedings of the Fifth Conference on International Language Resources and Evaluation, pages 229-233. European Language Resources Association (ELRA). May 2006.

D. De Roure, C. Goble, and R. Stevens 2008. "The Design and Realisation of the myExperiment Virtual Research Environment for Social Sharing of Workflows," Future Generation Computer Systems, vol. 25, pp. 561-567.

D. Hull, K. Wolstencroft, R. Stevens, C. Goble, M. Pocock, P. Li, and T. Oinn. 2006. "*Taverna: a tool for building and running workflows of services.*" Nucleic Acids Research, vol. 34, iss. Web Server issue, pp. 729-732.

U. Heid, H. Schmid, K. Eckart and E. Hinrichs. (2008). *A Corpus Representation Format for Linguistic Web Services: The D-SPIN Text Corpus Format and its Relationship with ISO Standards.* In: Proceedings of the 6th International Conference on Language Resources and Evaluation (LREC 2008). ELRA, Marrakech.

Nancy Ide, Patrice Bonhomme, Laurent Romary. 2000. "*XCES: An XML-based encoding standard for linguistic corpora*". In Proceedings of the Second International Language Resources and Evaluation Conference. Paris: European Language Resources Association (2000).

Nancy Ide, Harry Bunt. 2010. *Anatomy of Annotation Schemes: Mapping to GrAF.* Proceedings of the Fourth Linguistic Annotation Workshop, ACL 2010, pages 247-255.

Nancy Ide, Lauren Romary.2004. "*International Standard for a Linguistic Annotation Framework*". Journal of Nataural Language Engineering, 10:3-4, 211-225.

Nancy Ide, Keith Surderman. 2007. "*GrAF: A Graph-based Format for Linguistic Annotations*". In Proceedings of the Linguistic Annotation Workshop (June 2007), pp. 1-8.

K. Lee, J. Pustejovsky, H. Bunt, B. Boguraev, and N. Ide. 2007. *Language resource management - Semantic annotation framework (SemAF) - Part 1 :Time and events.* International Organization for Standardization, Geneva, Switzerland, 2007.

T. Oinn, M. Greenwood, M. Addis, N. Alpdemir, J. Ferris, K. Glover, C. Goble, A. Goderis, D. Hull, D. Marvin, P. Li, P. Lord, M. Pocock, M. Senger, R. Stevens, A. Wipat, and C. Wroe. 2006. "*Taver-*

na: lessons in creating a workflow environment for the life sciences," Concurrency and Computation: Practice and Experience, vol. 18, iss. 10, pp. 1067-1100.

M. Senger, P. Riceand T. Oinn. 2003. *"Soaplab - a unified Sesame door to analysis tools (2003)"* In UK e-Science All Hands Meeting.

Appendix A. Freeling output GrAF

```
<graph xmlns="http://www.xces.org/ns/GrAF/1.0/">
  <header> ... </header>
  <!-- la casa está en llamas -->

  <node xml:id="freeling-n1">
    <link targets="seg-r1"/></node>
  <a label="tok" ref="freeling-n1" as="xces">
    <fs>
      <f name="word" value="la"/>
      <f name="lemma" value="el"/>
      <f name="postag" value="DA0FS0"/>
      <f name="probability" value="0.972146"/>
    </fs>
  </a>

  <node xml:id="freeling-n2">
    <link targets="seg-r2"/></node>
  <a label="tok" ref="freeling-n2" as="xces">
    <fs>
      <f name="word" value="casa"/>
      <f name="lemma" value="casa"/>
      <f name="postag" value="NCFS000"/>
      <f name="probability" value="0.971264"/>
    </fs>
  </a>

  <node xml:id="freeling-n3">
    <link targets="seg-r3"/></node>
  <a label="tok" ref="freeling-n3" as="xces">
    <fs>
      <f name="word" value="está"/>
      <f name="lemma" value="estar"/>
      <f name="postag" value="VAIP3S0"/>
      <f name="probability" value="0.996032"/>
    </fs>
  </a>

  <node xml:id="freeling-n4">
    <link targets="seg-r4"/></node>
  <a label="tok" ref="freeling-n4" as="xces">
    <fs>
      <f name="word" value="en"/>
      <f name="lemma" value="en"/>
      <f name="postag" value="SPS00"/>
      <f name="probability" value="1"/>
    </fs>
  </a>

  <node xml:id="freeling-n5">
    <link targets="seg-r5"/></node>
  <a label="tok" ref="freeling-n5" as="xces">
    <fs>
      <f name="word" value="llamas"/>
      <f name="lemma" value="llama"/>
      <f name="postag" value="NCFP000"/>
      <f name="probability" value="0.875"/>
    </fs>
  </a>
</graph>
```

Appendix A. Tree Tagger output GrAF

```
<graph xmlns="http://www.xces.org/ns/GrAF/1.0/">
  <header> ... </header>
  <!-- La casa está en llamas -->

  <node xml:id="freeling-n1">
    <link targets="seg-r1"/></node>
  <a label="tok" ref="freeling-n1" as="xces">
    <fs>
      <f name="word" value="la"/>
      <f name="lemma" value="el"/>
      <f name="postag" value="AFS"/>
    </fs>
  </a>

  <node xml:id="freeling-n2">
    <link targets="seg-r2"/></node>
  <a label="tok" ref="freeling-n2" as="xces">
    <fs>
      <f name="word" value="casa"/>
      <f name="lemma" value="casa"/>
      <f name="postag" value="N5-FS"/>
    </fs>
  </a>

  <node xml:id="freeling-n3">
    <link targets="seg-r3"/></node>
  <a label="tok" ref="freeling-n3" as="xces">
    <fs>
      <f name="word" value="está"/>
      <f name="lemma" value="estar"/>
      <f name="postag" value="VDR3S-"/>
    </fs>
  </a>

  <node xml:id="freeling-n4">
    <link targets="seg-r4"/></node>
  <a label="tok" ref="freeling-n4" as="xces">
    <fs>
      <f name="word" value="en"/>
      <f name="lemma" value="en"/>
      <f name="postag" value="P"/>
    </fs>
  </a>

  <node xml:id="freeling-n5">
    <link targets="seg-r5"/></node>
  <a label="tok" ref="freeling-n5" as="xces">
    <fs>
      <f name="word" value="llamas"/>
      <f name="lemma" value="llama"/>
      <f name="postag" value="N5-FP"/>
    </fs>
  </a>
</graph>
```

Appendix A. Berkeley Tagger output GrAF

```
<graph xmlns="http://www.xces.org/ns/GrAF/1.0/">
  <header> ... </header>
```

```xml
    &lt;!-- the house is on fire --&gt;

    &lt;node xml:id="freeling-n1"&gt;
      &lt;link targets="seg-r1"/&gt;&lt;/node&gt;
    &lt;a label="tok" ref="freeling-n1" as="xces"&gt;
      &lt;fs&gt;
        &lt;f name="word" value="the"/&gt;
        &lt;f name="postag" value="DT"/&gt;
      &lt;/fs&gt;
    &lt;/a&gt;

    &lt;node xml:id="freeling-n2"&gt;
      &lt;link targets="seg-r2"/&gt;&lt;/node&gt;
    &lt;a label="tok" ref="freeling-n2" as="xces"&gt;
      &lt;fs&gt;
        &lt;f name="word" value="house"/&gt;
        &lt;f name="postag" value="NN"/&gt;
      &lt;/fs&gt;
    &lt;/a&gt;

    &lt;node xml:id="freeling-n3"&gt;
      &lt;link targets="seg-r3"/&gt;&lt;/node&gt;
    &lt;a label="tok" ref="freeling-n3" as="xces"&gt;
      &lt;fs&gt;
        &lt;f name="word" value="is"/&gt;
        &lt;f name="postag" value="VBZ"/&gt;
      &lt;/fs&gt;
    &lt;/a&gt;

    &lt;node xml:id="freeling-n4"&gt;
      &lt;link targets="seg-r4"/&gt;&lt;/node&gt;
    &lt;a label="tok" ref="freeling-n4" as="xces"&gt;
      &lt;fs&gt;
        &lt;f name="word" value="on"/&gt;
        &lt;f name="postag" value="IN"/&gt;
      &lt;/fs&gt;
    &lt;/a&gt;

    &lt;node xml:id="freeling-n5"&gt;
      &lt;link targets="seg-r5"/&gt;&lt;/node&gt;
    &lt;a label="tok" ref="freeling-n5" as="xces"&gt;
      &lt;fs&gt;
        &lt;f name="word" value="fire"/&gt;
        &lt;f name="postag" value="NN. "/&gt;
      &lt;/fs&gt;
    &lt;/a&gt;
&lt;/graph&gt;
```

Interoperability Framework: The FLaReNet action plan proposal

Nicoletta Calzolari, Monica Monachini, Valeria Quochi
Istituto di Linguistica Computazionale "A. Zampolli"
Consiglio Nazionale delle Ricerche
Via Moruzzi 1, Pisa, Italy
name.surname@ilc.cnr.it

Abstract

Standards are fundamental to ex-change, preserve, maintain and integrate data and language resources, and as an essential basis of any language resource infrastructure. This paper promotes an Interoperability Framework as a dynamic environment of standards and guidelines, also intended to support the provision of language-(web)service interoperability. In the past two decades, the need to define common practices and formats for linguistic resources has been increasingly recognized and sought. Today open, collaborative, shared data is at the core of a sound language strategy, and standardisation is actively on the move. This paper first describes the current landscape of standards, and presents the major barriers to their adoption; then, it describes those scenarios that critically involve the use of standards and provide a strong motivation for their adoption; lastly, a series of actions and steps needed to operationalise standards and achieve a full interoperability for Language Resources and Technologies are proposed.

1 Interoperability and Interoperability Framework

Today open, collaborative, shared data is at the core of a sound language strategy. Standards are fundamental to exchange, preserve, maintain and integrate data and Language Resources (LRs), to achieve interoperability in general; and they are an essential basis of any language resource infrastructure.

In the past, we used the notion of "reusability" that today has evolved into "interoperability". *Interoperability* means the ability of information and communication systems to exchange data and to enable the sharing of information and knowledge. Interoperability was declared one of the major priorities for the LT field at the first FLaReNet Forum in Vienna (Calzolari et al. 2009)

An *Interoperability Framework* can be defined as a dynamic environment of language (and other) standards and guidelines, where different standards are coherently related to one another and guidelines clearly describe how the specifications may be applied to various types of resources. Such a framework must be dynamic in several ways. First, as it is not feasible to define one single standard that can cover all the various linguistic representation levels and applications, a series of specific standards should continue to exist, but they should form a coherent system (i.e. coherence among the various standard specifications must be ensured so that they can "speak" to each other). Then, standards themselves must be conceived as dynamic, because they need to follow and adapt to new technologies and domains of application. As the Language Technology (LT) field is expanding, standards need to be periodically revised, updated and integrated in order to keep the pace of technological advancements.

An Interoperability framework is also intended to support the provision of language services interoperability.

Enterprises nowadays seem to need such a language strategy, and to be key players they must rely on interoperability, otherwise they are out of business. A recent report by TAUS (TAUS/LISA 2011) states that: "The lack of interoperability costs the translation industry a fortune", where the highest price is paid mainly for adjusting data formats.

2 The "History" of Standards

In the past two decades, because of the robustness and industrial applicability of some NLP technology, the need to define common practices and formats for linguistic data resources has been increasingly understood and sought. Language data resources, in fact, serve LT development in various ways. They are

- the data which is passed and exchanged among software components or applications;

Proceedings of Workshop on Language Resources, Technology and Services in the Sharing Paradigm, pages 41–49,
Chiang Mai, Thailand, November 12, 2011.

- the lexical, terminological and semantic resources needed to perform various tasks such as information extraction, machine translation (MT), question answering;
- the primary source for statistical language modelling, fundamental for example in statistical machine translation (SMT), or automatic speech recognition, and many other applications.

Several projects laid the foundations for standardisation of resource representation and annotation, e.g. the Expert Advisory Group on Language Engineering Standards (EAGLES 1996) within which also the Corpus Encoding Standard (CES and XCES, Ide 1998) was developed, and the International Standard for Language Engineering (ISLE, Calzolari et al. 2002). With these projects Europe in the '90s was at the forefront in establishing standards for LT.

All these efforts bring us to the current landscape where actual standardisation is on the move. Consensus has begun to emerge, and in certain areas stable standards have already been defined. However, for many areas work is still ongoing either because "the emergence of a solid body of web-based standards have dramatically impacted and re-defined many of our ideas about the ways in which resources will be stored and accessed over the past several years" (Ide and Romary 2007), or because there are new emerging technologies, such as multimodal ones, that have specific requirements not covered by existing formats and established practices.

We therefore observe a continuum of standardisation initiatives at various stages of consolidation and the rising on new proposals, as the various areas of LTs become mature. Also, while some standards are "official", that is designed and promoted by standardisation bodies - i.e. ISO, W3C and LISA - others emerged bottom-up. These are the so-called *de-facto* standards or *best practices*: formats and representation frameworks that have gained community consensus and are widely used: e.g. WordNet (Fellbaum 1998), PennTreeBank (Marcus et al. 1993), CoNLL[1] (Nivre et al. 2007).

2.1 The FLaReNet Landscape

Drawing on a previous report drafted by the CLARIN[2] project (Bel et al. 2009), together with FLaReNet, META-SHARE and ELRA the original document has been revised and updated with standards relevant for the broader LT community, also addressing those that are typically used in industry, at different levels of granularity. "The Standards' Landscape Towards an Interoperability Framework"[3] (Bel et al., to appear) thus lists both current standards and on-going promising standardisation efforts so that the community can monitor and actively contribute to them. This document is conceived like a "live" document to be adopted and updated by the community (e.g. in future projects and networks), so as not to restart similar efforts over and over.

It is meant to be a general reference guide for the whole community and particularly useful for LT initiatives such as the META-SHARE infrastructure, as it provides concrete indications about standards and best practices that are important for given tasks or media in LT. These standards are at different stages of development: some are already very well known and widely used, others more LR-specific standards, especially those developed in the framework of the ISO Technical Committee 37 devoted to LR management, are in the process of development or are being revised.

Currently, relatively small sets of basic standards (defined as foundational standards) can be identified that have gained wide consensus. These are not necessarily specific to language resources, but provide a minimum basis for interoperability: e.g. Unicode-UTF8 for character encoding, ISO639 for language codes, W3C-XML for textual data, PCM, MP3, ATRAC, for audio, etc.

On top of these we find standards specifically addressing LR management and representation that should also be considered as foundational - ISO 24610-1:2006 - Feature structure representation, TEI, and LMF for lexical resources (Francopoulo et al. 2006, 2008). They are increasingly recognized as fundamental for real-world interoperability and exchange.

A set of other standards focusing on specific aspects of linguistic and terminological representation are also currently in place and officially established, such as TMF (ISO 2002) for terminology, SynAF (Declerk, 2006) and MAF (Clément and de la Clérgerie, 2005) for morphological and syntactic annotation. These result from years of work and discussions among groups of

[1] http://ilk.uvt.nl/conll/#dataformat
[2] www.clarin.eu

[3] This document also collects input also from the LRE Map, Multilingual Web, the FLaReNet fora, LREC Workshops, ISO and W3C.

experts from various areas of language technology and are thought to be comprehensive enough to allow for the representation of most current annotations. Most of them address syntactic interoperability by providing pivot formats (e.g. LAF/GrAF, Ide and Suderman 2007), while today there is a greater need for semantic interoperability, which is still an actual challenge. Most of the more linguistically oriented standards are also periodically under revision in an attempt to make them ever more comprehensive as new technologies appear and new languages are being considered. Effort is still needed for their promotion and to spread awareness to a wider community.

Standards related to terminology management and translational technologies are probably the most widespread and consolidated, in part because of the real market behind the translation industry: we speak of TMF, TMX, TBX [4], XLIFF, an OASIS standard for the exchange of data for translation. A recent effort is the reference architecture OAXAL (Zydron, 2008), a standard component stack, made up of a number of core standards from W3C, OASIS and LISA.

Finally, the current situation witnesses a stream of on-going standardisation projects and initiatives focused mainly on recent mature areas of linguistic analysis and on emerging technologies such as semantic annotation which includes temporal and space annotation (ISO24617 – 1-6), emotion, i.e. EML (W3C, 2007) and multimodal annotation, i.e. EMMA (W3C, 2009). These are initiatives the community needs to monitor closely and actively participate in.

Along with the standards mentioned above, in specific communities there are established practices that can be considered *de-facto* standards, e.g. WordNet and the PennTreeBank. For these a number of tools exist that facilitate their usage. As these need not to change, at least not in the near future, it is recommended the development of mappers/converters from these best practices/common formats to the other endorsed/official standards.

LR standards become increasingly relevant for all industry branches where LRs are being produced and used, information technology, automation/robotics, telecommunications, data mining, information retrieval, and for all sectors supported by information technologies: eCommerce, eHealth, eLearning, eGovernment, eEnvironment

Concluding, we can safely state that today a number of standards exists that create a potentially useful framework, ready for adoption, and that efforts now should to spread their application.

2.2 Barriers and major problems

While the current picture of LTs presents a great potential for real interoperability, some problems or barriers have emerged that hamper the broad usability of the current standards framework.
The key issue is not so much a lack of standards, but, in particular for LT-specific standards, a *lack of (open) tools for an easy use* of them. This certainly is a major factor that hampers a broad standard usage. Another barrier is the lack of reference implementations and documentation, possibly open source, to enable others to understand what was done and how. A major problem has to do with lack of developer- and user education and culture in using standards. There is resilient tradition to use idiosyncratic schemes, which causes incompatibility of formats (even for minor differences), thus hampering the possibility of merging annotations or using them together. This in turn prevents easy reuse of available data.

Within ISO, general interest standards (like country codes) are free. But others are not, and this should be avoided. In fact, this may be one other major factor preventing a wider adoption of standards. There are now attempts – i.e. in ISO TC 37 – to overcome this situation by allowing direct application of standards free of charge through implemented databases with free access such as the new ISO 12620 ISOcat.

In W3C, full documentation of standards is free, so it is easy for W3C documents to be spread and largely applied. However, participation in the definition and decision-making process is costly.

Standards need to be built by consensus; therefore their creation is a slow process[5].

3 Motivations for standards

There are various scenarios that critically involve the need for standards and provide a strong motivation for their adoption and for investment in the development of the missing ones. This section briefly introduces some of them.

[4] First developed in the SALT project, TMF and TBX are now ISO standards

[5] This is also in line with all other recommendations from FLaReNet and also fits well to the strategies of META-NET.

[1]. ***Use of the same tools on different data; use of different tools on the same data***. Interoperability among software components is today a major issue. In architectures for knowledge mining, or for the creation of new resources, where the same data have to be used, enriched and queried by (chains of) different tools, common formats become crucial for their success, as for instance in the KYOTO project[6] where the KAF has been defined and adopted as a common representation format for textual data and related linguistic annotations (Bosma et al. 2009). Moreover, the use of different tools on the same data is relevant for testing and comparing tools, and also in collaborative situations to process the same corpus for different purposes.

[2]. ***Creation of workflows - Web Service Interoperability***. In cases where workflows need to be built chaining together tools not originally built to work in pipeline/together, standards will ensure their execution. As of today, in most cases workflows can be run with tools that were already designed to work together, or with the use of format converters. This is a major obstacle esp. in the context of web-based platforms for distributed language services. Experiences such as PANACEA (Bel 2010, Toral et al. 2011) show that using a common standardised format facilitates integration. If tools were built/modified to work directly on common/standard formats, workflows might be simpler, easier to design and quicker to run. While this is not possible at present, when the advantages are shown, new tools could naturally go in this direction. Workflow management should be generalised to cover both local processing and web service interfaces.

[3]. ***Integration/Interlinking of resources***. This has recently become an important trend also for companies that wish to provide composite services. In order to exploit the wealth of manual annotations already existing and developed within the years mostly by academic institutions, (legacy) resources must be integrated and interlinked. This is needed for example also for generating new training data, or for re-purposing already existing one. In order to achieve this goal broadly, we need not only standard formats but also common methodologies and best practices for resource management and update. The experience of linking Propbank and PennTreebank in SemLink[7] teaches us that changes/updates in one resource cause many problems to their mapping, resulting in a lot of manual work to be done. Data lifecycle issues thus enter into play here.

[4]. ***Mashing-up***. Also for the mash-up movement, i.e. web applications that allow developers with relatively little technical skills to combine, quickly and easily, existing content (geographic data, pictures, videos, news ...) and functionalities in new ways from different sources, standards are obviously critical to easily integrate data.

[5]. ***Documentation and metadata***. At a different level, documentation and adequate use of metadata is what makes resources (re-) usable in the first place. Standardising documentation in the form of standard templates would facilitate developers and users. Consensus on basic sets of Metadata agreed in the community is also of utmost importance for an easy identification and tracking of resources independently from their physical location. This is critical in the emerging infrastructures and there is a big interest and a movement towards metadata standardisation, not only in Europe and the USA, but also e.g. in Australia.

[6]. ***Validation of language resources***. In order to be able to establish a certified quality validation of LRs (an issue that is coming-up more and more often) conformity to an accepted standard is a requirement.

[7]. ***Evaluation campaigns: shared tasks***. If we want to evaluate and compare the results of different methods, approaches, or technologies, it is important to have data encoded and annotated according to a common format that different groups need to be able to process and use. Here standards clearly play a fundamental role. In fact, many de-facto standards find their origins in evaluation campaigns or shared tasks and then become commonly used in the related sub-community (e.g. CoNLL). Therefore, it must be recognised that such initiatives play an important role also in introducing/disseminating the use of standards

[8]. ***Collaborative creation of resources***. Collaborative ways of creating or updating/enhancing LRs represent a recent trend in

[6] www.kyoto-project.eu

[7] http://verbs.colorado.edu/semlink/

the LT community. To fully exploit the potential of web-based collaboration, again common formats and annotation schemes have to be employed, so that distributed annotation, editing and data aggregation tools can be easily developed.

[9]. ***Preservation***. As IT evolves, both data resources and tools need to be ported to new systems, encodings etc. Storing data and developing tools according to widely accepted or official standards should thus facilitate their portability and help avoiding mismatches. Also, standards would make preservation easier as they would allow resource structures and content to be accessible (and understandable) also in time.

4 Strategies and recommendations

This section leads to the identification of a number of strategies and actions recommended by FLaReNet for achieving full interoperability in the Language Resource/Technology sector.

4.1 Address Semantic/content interoperability

Until now we have mostly tackled the problem of syntactic interoperability, i.e. the ability of systems to process exchanged data either directly or via conversion. Pivot formats, such as GrAF, attempt to solve syntactic interoperability, enabling merging and easy transduction among formats. Semantic interoperability, i.e. ability of systems to interpret exchanged linguistic information in meaningful consistent ways (e.g. through reference to a common set of categories), still remains unattained, as it is much more difficult. Linguistic characteristics of different languages, as well as different linguistic theoretical approaches play a big role in this. Interoperability of content is however desperately needed in the current landscape (e.g. in the scenarios [1], [2], [3], [4], [8] above). A good and practical rule (already recognised as a basic principle in EAGLES) is to define the standard as the lowest common denominator, at the maximal level of granularity. But, to arrive at this point large confrontations among experts are required. A recent effort in this direction is represented by ISOCAT (Kemps-Snijders et al. 2009), but more initiatives should be brought forward in order to maximise and accelerate the process.

4.2 Push Linked Data and Open Data

Interoperability through Linked Data could mean to be able to link our objects of linguistic/semantic knowledge with corresponding knowledge in other fields, and therefore to converge both within the field and outside with other fields. This would be very beneficial in scenatrios like [3] and [4]. To achieve maximum results, data needs to be open as much as possible, or the potential exploitation advantages will be lost. We must therefore closely monitor and participate to the Linked Open Data[8] initiative, connected to issue of semantic interoperability, to understand and enhance the potentialities for our field.

4.3 Develop tools that enable the use of standards

In order to increase the availability of shareable/exchangeable data, we must foster the development and availability of tools that enable an easy use of standards.

4.4 Incentivise web services platforms

Web service platforms (as in scenario [2]) certainly offer an optimal test case for interoperability and possibly a good showcase to demonstrate the need and advantages of the adoption of standards. Such platforms need both syntactic and semantic interoperability and thus can also function as an evaluation ground for interoperability issues. Projects like Language Grid, U-Compare and PANACEA could thus be seen as models for platforms providing LT services. A possible concrete action in this direction could be to compel players to deploy results of (publicly funded) projects as web-services that can be used, tested and called by others.

Cloud-based service architectures could also be leveraged as enablers for LT development.

4.5 Experiment with collaborative and crowdsourcing platforms.

The use of the collaborative paradigm to create language resources (in [8]) may become a means to encourage or even compel standardisation and - as a consequence - to share all the more the burden and cost of resource creation. Also crowdsourcing for shared resources is somehow linked to interoperability, requiring commonly accepted specifications. Collaborative develop-

[8] http://linkeddata.org/

ment of resources would create a new culture of joint research.

4.6 Establish a collaborative multilingual annotation plan

A collaborative approach to the creation of multilingual, possibly parallel, annotated data would also help maximise the visibility, use and reuse of resources, while at the same time encouraging exploratory diversity. A huge multilingual annotation pool, where everyone can deposit data annotated at every possible different linguistic level for the same resources, or for diverse resources, should be defined as a specific type of collaborative initiative for resource annotation (Calzolari 2010). This could create a fruitful (community driven) exchange between most used annotation schemes and establishment of best practices. Such an initiative would also be extremely beneficial for infrastructures like META-SHARE.

4.7 Support evaluation and validation campaigns

As mentioned in [7], evaluation campaigns help in standardisation. The lack of a European evaluation body that coordinates and prioritises evaluation efforts is an issue that finally hampers interoperability. Shared tasks should therefore become more prominent as loci where interoperability is foregrounded, where standards are pushed forth and thus the occasion to make progress in standardising not only resources but components as well. The possibility of having official validators[9] for compliance to basic linguistic standards can/should also be investigated. This could be used to provide the community, through with validation services for the resources to be shared.

4.8 Set up Interoperability Challenges

Along with the previous proposal, the idea of organising interoperability challenges, discussed by Nancy Ide and James Pustejovsky at a SILT Workshop (April 2011), should be enforced and supported, as an international initiative to evaluate and possibly measure interoperability. This could speed up the dissemination of standards and drive interoperability forward[10]. The NLP community should be involved and an overall challenge should be defined that explicitly require the use and integration of multiple data formats, annotation schemes, and processing modules, so that players will be highly motivated to adapt, adopt, use standards and common format and could start seeing the advantages they offer.

4.9 Standards should be open and simple

As a basic rule standards should be open, simple, and relatively non-invasive to facilitate their adoption. For example, people should continue to be allowed to program/mark-up as they wish, but there should be well-formed points of contact that act as bridge between data and code that the community needs to come up with.

4.10 Maintain a repository of standards and best practices

Information on standards is essential. A repository of standards and best practices must be created and kept alive. A preparatory initiative was started within FLaReNet[11], but dedicated effort must be devoted to create and support a repository of standards and best practices so that it assumes also the effect of a cultural initiative. A repository of standards could obviously be linked to a repository of open data compliant with the them. This would maximise the benefits.

4.11 Organise awareness initiatives

Awareness about the existing standards and the motivations behind them is one of the key factor for enlarging their adoption. Educational programs should therefore be launched to explain, promote and disseminate standards especially to students and young researchers (e.g. through tutorials at conferences, summer schools, seminars...). Steps could be taken to include standardisation in regular university curricula. Also, effective ways to demonstrate the return of investment (ROI) of interoperability must be sought. Adapting one's tools and resources to standardised common formats in fact requires some investments that players may not be willing to make unless the clearly see advantages.

4.12 Set up a Standard Watch

At present, no mechanism is available to watch when a discipline deserves standardisation. We should create a permanent Observatory or Standard Watch. TAUS for example has announced an Interoperability Watchdog initiative that goes in the right direction. Examples of deficiencies

[9] http://validator.oaipmh.com/ or the OLAC validator http://www.language-archives.org/tools/xsv/
[10] https://sites.google.com/site/siltforum/files

[11] http://www.flarenet.eu/?q=FLaReNet_Repository_of_Standards_and_Guidelines

from the European side are the lack of support to official standardisation initiatives for important topics such as Space and Lexicon-Ontology, which have also an economic potential. As standardisation is a slow process and the ROI is not immediate, funding agencies should be more present in the initiatives. .

4.13 Establish a Quality Certificate

Work is needed towards the definition and establishment of some kind of Quality seal, on the model of the "Data Seal of Approval"[12], to be endorsed by the community. The Data Seal of Approval is a quality sign for resources (data) that provides a certification for data repositories to keep data visible and accessible and to ensure long term preservation. Similarly, efforts should be made to encompass not only data for archiving, but also for dynamic exchange and also for software components. For example, there is a requirement for CLARIN centres to comply with certain standards. This is linked to the concept of "preservation" and sustainability. Infrastructures like META-SHARE could introduce some mechanisms (possibly socially based) for assigning quality scores to resources and tools, also evaluating them for compliance to standards/best practices. Systems of "penalties" could be devised, as well, for not complying data resources.

4.14 Link up to web content-related standards

Collaboration and synergies must be enforced with ISO, W3C and other multilingual web content-related standards, which in the case of LT can be seen as more basic levels of representation that can to ensure the (potential) integration of LT/NLP technologies into present and future web content products. Multilinguality should be incorporated in standards, e.g. ISO standards should be instantiated/generalised for as many languages as possible, which does not always happen at present. A recommendation to standardisation bodies must be to test/apply standards multilingually.

4.15 International collaboration

In particular for standards it is important that initiatives are taken at a truly international level. This means going beyond European initiatives.

[12] http://www.datasealofapproval.org/

5 Conclusions: Operationalising Standards

A recurrent request from industrials in many recent meetings, such as the META-NET Vision Groups and the META-Council, is: "give me the standards and give me open data".

The major recommended step for an interoperability framework is operationalising standards, in the sense of making standards finally "operational" and come up with operational recommendations. Standards must be usable and actually used; otherwise they are of no relevance.

A step forward in this direction is to make standards open. However, there is no single definition of the term. The minimum requirements for open standards are availability and accessibility for all, detailed documentation and possibility to be implemented without restrictions. Publicly available standards with public specifications in fact promote their usage and adoption (Perens, 2010; Krechmer, 2006).

The basic pre-conditions to operationalise the standards and the essential steps to be taken need to be outlined. Some of these steps and conditions are summarised below.

5.1 Technical conditions

Common metadata. This is a commonly recognised pre-condition, in all the most important infrastructural initiatives: ELRA, LDC, CLARIN, META-SHARE.

Explicit semantics of metadata. Explicit semantics of annotation metadata/data categories is essential. A mechanism to be used can be ISOCat: even if there are still many problems, it is at the moment the only available instrument that allows the definition of data categories at a persistent web location and to reference them from any annotation scheme.

High level metadata is not the only set of values that are recorded in ISOCat. Until now, the linguistic categories within ISOCat have been mostly recorded from the EAGLES, MULTEXT-East and LIRICS projects (e.g. morpho-syntax, extended also to Semitic, Asian and African languages), and terminology starting from LISA and ISO-12620 sets of values. Recently ISOCat is enriched by the CLARIN project with the need of Social Sciences and Humanities (SSH) in mind. These metadata however are not enough for NLP. This gap (from SSH to NLP) is currently filled in META-SHARE and an effort must be done to involve a broad community of resource developers/users.

Creation of data category selections for the major standards/best practices would increase convergence towards common data categories. This would help taking a step towards semantic interoperability. Funding agencies could encourage entering data categories and selections in ISO-Cat, which could become a useful instrument if broadly used.

Tools that facilitate the use of standards. It is of utmost importance to develop (online) tools that hide the complexities of standard formats and allow for easy usage of standards and easy exportation/mapping to the standards. The development of converters from/to the major standards/best practices/common formats to other endorsed/official standards is thus recommended. This is true in particular for infrastructures like META-SHARE where best practices should be promoted also through tools.

5.2 Infrastructural conditions

A common (virtual) repository as an easy way to find the most appropriate standards. An international joint effort should take care of the indexing of different standards and best practices, to ease their finding and to keep track of the status and different versions and their history. This is critical for infrastructures like META-SHARE that should also be able to recommend standards and best practices for the resources made visible through them, in particular for the new ones.

Common templates for documentation. Currently, resource and tool documentation is often not adequate, ranging from too poor to too heavy. Nevertheless, documentation of resources is essential for reaching common understanding and practically for exchange and re-use. Therefore, a consensual set of templates for resource documentation should be devised and disseminated, with actions to facilitate their adoption.

Provide a framework that facilitates testing. Test scenarios to verify compliance are needed.

An interoperability framework for/of web services. Operationalising standards could also mean that they should be based on an interoperability framework for/of web services. We should therefore deploy linguistic services based on standards. A key point here is workflows (see the success of the KYOTO project).

"**Meta-interoperability**" among standards. We should also speak about "meta-interoperability" among standards and understand what it means operationally. Standards must constitute a coherent framework, i.e. they must be able to speak with each other. This refers to the LR specific ecology framework (as an integrated system).

5.3 Social and cultural conditions

Involvement of the community. The community as a whole must be involved in standardisation processes. It is recommended that researchers, groups and companies involved or interested in resource development/annotation/validation actively contribute to the definition of LT standards. Initiatives must be defined to change the community mentality into a "social network" for scientific collaboration, as community-level active participation is critical for attaining true interoperability. In fact, the wider the participation to such initiatives, the more robust and valid the standards would be. One possible way of making work on standardisation appealing could be to establish a framework for the citation of resources, like for publications, and measure their impact factor.

Dissemination (but not forcing). The potential and advantages of standardisation must be disseminated, standards pushed, incentives to the use of standards possibly devised, but people must not be obliged to conform. Standards must not be seen as an overhead, but people should feel that they want to use standards because it's in their own interest.

Interoperability as valid research area. Community mentality should be changed also to accept interoperability and standardisation as academically valid research areas.

Link to sustainability. In general, a virtuous circle must be established between standard-definition, adoption, feedback, and their interoperability.

Acknowledgements

This work has been supported by the FP7 FLaReNet project (ECP-2007-LANG-617001) and META-NET (FP7-ICT-4 – 249119: T4ME-NET).

We thank the whole FLaReNet community, which through participation to the meetings and discussions, considerably contributed to shaping the results and ideas reported in this paper.

References

Bel, N. et al. 2009. *CLARIN Standardisation Action Plan.* CLARIN http://www.clarin.eu/node/2841

Bel, N. et al. to appear. *The Standards' Landscape Towards an Interoperability Framework*

Bel, N. 2010. Platform for Automatic, Normalized Annotation and Cost-Effective Acquisition of Language Resources for Human Language Technologies: PANACEA. In *Proceedings of the 26th Annual Congress of the Spanish Society for Natural Language Processing (SEPLN)*, Valencia.

Bosma, W., et al. 2009. KAF: a generic semantic annotation format. In: *Proceedings of the 5th International Conference on Generative Approaches to the Lexicon* (GL 2009). Pisa.

Calzolari, N., et al. 2002. "Broadening the scope of the EAGLES/ISLE lexical standardization initiative". In *Proceedings of the 3rd workshop on Asian language resources and international standardization (COLING '02)*, vol. 12. pages 1-8, Taipei.

Calzolari N., et al. (eds.). 2009. *Shaping the Future of the Multilingual Digital Europe*, 1st FLaReNet Forum, Vienna.

Calzolari, N. 2010. Invited presentation at the COLING 2010 Panel. Beijing.

Declerk, T. 2006. SynAF: Towards a Standard for Syntactic Annotation. In *Proceedings of the 5th International Conference on Language Resources and Evaluation (LREC'06)*, pages 229-232, Genoa.

EAGLES 1996

http://www.ilc.cnr.it/EAGLES96/home.html

Fellbaum C. (ed.). 1998. *WordNet: An Electronic Lexical Database*. Cambridge, MA: MIT Press.

Francopoulo, G., et al. 2006. Lexical markup framework (LMF). In *Proceedings of the 5th International Conference on Language Resources and Evaluation (LREC'06)*, pages 233-236, Genoa.

Francopoulo G., et al. 2009. Multilingual resources for NLP in the lexical markup framework (LMF). *Language Resources and Evaluation*. 43(1): 57-70.

Ide, N. 1998. "Corpus Encoding Standard: SGML guidelines for encoding linguistic corpora." In *Proceedings of the First International Language Resources and Evaluation Conference (LREC'98)*, pages 463-470, Granada.

Ide, N and L. Romary. 2007 Towards International Standards for Language Resources. In Dybkjaer, L., Hemsen, H., Minker, W. (eds.), *Evaluation of Text and Speech Systems*, Springer, Dordrecht, 263-84.

Ide, N. and K, Suderman. 2007. GrAF: A graph-based format for linguistic annotations. In *Proceedings of the Linguistic Annotation Workshop at ACL 2007*, pages 1-8, Prague.

International Organization for Standardisation. 2002. *ISO:16642-2002. Terminological Markup Framework.* http://www.loria.fr/projets/TMF/

International Organization for Standardization. 2008. *ISO DIS 24611 Language Resource Management - Morpho-syntactic Annotation Framework (MAF).* ISO/TC 37/SC4/WG 2.

International Organization for Standardization. 2008. *ISO DIS 24611- (1,2,3,4,5,6) Language Resource Management - Semantic annotation framework (SemAF).* ISO/TC 37/SC4/WG 2.

Kemps-Snijders M., et al 2009. "ISOcat: Remodeling Metadata for Language Resources". *International Journal of Metadata, Semantics and Ontologies (IJMSO)*, 4(4): 261-276.

Krechmer K. 2006, Open Standards Requirements. *The International Journal of IT Standards and Standardization Research*, 4(1): 43-61.

Lionel C. and Éric de la Clergerie. 2005. Maf: a morphosyntactic annotation frame work. In *Proceedings of the 2nd Language and Technology Conference* (LTC'05), pages 90-94, Poznan.

Marcus, M. P., B. Santorini, M.A. Marcinkiewicz. 1993. Building a Large Annotated Corpus of English: The Penn Treebank. *Computational Linguistics* 19 (2): 313-330.

Nivre, J. et al. 2007. The CoNLL 2007 Shared Task on Dependency Parsing. In *Proceedings of the 2007 Joint Conference on Empirical Methods in Natural Language Processing and Computational Natural Language Learning (EMNLP-CoNLL)*, pages 915-932, Prague.

TAUS. 2011. *Annual Plan 2011: Translation Innovation Think Tank Interoperability Watchdog.* http://www.translationautomation.com/images/stories/pdf/taus-annual-plan-2011-extended.pdf

TAUS (2011) *Report on a TAUS research about translation interoperability*. February 25, 2011. http://www.translationautomation.com

Toral A., et al. 2011. "Towards a user-friendly webservice architecture for statistical machine translation in the PANACEA project". In: M. L. Forcada, H. Depraetere, V. Vandeghinste (eds.) *Proceedings of the 15th EAMT 2011*, pages 63-70, Leuven.

W3C 2007 EML: Emotion Incubator Group, W3C Incubator Group Report, 10 July 2007.

W3C 2009 EMMA: Extensible MultiModal Annotation markup language, W3C Recommendation, 10 February 2009.

Zydron A. 2008. OAXAL. What Is It and Why Should I Care? *Globalization Insider*. http://www.lisa.org/globalizationinsider/2008.

Promoting Interoperability of Resources in META-SHARE

Paul Thompson[1,2], Yoshinobu Kano[3], John McNaught[1,2], Steve Pettifer[1], Teresa Attwood[1,4], John Keane[1] and Sophia Ananiadou[1,2]
[1]Department of Computer Science, University of Manchester, UK
[2]National Centre for Text Mining, University of Manchester, UK
[3]Database Center for Life Science, University of Tokyo, Japan
[4]Faculty of Life Sciences, University of Manchester, UK
{paul.thompson, john.mcnaught, steve.pettifer, teresa.attwood, john.keane, sophia.ananiadou}@manchester.ac.uk
kano@dbcls.rois.ac.jp

Abstract

META-NET is a Network of Excellence aiming to improve significantly on the number of language technologies that can assist European citizens, by enabling enhanced communication and cooperation across languages. A major outcome will be META-SHARE, a searchable network of repositories that collect resources such as language data, tools and related web services, covering a large number of European languages. These resources are intended to facilitate the development and evaluation of a wide range of new language processing applications and services. An important aim of META-SHARE is the promotion of interoperability amongst resources. In this paper, we describe our planned efforts to help to achieve this aim, through the adoption of the UIMA framework and the integration of the U-Compare system within the META-SHARE network. U-Compare facilitates the rapid construction and evaluation of NLP applications that make use of interoperable components, and, as such, can help to speed up the development of a new generation of European language technology applications.

1 Introduction

The two dozen national and many regional languages of Europe present linguistic barriers that can severely limit the free flow of goods, information and services. The META-NET Network of Excellence has been created to respond to this issue. Consisting of 44 research centres from 31 countries, META-NET aims to stimulate a concerted, substantial and continent-wide effort to push forward language technology research and engineering, in order to ensure equal access to information and knowledge for all European citizens.

The success of META-NET is dependent on the ready availability of data, tools and services that can perform natural language processing (NLP) and text mining (TM) on a range of European languages.

These will form the building blocks for constructing language-technology applications that can help European citizens to gain easy access to the information they require. Among these applications will be semantic search systems to provide users with fast and efficient access to precisely the information they require, and voice user interfaces that allow easy access to information and services over the telephone, e.g., booking tickets, etc.

One of the major outcomes of META-NET will be the META-SHARE infrastructure, an open, distributed facility for sharing and exchange of language resources (LRs), consisting of a sustainable network of repositories of language data, tools and related web services for a large number of European languages. LRs will be documented with high-quality metadata and aggregated in central inventories, allowing for uniform search and access to resources. A further aim of META-SHARE is to promote the use of widely acceptable standards for LR building, in order to ensure the greatest possible interoperability of LRs.

META-SHARE shares some goals with related initiatives, such as the Open Language Archives Community (OLAC) (Hughes & Kamat, 2005), which is developing a virtual library of LRs augmented with metadata; the PANACEA project (Bel, 2010), which is creating a library of interoperable web services that automate the stages involved in the production and maintenance of LRs required by MT systems; and the Common Language Resources and Technology Infrastructure

Proceedings of Workshop on Language Resources, Technology and Services in the Sharing Paradigm, pages 50–58, Chiang Mai, Thailand, November 12, 2011.

(CLARIN) (Váradi et al., 2008), which is establishing an integrated and interoperable research infrastructure of LRs and technology. A memorandum of understanding between META-NET and CLARIN recognizes that they are complementary initiatives with harmonisable goals. Whilst CLARIN is largely oriented towards the social sciences and humanities research community, META-NET aims at supporting Human Language Technology (HLT) development, and thus will target HLT researchers and developers, language professionals (translators, interpreters, etc.), as well as industrial players, with a particular emphasis on cross-lingual technologies.

Advanced language technology applications are usually built from a number of component technologies, which are often common across a large number of different applications. For example, text-based applications frequently make use of tools such as tokenisers, part-of speech taggers, syntactic parsers, named entity recognisers, etc. Through its central inventories and detailed meta-data, META-SHARE will help application developers by facilitating accurate searches to be carried out over a large set of reusable tools, as well as over data on which they can be re-trained and evaluated.

In addition to reusability, a further issue that must be considered is the ease with which component tools can be combined together to create complete applications. Only if this combination can occur with minimal, or no, configuration, can the tools be said to be *interoperable*.

It is often the case that interoperability can be problematic to achieve, especially for resources that have different developers or creators. Reasons for this include the following:

- Use of different programming languages to implement the tools.
- Different input and output formats of the tools (e.g., plain text vs. XML).
- Incompatible data types produced by the tools (e.g., different tag sets).

Having to deal with such issues can be both time-consuming and a source of frustration for the developer, often requiring program code to be rewritten or extra code to be produced in order to ensure that data can pass freely and correctly between the different resources used in the application.

One way to overcome some of the problems of interoperability is to adopt the use of the Unstructured Information Management Architecture (UIMA)[1] (Ferrucci et al., 2006), which aims to facilitate the seamless combination of LRs into workflows that can carry out different natural language processing (NLP) tasks. U-Compare (Kano et al., 2009; Kano et al., 2011), which is built on top of UIMA, provides additional means for ensuring more universal interoperability between resources, as well as providing special facilities that allow the rapid construction and evaluation of natural language-processing/text-mining applications using interoperable UIMA-compliant resources, without the need for any additional programming.

METANET4U is one of a set of projects (together with META-NORD and CESAR), which are preparing LRs that operate on a wide range of different European languages for inclusion within META-SHARE. Part of the contribution of the METANET4U project is to encourage LR providers to make their resources UIMA-compliant. This is partly being achieved through the creation of a pilot version of META-SHARE, in which standard functionality is enhanced through the integration of U-Compare. As an initial step, UIMA-compliant LRs are currently being created for a subset of European languages, based on the resources that will be made available by the METANET4U partners. This will allow us to demonstrate that META-SHARE has the potential to serve not only as a useful tool to locate resources for a range of languages, but also to act as an integrated environment that allows for rapid prototyping and testing of applications that make use of these resources.

2 UIMA

In recent years, the issue of interoperability has been receiving increasing attention, e.g., Copestake et al. (2006); Cunningham et al. (2002); Laprun et al. (2002). UIMA provides a flexible and extensible architecture for implementing interoperability, which is achieved largely by virtue of a standard means of communication between resources when they are combined together into workflows.

2.1 Wrapping resources

At the heart of the UIMA framework is a data structure called the Common Analysis Structure (CAS). During the execution of a workflow, the

[1] http://uima.apache.org/

CAS is accessible by all resources, and stores all annotations, e.g., tokens, part-of-speech tags, syntactic parse trees, etc., that have been produced by the different resources. Each resource to be used within the UIMA framework must be "wrapped" as a UIMA component. This means that it must be specifically configured to obtain its input by reading data from the CAS. As output, UIMA components should add new annotations to the CAS, or update annotations already contained within it. For example, a tokeniser tool may add *Token* annotations to the CAS. A POS tagger may read *Token* annotations, and add a *POS* feature to them.

A standard way of reading, writing and updating the CAS, which must be followed by all UIMA components, means that differences in input/output formats of resources are essentially hidden, once the wrapper has been written. It is this feature that allows flexible and seamless combination of UIMA components into pipelines/workflows.

In order to facilitate such interoperability, a certain amount of overhead is required to create the wrapper code. Given that resources differ in their input/output format and parameters, a specialised wrapper must normally be produced for each different resource, although the general structure of the wrapper code is usually similar. The basic steps are as follows:

1. Read appropriate annotations from the CAS.
2. Convert the UIMA annotations to input format required by the tool (e.g., plain text, XML, standoff annotations, inline annotations, etc.)
3. Execute the tool, passing the correctly formatted input to it.
4. Convert the output of the tool to UIMA annotations.
5. Write or update the CAS with the newly generated UIMA annotations.

An example of a possible workflow for carrying out named entity recognition is the following:

Sentence Splitter →Tokeniser → POS Tagger → Syntactic Parser →Named Entity Recogniser

In combining resources together, it is only necessary to ensure that the types of annotation required as input by a particular component are present in the CAS at the time of execution of that component. For example, tokenisers generally require text that has been split into sentences as input. Thus, if such a tokeniser is to be included in a workflow, one of the components executed earlier in the workflow should produce output corresponding to sentence annotations. The UIMA framework makes this process quite straightforward, since each UIMA component must declare its input/output annotation types in a separate descriptor file.

The UIMA framework also deals with another issue of interoperability, in that after resources are wrapped as UIMA components, the original programming language is hidden and thus becomes irrelevant. Writing the UIMA wrapper is fairly straightforward when the resource is implemented in either Java or C++, or if the tool is available as a web service or as a binary.

2.2 Compatibility of data types

As mentioned above, each UIMA component must declare its input and output annotation types. Annotation types are separately declared in a *type system* descriptor file, and may be hierarchically structured. For example, a type *SemanticAnnotation* may specify *NamedEntity* and *Coreference* as subtypes. Each annotation type may additionally define features, e.g., a *Token* type may have a *PartOfSpeech* feature.

The UIMA framework itself does not impose or recommend the use of a particular type system. Accordingly, the various existing repositories of UIMA components (e.g., the BIONLP UIMA Component Repository (Baumgartner et al., 2008), the CMU UIMA component repository[2] and the UIMA-fr consortium (Hernandez et al., 2010)) generally make use of different type systems. This can be a major barrier to universal interoperability of resources. Although resources chosen from the same repository are likely to be interoperable, the same cannot be said for resources chosen from multiple repositories. This is because the individual type systems may use different package names, different names for annotation types or have different hierarchical structures, even though functionalities of the components across different repositories may be similar.

Ideally, in order to achieve maximum interoperability, a single, common type system would be imposed, to be followed by all developers of UIMA components. However, this is not considered a viable option, as it would be difficult to achieve consensus on exactly which types should be present, given, for example, the various different syntactic and semantic theories on which different tools are based.

[2] http://uima.lti.cs.cmu.edu

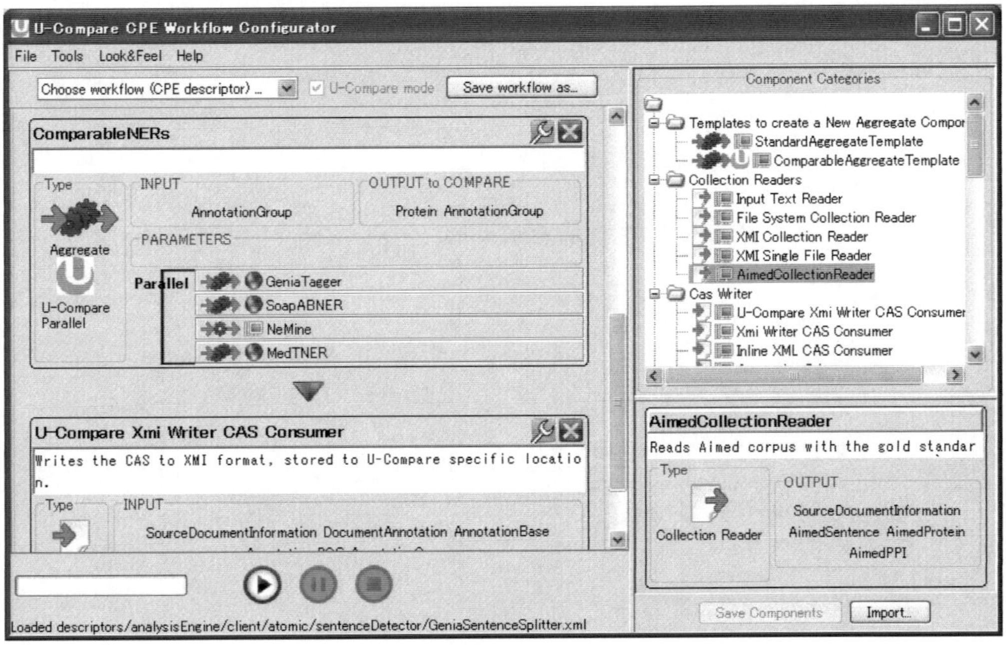

Figure 1: U-Compare interface

3 U-Compare

U-Compare (Kano et al., 2009; Kano et al., 2011) is a system built on top of UIMA. The main goals of U-Compare are to allow rapid and flexible construction of NLP applications and evaluation of these applications against gold-standard annotated data, without the need for any additional programming.

U-Compare builds upon the core elements of UIMA to provide a graphical user interface, which allows users to construct and configure workflows of UIMA components, using simple drag-and-drop actions, and to apply the workflow to a corpus of documents at the click of a button.

U-Compare includes several built-in annotation viewers, making it easy to visualise the various annotations produced by workflows, including more complex annotation types, such as syntactic trees and feature structures. The main U-Compare interface is shown in Figure 1, with the library of available components on the right, and the workflow builder on the left.

The rapid construction of NLP workflows is reliant on the ready availability of component resources. U-Compare is distributed with a library of over 50 UIMA components, constituting the world's largest type-compatible UIMA repository. A particular emphasis on biomedical text processing allows specialised, complex workflows to be constructed, e.g., to disambiguate species of biomedical named entities (Wang et al., 2010).

3.1 Evaluation in U-Compare

U-Compare additionally provides special facilities for evaluating the performance of workflows. For each step of a workflow (e.g., part-of-speech tagging, parsing, etc.) there are often several tools that could be used. U-Compare can compare the performance of each possible combination of tools against a gold standard annotated corpus, i.e., a corpus in which information of the type produced by the tool has been marked-up manually by human annotators. Such a comparison allows the best performing workflow for one's particular task to be determined. Results are reported in terms of performance statistics, precision, recall and F-score. The U-Compare evaluation interface is shown in Figure 2. On the left are the performance statistics and on the right are the annotations produced by the various tools under evaluation.

The power of U-Compare's evaluation framework has recently been demonstrated in the recognition of chemical named entities in scientific texts (Kolluru et al., 2011). A well–established named entity recogniser for the chemistry domain, Oscar3 (Corbett & Murray-Rust, 2006), had a rigid structure, which made it difficult to modularise and to adapt to new and emerging trends in annotation and corpora.

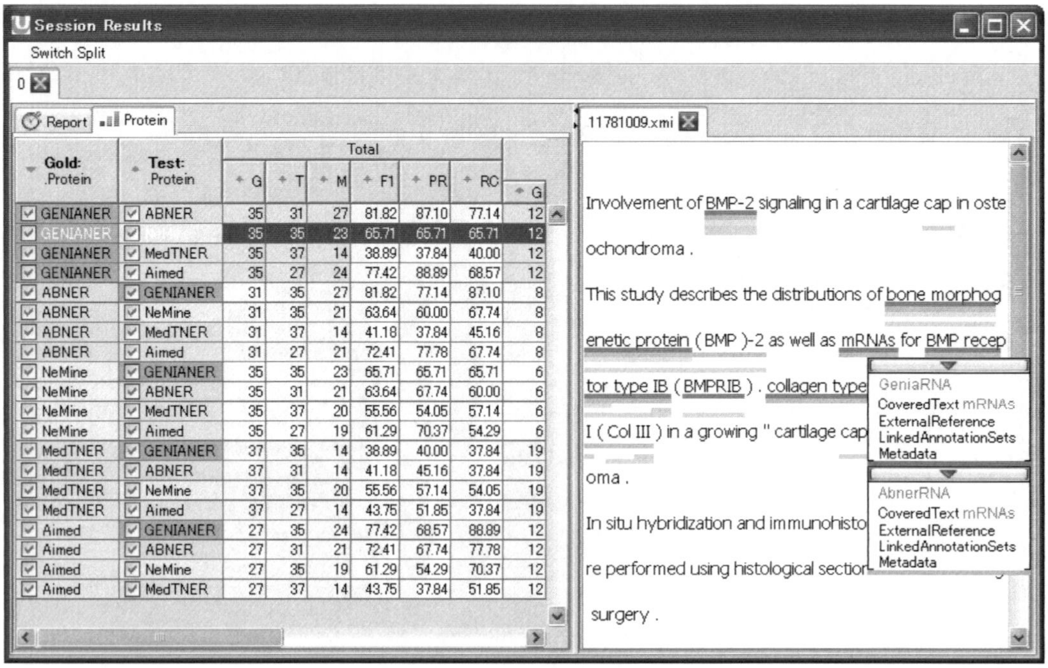

Figure 2: Evaluation in U-Compare

Oscar3 was refactored into a number of separate, reconfigurable U-Compare components, and experiments showed that the substitution of a new tokeniser into the workflow could improve performance over the original system. The new, modularised version of Oscar (OSCAR4[3]) has recently been released.

A similar approach could also be used to improve the performance of other types of applications relevant to language technology, e.g., machine translation systems such as Apertium (Armentano-Oller et al., 2006), which also has a modular architecture.

3.2 U-Compare type system

U-Compare's current inventory of components has been drawn from a number of different sources, including existing UIMA repositories that use their own type systems. This meant that issues of type system compatibility had to be faced. As a partial solution to the type system interoperability problem, U-Compare has defined a *sharable* type system.

The aim of the U-Compare sharable type system is to act as a kind of bridge, to facilitate the construction of workflows containing almost any UIMA components, regardless of their source, or the original type system that they use. Communication between existing UIMA components is made possible by mapping their original input and output types to appropriate types in the U-Compare type system. Newly wrapped components directly use types belonging to the sharable type system. However, such components may define their own type system extensions, as long as any new types defined extend existing types in the hierarchy. It is hoped that the U-Compare type system will eventually be adopted as a standard, which will help to ensure greater interoperability between UIMA components in the future.

As mentioned previously, defining an exhaustive, common type system sufficient for all possible UIMA components would be a virtually impossible task. According to this, the aim of the U-Compare type system is to define a set of types that on the one are hand fairly general, but on the other hand are fine-grained enough to allow the most common types of annotation produced by NLP applications to be represented. The currently defined types correspond to syntactic, semantic and document-level concepts, as illustrated in Figures 3, 4 and 5, respectively.

When mapping between a particular type system and the U-Compare sharable type system, it is inevitable that in certain cases, information loss will occur. This is because the general types of the U-Compare type system cannot encode all the subtleties of information produced by many different components. Therefore, certain aspects of the functionality of a particular resource may

[3] https://bitbucket.org/wwmm/oscar4/

be hidden by the U-Compare type system. However, since one of the aims of U-Compare is to provide as large a library as possible of interoperable NLP components, such a trade-off is sometimes necessary to guarantee such interoperability.

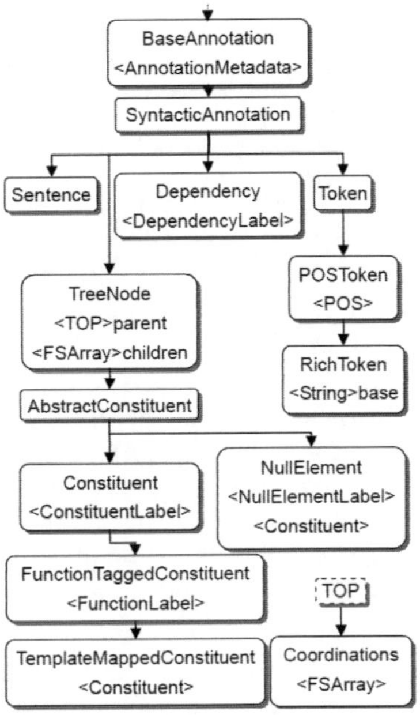

Figure 3: Syntactic types in the U-Compare type system

Despite the possible loss of information when using the U-Compare type system, two important points should be noted. Firstly, the hierarchical nature of the type system aims to minimise information loss as much as possible. Types from exisiting, external systems can be mapped to the most specific type possible in the U-Compare hierarchy. Secondly, since the U-Compare type system is still considered as work in progress, the addition of further well-motivated types will be considered, which could further decrease levels of information loss.

A further advantage of the hierarchical structure of the type system is that it can help to expose clearly the capabilities of a particular resource. Consider, for example, a resource that outputs annotations of type *RichToken* (see Figure 3). These annotations constitute a token whose base form is recorded in the *base* feature. As such, they could be used to store the output of a morphological analyser.

The type system hierarchy tells us that *RichToken* is a subtype of *POSToken,* which stores a token, along with part-of-speech information. Thus, annotations of type *RichToken* will specify not only the base form of the token, but also its part-of-speech. Therefore, if a particular tool requires part-of-speech tagged tokens as input, then it can be executed in a workflow following a tool whose output is *either POSToken* or *RichToken*, since both of these tool types will output token annotations with part-of-speech information. Even though tools outputting *RichToken* information would contain some redundant information in this case, this does not matter, as long as the required information is also present in the CAS.

4 U-Compare and META-SHARE

The utility of U-Compare has already been amply demonstrated through its use in many tasks by both NLP experts and non-expert users, from the individual level to worldwide challenges. These include the BioNLP'09 shared task (Kim et al., 2009) for the extraction of bio-molecular events (bio-events) that appear in biomedical literature, in which U-Compare served as an official support system; the CoNLL-2010 shared task on the detection of speculation in biomedical texts (Farkas et al., 2010); the BioCreative II.5 challenge (Sætre et al., 2009) of text-mining and information-extraction systems applied to the biological domain; and linking with Taverna (Kano et al., 2010), a generic workflow management system.

Mostly, these usages have been limited to the processing of biomedical texts in the English language. Integration within META-SHARE will additionally allow the utility of U-Compare to be demonstrated in a multilingual scenario, where it will help to facilitate the rapid expansion of NLP applications covering a range of European languages. In order to ensure the success of this, a number of different areas have to be addressed.

4.1 Expansion of U-Compare component library

In order to meet with the multilingual and multimodal goals of META-SHARE, the current library of U-Compare components must be expanded. As an initial step, we have identified around 40 resources (both tools and corpora) that concern languages other than English (namely Catalan, French, Maltese, Portuguese, Romanian and Spanish), and which our METANET4U project partners are planning to make available in META-SHARE.

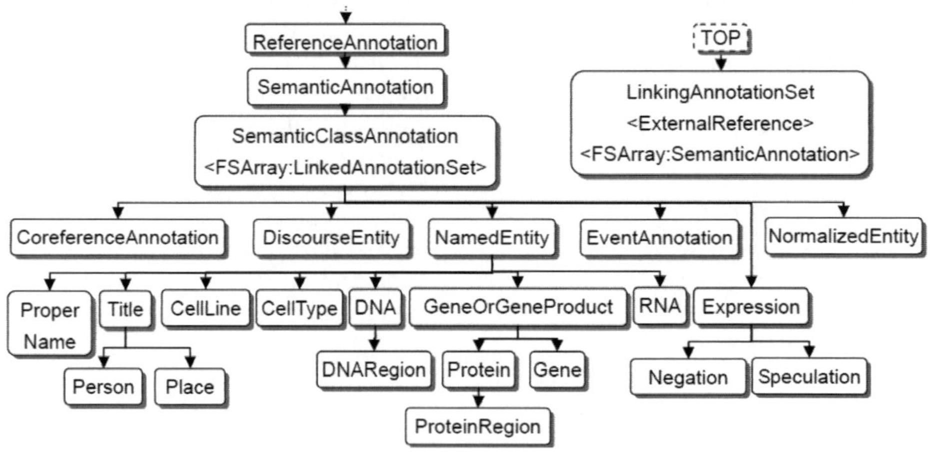

Figure 4: Semantic types in the U-Compare type system

The resources are a mixture of monolingual and multilingual, and concern different modalities (both written and spoken language). As an ongoing task, these resources are being wrapped as UIMA components that comply with the U-Compare type system.

4.2 Evaluation and consolidation of the U-Compare type system

Once completed, the new set of U-Compare compatible UIMA components will almost double the size of the current library, and in creating them, we will be able to consolidate and evaluate the utility of the U-Compare type system in scenarios other than the processing of English biomedical text. This will help us to work towards the goal of defining a sharable-type system that can be applied regardless of language or domain, and which could be promoted as a standard to be followed both in META-SHARE, and beyond.

An initial analysis of the selected resources suggests that, to a large extent, the existing type system is sufficient to describe their inputs and outputs, with no language-specific issues becoming immediately apparent. However, some types of tool that are not currently available in the U-Compare library, such as discourse parsers and semantic role labellers, will motivate a small number of additions to the type system. Since the current version of the type system was created only for written resources, further extensions will need to be made for spoken resources.

4.3 Extending U-Compare functionality

The functionality of the U-Compare software must also be extended to handle the new types of components that will be made available, in particular to provide support for multilingual and speech-based components. As mentioned previously, U-Compare provides annotation viewers that allow annotations produced by workflows to be easily visualised. Since multilingual components will often produce annotations in multiple languages, a new type of viewing component should be developed that allows both source and target language information to be displayed. Viewers for speech-based output will allow speech files to be played and corresponding waveforms to be displayed.

4.4 Specification of workflows

As a final step, we will implement a number of workflows that make use of the newly wrapped components in various ways. Through integration within META-SHARE, these workflows can act as templates for carrying out important language-processing tasks, which may be changed or configured according to the requirements of different types of application.

We have designed workflows for over 20 different tasks, which will be implemented after the appropriate resources have been wrapped. Some of these are fairly simple tasks, which may be considered as building blocks to be used in the construction of more complex workflows (e.g., sentence splitting and POS tagging, etc), whilst others may be considered complete tasks in themselves (e.g., discourse parsing, translation of text, ontology building, etc.), involving 10 or more processing steps.

According to the set of LRs that are currently being wrapped as UIMA components, most of the tasks will be accomplishable in a number of different languages, through the substitution of appropriate alternative components.

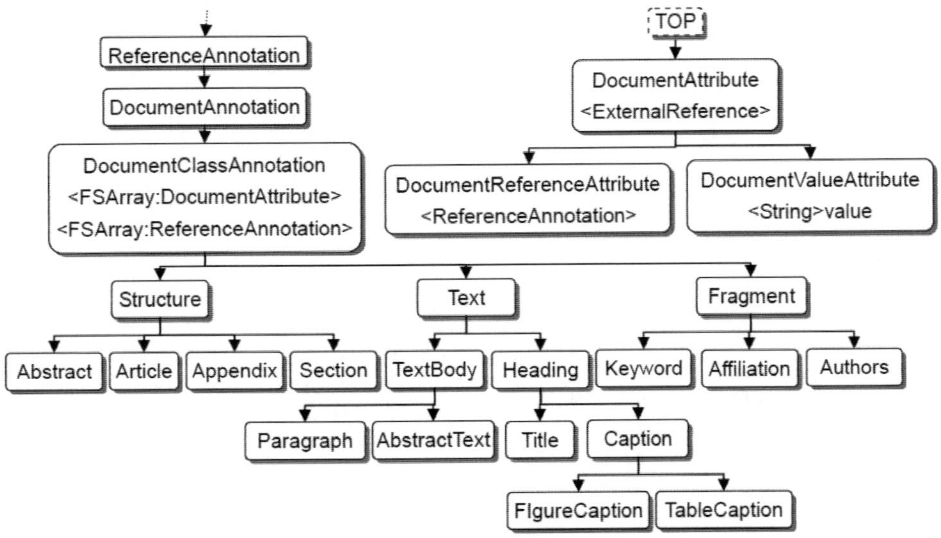

Figure 5: Document-level types in the U-Compare type system

Often, there are several paths that can be taken to complete a given task for each language. For example, some tools perform *both* part-of speech tagging and lemmatization, whilst in other cases, different tools exist to perform each step separately.

Since a number of gold-standard annotated corpora will be made available as U-Compare components, an evaluation of which path produces the best results will often be possible, using U-Compare's evaluation functionalities, as described earlier. By providing facilities for META-SHARE users to make their own workflows available to other users, and to provide feedback about existing workflows, the process of creating new applications could become even easier.

5 Conclusion

The speed and ease with which new applications can be developed using component language resources is heavily dependent on the amount of work that must be performed by system developers to allow such components to communicate with each other in the correct manner. We have described how, by wrapping resources as UIMA components whose annotation types conform to the U-Compare type system, greater interoperability of the resources, and with it, easier reuse and more flexible combination, can be achieved.

It is hoped that the planned integration of the U-Compare system within META-SHARE will contribute to a more rapid and straightforward expansion of the European language technology landscape. The integration will allow users to benefit from running and configuring existing workflows, as well as creating new workflows, with only a few mouse clicks, and without the need to write any new program code.

Acknowledgements

The work described in this paper is being funded by the DG INFSO of the European Commission through the ICT Policy Support Programme, Grant agreement no. 270893 (METANET4U).

References

Armentano-Oller, C., Carrasco, R., Corbí-Bellot, A., Forcada, M., Ginestí-Rosell, M., Ortiz-Rojas, S. (2006). Open-source Portuguese–Spanish machine translation. *Computational Processing of the Portuguese Language*, 50-59.

Baumgartner, W. A., Cohen, K. B., & Hunter, L. (2008). An open-source framework for large-scale, flexible evaluation of biomedical text mining systems. *Journal of Biomedical Discovery and Collaboration, 3*, 1.

Bel, N. (2010). Platform for Automatic, Normalized Annotation and Cost-Effective Acquisition of Language Resources for Human Language Technologies: PANACEA. In *Proceedings of XXVI Congreso de la Sociedad Española para el Procesamiento del Lenguaje Natural (SEPLN-2010).*

Copestake, A., Corbett, P., Murray-Rust, P., Rupp, C. J., Siddharthan, A., Teufel, S. (2006). An architecture for language processing for scientific texts. In *Proceedings of the UK e-Science All Hands Meeting 2006.*

Corbett, P., & Murray-Rust, P. (2006). High-throughput identification of chemistry in life science texts. *Computational Life Sciences II*, 107-118.

Cunningham, D. H., Maynard, D. D., Bontcheva, D. K., & Tablan, M. V. (2002). GATE: A framework and graphical development environment for robust NLP tools and applications. In *Proceedings of the 40th Anniversary Meeting of the Association for Computational Linguistics (ACL'02)*, pp. 168-175.

Farkas, R., Vincze, V., Móra, G., Csirik, J., & Szarvas, G. (2010). The CoNLL-2010 shared task: learning to detect hedges and their scope in natural language text. In *Proceedings of the Fourteenth Conference on Computational Natural Language Learning---Shared Task*, pp. 1-12.

Ferrucci, D., Lally, A., Gruhl, D., Epstein, E., Schor, M., Murdock, J. W. (2006). Towards an Interoperability Standard for Text and Multi-Modal Analytics. *IBM Research Report RC24122.*

Hernandez, N., Poulard, F., Vernier, M., & Rocheteau, J. (2010). Building a French-speaking community around UIMA, gathering research, education and industrial partners, mainly in Natural Language Processing and Speech Recognizing domains. In *LREC 2010 Workshop on New Challenges for NLP Frameworks*, pp. 41-45.

Hughes, B., & Kamat, A. (2005). A metadata search engine for digital language archives. *D-Lib Magazine, 11*(2), 6.

Kano, Y., Baumgartner, W. A., Jr., McCrohon, L., Ananiadou, S., Cohen, K. B., Hunter, L. (2009). U-Compare: share and compare text mining tools with UIMA. *Bioinformatics, 25*(15), 1997-1998.

Kano, Y., Dobson, P., Nakanishi, M., Tsujii, J., & Ananiadou, S. (2010). Text mining meets workflow: linking U-Compare with Taverna. *Bioinformatics, 26*(19), 2486-2487.

Kano, Y., Miwa, M., Cohen, K. B., Hunter, L. E., Ananiadou, S., & Tsujii, J. (2011). U-Compare: A modular NLP workflow construction and evaluation system. *IBM Journal of Research and Development, 55*(3), 11:1-11:10.

Kim, J.-D., Ohta, T., Pyysalo, S., Kano, Y., & Tsujii, J. (2009). Overview of BioNLP'09 Shared Task on Event Extraction. In *Proceedings of the BioNLP 2009 Workshop Companion Volume for Shared Task*, pp. 1-9.

Kolluru, B., Hawizy, L., Murray-Rust, P., Tsujii, J., & Ananiadou, S. (2011). Using Workflows to Explore and Optimise Named Entity Recognition for Chemistry. *PLoS ONE, 6*(5), e20181.

Laprun, C., Fiscus, J., Garofolo, J., & Pajot, S. (2002). A practical introduction to ATLAS. In *Proceedings of the 3rd LREC Conference*, pp 1928–1932.

Sætre, R., Yoshida, K., Miwa, M., Matsuzaki, T., Kano, Y., & Tsujii, J. (2009). AkaneRE Relation Extraction: Protein Interaction and Normalization in the BioCreAtIvE II. 5 Challenge. In *Proceedings of BioCreative II. 5 Workshop 2009 special session| Digital Annotations*, p 33.

Váradi, T., Krauwer, S., Wittenburg, P., Wynne, M., & Koskenniemi, K. (2008). CLARIN: Common language resources and technology infrastructure. In *Proceedings of the 6th International Conference on Language Resources and Evaluation (LREC 2008)*, pp. 1244-1248.

Wang, X., Tsujii, J., & Ananiadou, S. (2010). Disambiguating the Species of Biomedical Named Entities Using Natural Language Parsers. *Bioinformatics, 26*(5), 661-667.

Federated Operation Model for the Language Grid

Toru Ishida[1], Yohei Murakami[2], Yoko Kubota[1], Rieko Inaba[1]
[1]Department of Social Informatics, Kyoto University
[2]National Institute of Information and Communications Technology
ishida@i.kyoto-u.ac.jp, yohei@nict.go.jp,
{yoko, inaba}@i.kyoto-u.ac.jp

Abstract

The concept of collective intelligence is contributing significantly to knowledge creation on the Web. While current knowledge creation activities tend to be founded on the approach of assembling content such as texts, images and videos, we propose here the service-oriented approach. We use the term *service grid* to refer to a framework of collective intelligence based on Web services. This paper provides an institutional design mainly for non-profit service grids that are open to the public. In particular, we deepen the discussion of 1) intellectual property rights, 2) application systems, and 3) federated operations from the perspective of the following stakeholders: *service providers*, *service users* and *service grid operators* respectively. The Language Grid has been operating, based on the proposed institutional framework, since December 2007.

1 Introduction

Based on scalable computing environments, we propose a service-oriented approach to developing collective intelligence. This approach requires institutional design to share services among participants. In this paper, we call the infrastructure to form service-oriented collective intelligence the *service grid*[1]. The service grid has three stakeholders: *service providers*, *service users* and *service grid operators*. For the institutional design, we should consider the following issues related to each stakeholder:

- How to protect intellectual property rights of service providers and to motivate them to provide services to the service grid. To this end, service providers should be allowed to define for what purpose or purposes their services can be used and to define usage rights accordingly.
- How to encourage a wide variety of activities of service users to increase their use of the provided services. To this end, service users should be allowed to run application systems that employ the services permitted for such use.
- How to reduce the load on service grid operators, while allowing them to globally extend their service grids. To this end, federated operation should be facilitated, where several operators collaboratively operate their service grids by connecting them in a peer-to-peer fashion.

In this paper, we describe our institutional design for a public service grid typically operated by non-profit organizations such as universities and research institutes. Based on this discussion, we have already developed the *service grid server software* and started the Language Grid that focuses on language services (Ishida, 2006). The rest of this paper describes the concept of service-oriented collective intelligence, the institutional design considering stakeholders including service providers, service users and service grid operators, and our experience in operating the Language Grid.

2 Stakeholders

To simplify the following discussions in this paper, the main stakeholders are classified into three groups:

[1] Service grid is a generic term meaning a framework where "services are composed to meet the requirements of a user community within constraints specified by the resource provider" (Furmento et al., 2002) (Krauter et al., 2002).

Proceedings of Workshop on Language Resources, Technology and Services in the Sharing Paradigm, pages 59–66,
Chiang Mai, Thailand, November 12, 2011.

- *Service provider* provides all kinds of services to the service grid.
- *Service user* invokes and uses the services provided to the service grid.
- *Service grid operator* is provided with services from the service providers, and allows the service users to invoke and use the provided services.

Service providers and service users are collectively called *service grid users*. A service grid user can act as a service provider as well as a service user. The role of the service grid operator is to stand between service grid users (typically between a service provider and a service user) and support their provision and use of the services. In the following sections, we discuss institutional design in terms of the contracts between a service grid operator and a service grid user.

Note that Web services are classified into *atomic services* and *composite services*. An atomic service means a Web service that enables service users to access the provided resources. Such provided resources include data, software, and human resources that are shared in the service grid as atomic services. On the other hand, a composite service means a Web service that is realized by a procedure called *workflow* that invokes atomic services.

To handle the intellectual properties present in the services and resources, the service grid operator may propose a unified license (GPL, Creative Commons etc.) to the service providers to register their services with the service grid. While a unified license will simplify the operation and promote the use of the service grid, it could cause the service providers to lose some or all of their incentives. Therefore, to better support the service providers, the institutional design of the service grid will not be based on the premise of a unified license.

The operation of the service grid discussed in the rest of this paper assumes that it is operated publicly mainly by non-profit organizations such as universities and research institutes. It does not assume the case of the service grid in a business firm, where service grid operators can completely or partially control the incentives of service grid users.

3 Service Provider

3.1 Purpose of the Service Use

From the service provider's standpoint, any discussion of the protection of their intellectual property must address the purpose intended in using their services. In fact, many research institutes and public organizations clearly specify that their services are for *non-profit or research use only*. To reflect such service providers' concerns, we classify the purpose of service use into the following three categories and allow each service provider to permit one or more of the categories:

- *Non-profit use* means 1) use by public institutions and non-profit organizations for their main activities, or 2) use by companies and organizations other than public institutions and non-profit organizations for their *corporate social responsibility* activities.
- *Research use* means the use for research that does not directly contribute to commercial profit.
- *Commercial use* means the use for purposes intended to directly or indirectly contribute to commercial profit.

The above classification can be applied to organizational use as well as personal use. However, when personal use only means private use, personal use can be classified as non-profit use. Note that activities by public institutions and non-profit organizations other than their main activities are excluded, aiming to prohibit service use to obtain funding. Meanwhile, corporate social responsibility activities are included in non-profit use because such activities are often operated in collaboration with public institutions or non-profit organizations.

If a service provider is already selling its service to organizations like local governments, it may not wish to allow non-profit use through the service grid. If service users want to use services, the specified purpose of service use must comply with the terms of use specified by the service provider.

3.2 Control of Service Use

When service providers register their services in the service grid, they are required to provide information on copyright and other intellectual property rights of the resources included in their services. In the event that the service provider has been granted a license to the resource by a third party, such information shall also be included. The service provider is required to own the resources or the authority to allow third parties to use the resources. This prevents the service users from accidentally violating the third party's intellectual property rights.

Now, who should register and manage the services in the service grid? If we stand on the premise that the collective intelligence is autonomously formed by the service providers, the service providers should be responsible for the maintenance of their resources, and the process of developing the resources into an atomic service, which we call *wrapping*. The service providers also have to maintain their services and the connection between the services and the service grid. On the other hand, to guarantee the service's quality and safety, the registration and maintenance of services should be done by the operator or with the operator's approval. Therefore, the decision about who should register and manage the services needs to be made considering the trade-off between stimulating the autonomous activities of the service provider and ensuring the quality and safety of the service grid.

Likewise, we need to consider whether to leave the service deregistration process to the service provider or the operator. When focusing on the quality and the safety of the service grid, at least to cover the case of emergencies, the operator needs to be able to deregister a service.

For the service provider, it is desirable that there be flexibility in setting out the terms of use of their services. For example, the possible conditions are as follows:

- Restrictions on the service users who may be licensed to use the services;
- Restrictions on the purpose for which the services may be used;
- Restrictions on the application systems that use the services;
- Restrictions on the number of times that the services may be accessed and the amount of data that may be downloaded from the services.

By setting out conditions of their services employing the same resource, the service provider can provide their services under dual license. For example, one is provided to every user under several restrictions on access counts and data transfer size without any charge. Meanwhile, the other is provided to the users who pay a fee without any restrictions.

In general, when the service grid allows the terms of use to be set in detail, it will increase the service provider's satisfaction, while forcing greater overhead on the service users to comply with the detailed terms of use. Moreover, when the service users use a composite service, they need to satisfy all terms of use of every atomic service in the composite service. If we try to assure that automatically, the operator must provide technical measures to ensure that the service users will not violate the terms of use. Therefore, we must trade the service provider's flexibility off against the service user's convenience and the operator's cost.

4 Service User

4.1 Service Use through Application System

When service users use the service grid for purposes other than personal use, many of them provide an *application system* using services to other users. Here *application system* means, as shown in Fig. 1, a system that is provided by a service user and that allows users of the system to indirectly access the service grid without being personally authorized by the service grid. In this case, the service user is responsible for ensuring that the application system users comply with the terms of use of each service that is used through the application system.

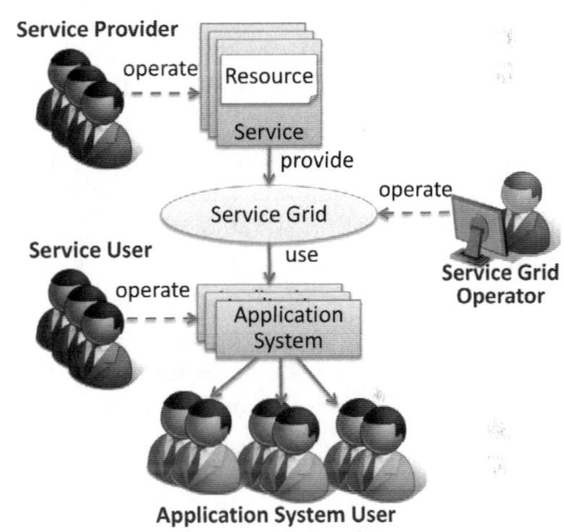

Fig. 1. Service Use through Application System

4.2 Control of Application System

A service user may operate different types of application systems; for example, one provides an application system to the general public through the Web, and another provides an application system through a particular terminal in a certain location like a reception counter. This paper focuses on how an application system can be controlled by the service user and classifies the control of application systems into two types: *under client control* and *under server control*.

- *Under client control* means the status where the users of an application system are under the control of the service user who provides the application system.

More specifically, it means the status where the terminals of application system users are under the control of the service user or where the service user is able to identify each application system user. In all cases, the service user who provides the application system must be able to fully grasp at any time the status of use of the application system at each terminal and/or by each user, and have the technical and legal authority to suspend use as necessary.

- *Under server control* means the status where the server on which the application system runs is under the control of the service user, while application system users are not under the control of the service user. In this case, the service user must be able to fully grasp at any time the status of use of the application system server and have the technical and legal authority to suspend the server as necessary.

Two examples of the operation of an application system are shown in Fig. 2. When an application system provided through the Web can be accessed by users from home without authentication, the status is not *under client control*; however, if the service user controls the Web server, the status is *under server control*. When an application system is provided through a terminal at a reception counter and the terminal is under the control of the service user, the operation is classified as *under client control*.

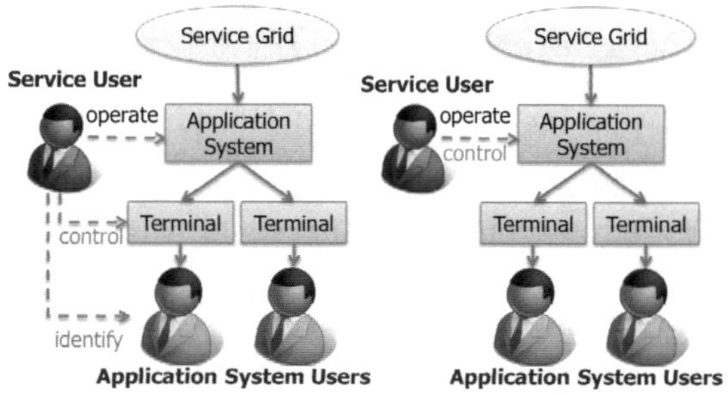

(1) Client Control (2) Server Control

Fig. 2. Service Use through Application System

The classification aims to allow service users to develop their own application system and select properly the range of the application system to be offered. Furthermore, the service provider can limit the range of application system users by specifying which type of application system control the provided service must adopt. For example, when a service provider sells a service to local governments, the service provider may agree to provide the service to patients at a reception counter in a hospital (*under client control*) but may refuse to provide the service to the public through a local government's Web server (*under server control*).

4.3 Return for Service Providers

Where is the service provider's incentive for providing their services? When the service providers provide their services for free, the service grid operator is required to provide statistical information on the use of the services to the service providers. The statistical information shows who used or is using which service and to what extent. Such information stimulates the interaction between the service providers and the service users. However, the statistical information should not include any transferred data or personal information regarding the senders of data. In case the service providers wish to obtain information on the use of the services other than statistics, the provider should conclude an agreement that establishes the provision of such information with the service user. The service grid operator is not involved in such an agreement.

When service providers provide their services for profit, they will receive fees from the service users by concluding a contract for the payment of such fees. Again, the operator is not involved in such contracts.

5 Service Grid Operator

To globally disseminate the service grid, which is centered on non-profit organizations like universities and research institutes, multiple operator organizations need to create/join an affiliation. We call this *federated operation*. The reasons driving federated operation include not only the limited number of users that a single operator can handle, but also the locality caused by geographical conditions and application domains.

There are two types of federated operation. One is *centralized affiliation*, where the operators form a federal association to control the terms of affiliation based on mutual agreement. This yields flexibility in deciding affiliation style, but incurs a lot of cost in maintaining the federal association. The other is *decentralized affiliation*, which allows a service grid user to create and become the operator of a new service grid that reuses the agreements set by the first service grid. This type of operation promotes forming peer-to-peer networks by the operators. The type of affiliation is defined by reuse of agreements, but the formation of the peer-to-peer network by the operators is flexible and no maintenance cost is necessary. In the following section, we further discuss decentralized affiliation since it suits non-profit organizations like universities and research institutes.

Let an *affiliated operator* be a service grid user who operates its own service grid that reuses the agreements of the original service grid. Let an *affiliated user* be a user who is licensed to use the affiliated operator's service grid. In such a case, as shown in Fig. 3, the affiliated user can use the original service grid, in which the affiliated operator takes the role of a service grid user. That is the key idea of the peer-to-peer federated operation. Even in such case, service providers still have the right to choose whether to allow the affiliated user to use their services or not.

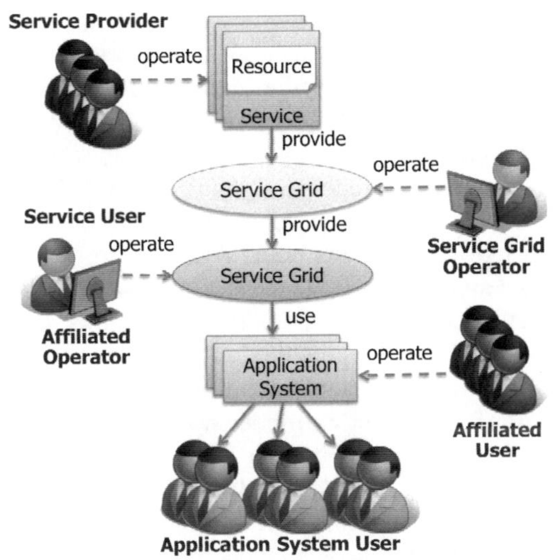

Fig. 3. Federated operation of service grid

Two service grids in equal partnership are likely to establish a *bidirectional affiliation,* where both operators become users of the other service grid. *Unidirectional affiliation* is also possible. For example, if one service grid provides only basic services and the other provides only applied services, the latter can be a user of the former service grid.

Sometimes it is impossible for different service grids to use exactly the same agreements. A typical problem is the governing law. For international affiliation, a possible idea is to adopt a common law like New York State law, but operators may wish to adopt the governing law of their own locations. In such a case, operators will use the same agreements except for the governing law. In that case, the service providers would need to accept the use of the different governing law to handle the affiliated users in that location.

6 Operation of the Language Grid

6.1 Language Grid Service Manager

The Language Grid is a service grid for language resources. Its concept was developed in 2005, and the project was launched in April 2006 (Ishida, 2006). The fundamental software forming the service grid was developed and has been released by the National Institute of Information and Communications Technology (NICT).

In designing the Language Grid system, it was important to deal with service providers, who had various incentives. For example, some language services may already be sold for profit. If the service grid failed to allow the service provider to receive fees for their services, it would be hard to realize a service grid that truly satisfied service users. Furthermore, since each of the existing dictionaries and language processing software had various types of licenses, the operator could not unify those licenses. Many research institutes that develop language resources can provide their resources as long as they are used only for research. However, if they are used by non-profit organizations for their activities, the research institutes may need to know by who, when, and how much their resources are being used. Such various incentives and conditions form the background of our institutional design prioritizing the intellectual property rights of the service providers. In our operation model (Ishida et al., 2008), language service providers can fully control access to their language services using the Language Grid. Language service providers can select users, restrict the total number of accesses per year/month/day, and set the maximum volume of data transfer per access. Providers can set those conditions via the Language Grid Service Manager (see Fig. 4). This software provides the registration of services, measurement of service usage frequency, access control of services, and always monitors the Language Grid.

On the other hand, service users wish to use the provided language resources in their various activities. At a school with multi-national students, teachers and parents as well as students will use language services. To allow a large number of people to use the services, the school is required to identify their registered users properly. At the reception counter of a hospital, however, it is difficult to ask patients to register themselves to the reception support system. It is more real-

Fig. 4. Language Grid Service Manager

istic to identify the terminals to permit service access. In this way, the system must be designed to allow many application system users to use language services in their different environments. To avoid the fraudulent usage of language services, however, service users should not allow the application system users to discover the ID and password of the Language Grid. For example, in the case of an NPO offering medical interpreter services to foreign patients, the NPO is required to enter their Language Grid ID and password in such a way that they do not become public; one solution is to embed the ID and password in their patient support systems.

6.2 Centralized Operation

The *service grid server software* has been developed and released as open source software. Using this source code, universities and research institutes can operate any kind of service grid. The Department of Social Informatics of Kyoto University started operation of the Language Grid for nonprofit purposes in December 2007. As of June 2011, 139 groups in 17 countries had joined the Language Grid: research institutes include Chinese Academy of Sciences, the National Research Council (CNR), German Research Center for Artificial Intelligence (DFKI), and National Institute of Informatics (NII), universities include Stuttgart University, Princeton University, Tsinghua University and a number of Japanese universities, NPO/NGOs and public sector bodies. Companies have also joined: Nippon Telegraph and Telephone Corporation (NTT), Toshiba, Oki and Google are providing their services without any charge.

We first expected that NPO, NGO and public sectors would become the major users, but universities are using the Language Grid more intensively at this moment; researchers and students who are working on Web analyses, CSCW, and multicultural issues are using language services for attaining their research goals. This trend is natural in the early stage of introducing a new Internet technology. Fig. 5 shows the recent statistics of member organizations.

Research institutes, universities, and companies are providing atomic language services such as dictionaries and machine translators. The number of shared language resources now totals 67. Organizations that provided language resources include Chinese Academy of Sciences, Stuttgart, Princeton, Kookmin, and Kyoto Universities, NICT, NII, NTT, Google, Toshiba, Oki, Kodensha, Asian Disaster Reduction Center and a number of public sector groups and NPO/NGOs. When providing atomic language services, providers specify copyright notices and license information in the profiles of the resources. To create composite services that involve the combination of atomic services, many workflows are being written and released. Currently more than 100 services are registered in the Language Grid.

The operation model designed by the authors reflects the intentions of user groups around the world like research institutes and non-profit organizations (Ishida et al. 2008). We were only able to attract such participants because we developed the Language Grid with a strong bias towards formalizing the obligations of all parties. Design of the operation model was conducted in parallel with development of the service grid server software. It took more than six months to achieve consensus on the model. It is probably fair to say that the software was written to realize the operation model.

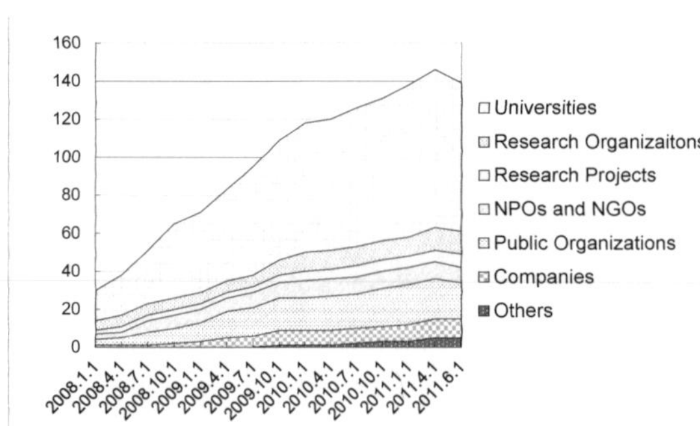

Fig. 5. Number of participant organizations

6.3 Federated Operation

From operating the Language Grid over two years, we have gained many insights. One of them is the importance of federated operation. Since the operation center in Kyoto cannot reach local organizations in other countries, over 70 percent of participating organizations are in Japan. Since we need global collaboration, even for solving language issues in local communities, this imbalance should be overcome: the Language Grid operators need to be dispersed into different organizations globally and to collaborate with each other. The federated operation model was invented to realize such collaboration. In fact, the National Electronics and Computer Technology Center (NECTEC) in Thailand launched the Bangkok Operation Center in October 2010, and is now federated with the Kyoto Operation Center. The Bangkok Operation Center has a plan to provide a collection of atomic services for language processing i.e. LEXiTRON for a Thai-English dictionary, Parsit for English to Thai machine translation, Vaja for Thai text to speech conversion, and morphological analysis utilities. Those services can be accessed by users of the Kyoto Operation Center.

So far, we have described the federated operation of the same kind of service grids. In fact, we had an opportunity to realize the collaboration of different kinds of service grids. The joint research between Tsinghua University's Smart Classroom and the Language Grid is a typical achievement (Suo *et al.*, 2009). We rebuilt Tsinghua University's Smart Classroom as a collection of pervasive computing services. That allowed easier connection between the Smart Classroom and the Language Grid to develop Open Smart Classroom, which connects classrooms in different countries. NECTEC also needs the collaboration of different kinds of service grids provided by neighboring interest groups. These services will soon be extended to cover other media resulting from NECTEC's initiative called the Digitized Thailand Project.

7 Conclusion

In this paper, we named an infrastructure that forms collective intelligence based on Web services a *service grid*, and designed an institutional framework for a public service grid operated by non-profit organizations such as universities and research institutes. From a consideration of the different standpoints of *service providers*, *service users* and *service grid operators*, which constitute the service grid, we proposed the following framework:

- To protect the intellectual property rights of service providers, the purposes of service use are classified into *non-profit use*, *research use*, and *commercial use*. The service providers can set the terms of service use for each purpose.
- The type of control employed by application systems are classified into *client control* and *server control*. This flexibility allows service users to employ different types of application systems to support their activities.
- To decrease the cost of service grid operators and extend service grid operation globally, the framework allows service grid operators to conduct *federated operation*. The collaboration is realized in a peer-to-peer fashion by introducing the concepts of *affiliated operators* and *affiliated users*.

The institutional design discussed in this paper is based on our three-year experience of operating the Language Grid. We hope that our experiences will promote the accumulation of knowledge about designing institutional frameworks and contribute to the development of service-oriented collective intelligence.

Acknowledgments

We acknowledge the considerable support of National Institute of Information and Communications Technology, and Department of Social Informatics, Kyoto University. A part of this work was supported by Strategic Information and Communications R&D Promotion Programme from Ministry of Internal Affairs, a Grant-in-Aid for Scientific Research (A) (21240014, 2009-2011) from Japan Society for the Promotion of Science (JSPS), and Kyoto University Global COE Program: Informatics Education and Research Center for Knowledge-Circulating Society.

References

Nathalie Furmento, William Lee, Anthony Mayer, Steven Newhouse, John Darlington. 2002. ICENI: an open grid service architecture implemented with Jini. *International Conference on High Performance Networking and Computing*:1-10.

Toru Ishida. 2006. Language Grid: an infrastructure for intercultural collaboration. *2006 IEEE/IPSJ Symposium on Applications and the Internet (SAINT-06)*: 96-100.

Toru Ishida, Akiyo Nadamoto, Yohei Murakami, Rieko Inaba, Tomohiro Shigenobu, Shigeo Matsubara, Hiromitsu Hattori, Yoko Kubota, Takao Nakaguchi, Eri Tsunokawa. 2008. A non-profit operation model for the language grid. *International Conference on Global Interoperability for Language Resources*: 114-121.

Klaus Krauter, Rajkumar Buyya, Muthucumaru Maheswaran. 2002. A taxonomy and survey of grid resource management systems for distributed computing. *Software: Practice & Experience* 32(2): 135-164.

Paul P. Maglio, Savitha Srinivasan, Jeffrey T. Kreulen, Jim Spohrer. 2006. Service systems, service scientists, SSME, and innovation. *Communications of the ACM* 49(7): 81-85.

Yue Suo, Naoki Miyata, Hiroki Morikawa, Toru Ishida, Yuanchun Shi. 2009. Open smart classroom: extensible and scalable learning system in smart space using web service technology. *IEEE Transactions on Knowledge and Data Engineering* 21(6): 814-828

Open-Source Platform for Language Service Sharing

Yohei Murakami, Masahiro Tanaka, Donghui Lin
National Institute of Information and Communications Technology
{yohei, mtnk, lindh}@nict.go.jp

Toru Ishida
Department of Social Informatics
Kyoto University
ishida@i.kyoto-u.ac.jp

Abstract

The Language Grid is an infrastructure for enabling users to share language services developed by language specialists and end user communities. Users can also create new services to support their intercultural/multilingual activities by composing various language services. In the Language Grid, there are several stakeholders with different incentives: service users, service providers, and a Language Grid operator. For enhancing the language service sharing, it is significant that the Language Grid can coordinate them to match their incentives. However, their incentives vary with the operation model of the Language Grid. To support the various operation models, the Language Grid should employ not a general platform dealing with various types of operation models, but a customizable platform. To this end, we have developed an open-source platform consisting of two types of components: core components and optional components. The former assures interoperability of Language Grids, while the latter provides flexibility of system configuration. It allows developers to extend the platform, and each operator to adapt the platform to his/her operation model by selecting the components. To validate the customizability, we have constructed the private Language Grid for Wikimedia using the same platform as public Language Grid.

1 Introduction

Although there are many language resources (both data and programs) on the Internet (Choukri, 2004), most intercultural collaboration activities still lack multilingual support. To overcome language barriers, we aim to construct a novel language infrastructure to improve accessibility and usability of language resources on the Internet. To this end, the Language Grid has been proposed (Ishida, 2006). The Language Grid takes a service-oriented collective intelligence approach to sharing language resources and creating new services to support intercultural/multilingual activities by combining language resources.

In previous work, many efforts have been made to combine language resources, such as UIMA (Ferrucci and Lally, 2004), GATE (Cunningham et al., 2002), D-Spin (Boehlke, 2009), Hart of Gold (Callmeier et al., 2004), and CLARIN (Varadi et al., 2008). Their purpose is to analyze a large amount of text data by linguistic processing pipelines. These pipelines consist of language resources, most of which are provided as open source by universities and research institutes. Users can thus collect language resources and freely combine them on those frameworks without considering other stakeholders.

Different from the above frameworks, the purpose of the Language Grid is to multilingualize texts for supporting intercultural collaboration by service workflows. PANACEA (Toral et al., 2011) is also a project to overcome language barriers by automatically acquiring, producing, updating, and maintaining language resources for MT by service workflow. The difference of them is that a workflow in the Language Grid combines language resources associated with complex intellectual property issues. These resources are provided by service providers who want to protect their ownership, and used by service users who need a part of the resources. Therefore, the Language Grid must coordinate these stakeholders' motivations. However, their incentives

Proceedings of Workshop on Language Resources, Technology and Services in the Sharing Paradigm, pages 67–74,
Chiang Mai, Thailand, November 12, 2011.

vary with the operation model of the Language Grid. To support the various operation models, we proposes open-source platform that enables developers to implement several modules and Language Grid operators to adapt their platforms to their operation models by selecting the modules. Moreover, by connecting their platforms, we can enhance language service sharing among different platforms.

The rest of this paper is organized as follows. Section 2 explains the design concept of the platform considering stakeholders' needs. Section 3 presents system architecture to satisfy requirements of the design concept. Section 4 illustrates how to extend and customize the platform. Section 5 introduces two types of system configurations to realize a public Language Grid and a private Language Grid. To validate the customizability, we show the case study of constructing the Language Grid for Wikimedia in Section 6.

2 Design Concept

The purpose of Language Grid is to accumulate language services and compose them. To realize Language Grid, system architecture should be designed to satisfy requirements of different operation models. Therefore, this section summarizes requirements of each of the operation models, and clarifies the required functions of Language Grid.

2.1 Requirements

Language Grid operators require flexibility of system configuration so that they can adapt the configuration to their two types of operation models: public Language Grid and private Language Grid. The former model is more open than the latter one. Every stakeholder is different organization in the public one, while an operator operates Language Grid for his/her use in the private one. For example, an operator operates a private Language Grid on a single cluster of machines and deploys on the cluster services, the provision policies of which are relaxed. Meanwhile, another operator operates a public Language Grid in a distributed environment by deploying services on each provider's server because the provision policies of the services are too strict. In the former case, the operator places high priority on performance of services. In the latter case, the other operator puts priority on resource security. Further, both of them may want to expand available services by allowing their users to access services on other Language Grids.

2.2 Functions

The Language Grid platform should provide the following functions extracted from the requirements in the previous subsection.

1. Modularization of system components: Language Grid operators can change implementations of each component in Language Grid platform in order to build their own Language Grids compliant with their operation models. In particular, it is necessary to switch communication components so that they can operate the platform both in a centralized environment and a distributed environment. The platform combines implementations of each component based on a configuration file defined by operators.
2. Language Grid composition: Language Grid operators can compose several Language Grids in order to increase the number of language services. The Language Grid platform realizes information sharing among Language Grids, and service invocation across Language Grids.

In designing the Language Grid architecture that provides the above functions, there are several technical constraints. For example, the architecture should be independent of service interfaces because language service interfaces vary depending on operators. In addition, the architecture should be independent of specifications of service invocations because there are several such specifications over HTTP, such as SOAP, REST, JSON, and Protocol Buffers. Moreover, it is necessary to distribute the platform to handle physically distributed services if the services are deployed on their providers' severs. In the next section, we explain the system architecture of the Language Grid platform considering these constraints.

3 System Architecture

3.1 Overview

The Language Grid architecture consists of six parts: *Service Manager*, *Service Supervisor*, *Grid Composer*, *Service Database*, *Composite Service Container*, and *Atomic Service Container*. Figure 1 (a) focuses on the first four parts, and Figure 1 (b) focuses on the last two parts.

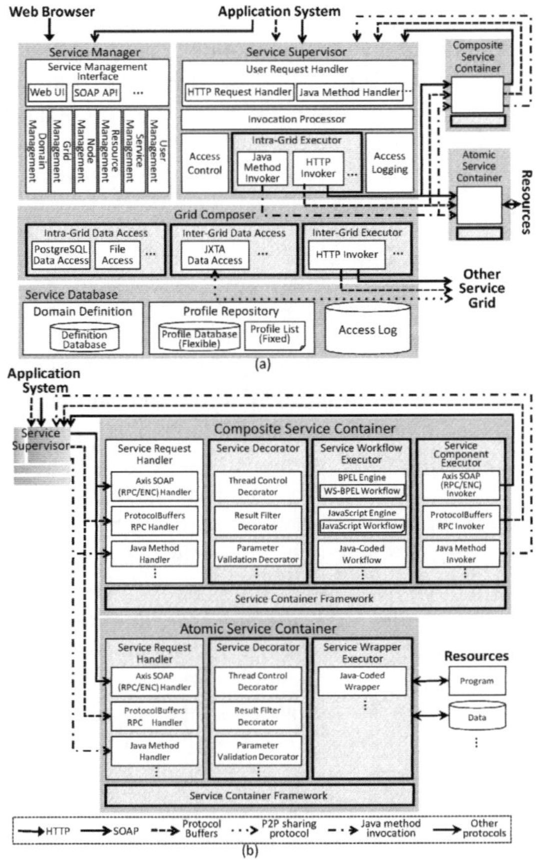

Figure 1. Language Grid Architecture

The *Service Manager* manages domain definition, grid information, node information, user information, service information and resource information registered in Language Grid. The service information includes access control settings and access logs. Since the information is registered through the *Service Manager*, it plays a front-end role for any functions other than service invocation. The *Service Supervisor* controls service invocations according to the requirements of the service providers. Before invoking the services on the *Composite Service Container* and *Atomic Service Container*, it validates whether the request satisfies providers' policies. The *Grid Composer* connects its Language Grid to other Language Grids to realize Language Grid composition for operators. The connection target is set through the *Service Manager*. The *Service Database* is a repository to store various types of information registered through the *Service Manager* and service invocation logs. The *Composite Service Container* provides composite service deployment, composite service execution, and dynamic service binding so that service users can customize services. The *Atomic Service Container* provides several utilities that service providers need in deploying atomic services.

In the remaining parts of this section, we provide the details of the *Service Manager*, *Service Supervisor*, *Grid Composer*, and *Composite/Atomic Service Container*.

3.2 Service Manager

The *Service Manager* consists of components managing various types of information necessary for Language Grid, such as domain definition, and grid, node, resource, service, and user information.

The *Domain Management* handles a domain definition that defines language service types, standard interfaces of language services, and attributes of language service profiles.

The *Grid Management* sets a target Language Grid connected by the *Grid Composer*. Based on the settings, the *Grid Composer* determines available services on other Language Grids. The *Node Management* handles information of nodes constituting its Language Grid and the connected Language Grid. Based on this information, the *Grid Composer* decides whether to save information registered on other nodes, and whether to distribute information to other nodes.

The *Resource Management* and *Service Management* handle language resource and language service information registered on Language Grid and the connected Language Grid. The information includes access control settings, service endpoints, intellectual properties associated with the language resources, and access logs. Based on this information, the *Service Supervisor* validates service invocation, locates service endpoints, and attaches intellectual property information to service responses.

Finally, the *User Management* manages user information registered on Language Grid. Based on this information, the *Service Supervisor* authenticates users' service requests.

3.3 Service Supervisor

The *Service Supervisor* controls service invocation by service users. The control covers access control, endpoint locating, load balancing, and access logging. To realize architecture independent of service specifications such as SOAP and REST, the *Service Supervisor* conducts such service invocation control based on an HTTP header.

The *User Request Handler* extracts information necessary to invoke a service from the service request over HTTP, and then authenticates the requester. The extracted information is sent to the *Invocation Processor*. Using the information, the *Invocation Processor* executes a sequence of pre-process, service invocation, post-process, and logging process. The access control is implemented as the pre-process, or the post-process.

After passing the access control, the *Intra-Grid Executor* invokes the service within its Language Grid. To invoke the service, the *Intra-Grid Executor* locates the service endpoint using the service ID. If there are multiple endpoints associated with the service ID, it chooses the endpoint with the lowest load. Finally, it invokes the service using *Java Method Invoker* implementation or *HTTP Invoker* implementation, which are selected according to the endpoint location.

3.4 Grid Composer

The *Grid Composer* not only creates a P2P grid network within its Language Grid, but also connects to other Language Grids. The former is needed to improve latency if the services are physically distributed. The latter is necessary to realize composition of Language Grids operated by different operators.

The *Intra-Grid Data Access* provides read/write interfaces for the *Service Database* within its Language Grid. In writing data, the *Intra-Grid Data Access* broadcasts the data to other nodes using a P2P network framework so that it can share the data with other nodes in the same Language Grid. As a result, service users can improve latency by sending their requests to a node located near the service. In this way, usage of the P2P network framework contributes to scalability of Language Grid.

On the other hand, the *Inter-Grid Data Access* shares various types of information with other Language Grids. The *Inter-Grid Data Access* also uses the P2P network to share information with other nodes across Language Grids. However, based on grid information registered through the *Service Manager*, the *Inter-Grid Data Access* saves only information related to the connected Language Grids.

The *Inter-Grid Executor* invokes services registered on a different Language Grid. To invoke a service across Language Grids, it replaces a requester's ID with the operator's user ID because the different Language Grid does not store user information of the requester, but rather of the operator as a Language Grid user. In addition, to control access to the services on a different Language Grid, the *Inter-Grid Executor* inserts the user ID of the requester into the request in invoking the service. By separating Language Grid that performs user authentication from the different Language Grid that performs access control, the two Language Grids do not have to share users' passwords.

3.5 Service Container

The *Service Container* executes composite services and atomic services. The *Composite Service Container* that executes composite services provides service workflow deployment and execution, and dynamic service binding. The *Atomic Service Container* that executes atomic services wraps language resources of service providers as language services with standard interfaces.

The *Service Request Handler* has multiple implementations according to service invocation protocols. If the *Service Container* is deployed on the same server as the *Service Supervisor*, the *Java Method Handler* implementation can be selected. When receiving a service request, the *Service Request Handler* receives from the *Service Container Framework* a chain of *Service Decorator*, *Service Workflow/Wrapper Executor*, and *Service Component Executor*, and executes the chain.

In invoking a component service of a composite service, the *Service Workflow Executor* can select a concrete service based on binding information included in a service request. This dynamic service binding is realized because language service interfaces are standardized.

4 Open Source Customization

The stakeholders' incentives vary depending on the operation model of Language Grid. If a Language Grid operator operates a public Language Grid, the operator promotes various users to join the Language Grid and most service providers may demand intellectual property protection. To satisfy these requirements, services are deployed on providers' servers and the Language Grid platform should provide access control functions. That is, priority is placed on security of resources. On the other hand, if a Language Grid operator operates a private Language Grid, the operator may gather language resources published under open source license to reduce the operation cost. To this end, services are aggregated and deployed on a cluster of machines, and the Language Grid platform does not have to provide user authentication and access control. That is, priority is placed on service performance.

Thus, the types of stakeholders rely on Language Grid operators. This implies that it is impossible to develop a general platform dealing with various types of operation models beforehand. Therefore, we selected open-source style customization so that each operator can adapt the platform to his/her operation model.

We have published the source codes of the Language Grid platform under an LGPL license and begun an open source project wherein each operator can freely customize the platform. In the project, the source codes are classified into a core component and optional component with different development policies because unregulated derivatives prevent interoperability of Language Grids. The specifications of core components are decided by core members in the open source community. On the other hand, the specifications of optional components can be freely changed by developers in the open source project, and derivatives can be created. This classification is done to improve the interoperability of Language Grids. As shown in Figure 1, the core components are thick-frame rectangles, and optional components thin-frame ones. In nested rectangles, outside ones are APIs and in-side ones are their implementations. These implementations can be changed.

The Intra-Grid Data Access, Inter-Grid Data Access, Intra-grid Service Executor, and Inter-Grid Service Executor are core components because they are used to communicate with other Language Grids, and they share information with other Language Grids. In addition to this, Service Decorator, Service Workflow/Wrapper Executor, Service Component Executor, and Service Container Framework in Composite/Atomic Service Container are also core components because the implementations of the components are interleaved in atomic services or composite services by the Service Container Framework. On the other hand, the Service Supervisor and Service Manager are optional components so that operators can extend them according to their operation model, because their functions are used only within the single Language Grid.

5 Configuration of the Language Grid

In this section, we introduce the system configuration of a public Language Grid and private Language Grid. In the public Language Grid, third parties are expected to join it and every stakeholder is different from the operator. In the private Language Grid, the operator uses language services for its private use. The operator often employs language resources published under open source license to reduce the operation cost and increase the performance. Moreover, the operator of the private Language Grid may connect the private Language Grid with a public Language Grid in order to use more language services on the private Language Grid.

5.1 Public Language Grid

The Department of Social Informatics in Kyoto University operates a public Language Grid. Service providers may have several provision policies to protect their language resources. Therefore, the Language Grid prefers security of language resources to performance of language services. For this reason, the Language Grid enables service providers to protect their resources on their servers, and therefore should coordinate the resources deployed on the providers' servers. To realize these functions on the Language Grid, we construct it with two different types of server nodes: the service node and core node.

The service node provides only atomic services by deploying service wrappers to standardize interfaces of language resources. The service nodes are distributed to their service providers. On the other hand, the core node controls access to services and composes services. Moreover, it communicates with other core nodes in other Language Grids to realize federated operation of the Language Grid.

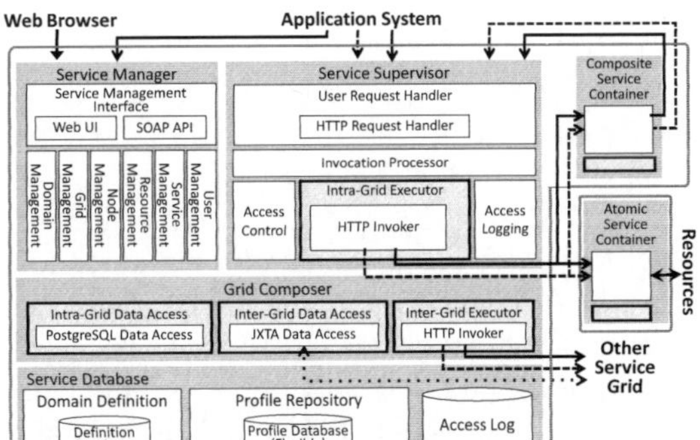

Figure 2. System Configuration of Public Language Grid

To instantiate the service node and core node, the Language Grid is configured as shown in Figure 2. The components surrounded by gray lines in the figure are deployed on the same server. The server on which the *Service Manager*, *Service Supervisor*, *Composite Service Container*, *Grid Composer*, and *Service Database* are deployed is called the core node, while that on which the *Atomic Service Container* is deployed is called the service node. This system configuration employs an HTTP invoker as the *Intra-Grid Executor* to communicate with language services on the *Atomic Service Container* physically distributed. Furthermore, the core node includes the *Inter-Grid Data Access* to share language services with other Language Grids and the *Inter-Grid Executor* to invoke language services on other Language Grids.

5.2 Private Language Grid

Unlike the system configuration of the public Language Grid, a private Language Grid prioritizing performance of language services is sometimes required.

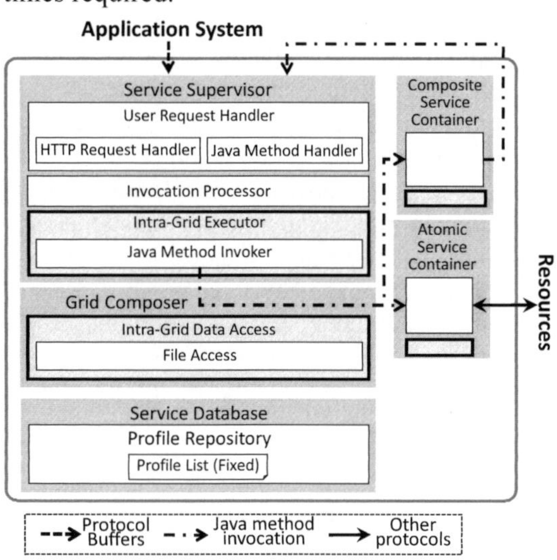

Figure 3. System Configuration of Private Language Grid

Figure 3 shows the system configuration of private Language Grid to satisfy the operator preferring performance and simplicity. The system configuration excludes the *Service Manager*, *Access Control*, and *Access Logging* components because the private Language Grid handles only language services associated with simple licenses. The *Inter-Grid Data Access* and *Inter-Grid Executor* are also removed if necessary language services can be aggregated into a single location. Moreover, the system configuration employs Java method invocation for communication between the *Service Supervisor* and *Composite/Atomic Service Container* to improve the latency of communication.

6 Case Study: Multilingual Environment for Wikimedia

In the case of employing a Language Grid to multilingualize Wikipedia, one of Wikimedia projects, by supporting multilingual discussion for Wikipedia translation community, the performance of language services should be given higher priority due to the huge amount of articles and users. Furthermore, the smaller the code size of the platform is, the more the Wikipedia operator likes it due to the low maintenance cost. We designed multilingual environment for Wikimedia considering technical requirements of the existing Wikimedia systems.

6.1 Technical Requirements

Numerous MediaWiki Extensions are available to add new features or enhance the functionality of the MediaWiki software from the users' point of view. Our goal in the development was that the actual Wikipedia community, which has a great number of users internationally, would accept the multilingual support system. From a technical point of view, as in any system development project, there are some technical requirements raised by the open-source community.

The first one is performance. Because Wikimedia projects such as Wikipedia are viewed by a great number of people every day, in particular a short response time is one of the very critical elements of the system design.

The second is usability. MediaWiki has its own look and feel, which should be consistent throughout any other MediaWiki extensions. Since Wikimedia projects are viewed by a variety of people of different age and computer skill, usability is one of the key elements to attract users.

Lastly, neutrality and independence is important for the Wikipedia community. The community does not depend too much on specific vendors, services or influence of third parties, but employs open source software and services.

6.2 System Design

Figure 4 shows the system architecture of multilingual environment using the Language Grid for Wikimedia. From the software point of view, the architecture consists of MediaWiki, the Language Grid for Wikimedia, the Language Grid Extension and Multilingual LiquidThreads Extension.

In order to develop a multilingual support system for Wikipedia discussion, we have introduced a private Language Grid, called Language Grid for Wikimedia. This employs the same system configuration as Figure 3 to prioritize performance and maintainability described in the first technical requirement. Wikimedia administrator operates the private Language Grid and aggregates several language services provided by volunteers for Wikimedia such as Microsoft and Google. Locating the Language Grid between MediaWiki and language services, we have prevented strong dependency to the language services described in the third technical requirement. Since the Language Grid is a multilingual service infrastructure, the Language Grid services should allow access via Language Grid Extension by any other MediaWiki extensions for general purposes. By unifying the access to the Language Grid, MediaWiki extensions can employ language services by invoking PHP function on the Language Grid Extension same as other MediaWiki extensions. This allows MediaWiki developers to use language services with MediaWiki's look and feel, as described in the second technical requirement.

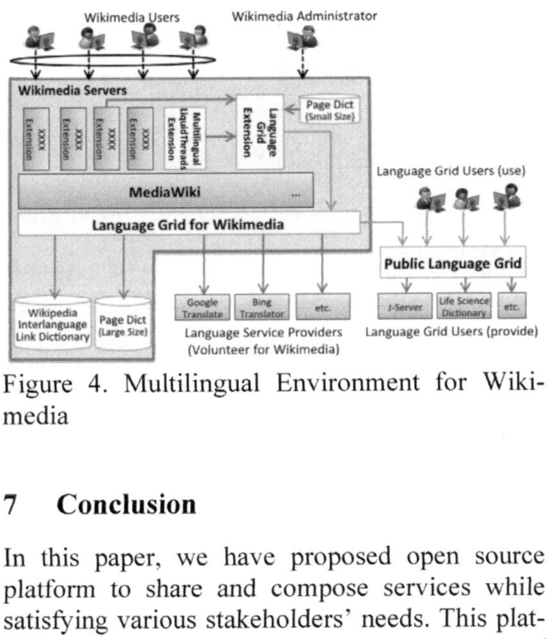

Figure 4. Multilingual Environment for Wikimedia

7 Conclusion

In this paper, we have proposed open source platform to share and compose services while satisfying various stakeholders' needs. This platform allows an operator to operate two types of Language Grid: private Language Grid and public Language Grid. The former prioritizes performance and maintainability, while the latter prioritizes intellectual property management. Moreover, combination of two types of Language Grid can complement language services on the private Language Grid with language services on the public Language Grid.

This diversity and interoperability of Language Grids are realized by classifying system architecture of Language Grid into two types of components: core components that guarantee the interoperability and optional components that provide alternative implementations. An open source project of Language Grid is expected to accelerate the diversity of Language Grid and produce other types of operation models of Language Grid.

Acknowledgments

We acknowledge the considerable support of National Institute of Information and Communications Technology, and Department of Social Informatics, Kyoto University. A part of this work was supported by Strategic Information and Communications R&D Promotion Programme from Ministry of Internal Affairs.

References

Volker Boehlke. 2009. A prototype infrastructure for D-spin-services based on a flexible multilayer architecture. Text Mining Services Conference (TMS'09)

Ulrich Callmeier, Andreas Eisele, Ulrich Schäfer, Melanie Siegel. 2004. The Deep Thought core architecture frame-work. The Fourth International Conference on Language Resources and Evaluation (LREC'04): 1205-1208.

Khalid Choukri. 2004. European Language Resources Association history and recent developments. SCALLA Working Conference KC 14/20.

Hamish Cunningham, Diana Maynard, Kalina Bontecheva, Valentin Tablan. 2002. GATE: an architecture for devel-opment of robust HLT applications. The Fortieth Annual Meeting of the Association for Computational Linguistics (ACL'02): 168-175.

David Ferrucci, Adam Lally. 2004. UIMA: an architectural approach to unstructured information processing in the corporate research environment. Journal of Natural Language Engineering 10: 327-348.

Toru Ishida. 2006. Language Grid: an infrastructure for intercultural collaboration. The IEEE/IPSJ Symposium on Applications and the Internet (SAINT'06): 96-100.

Antonio Toral, Pavel Pecina, Andy Way, Marc Poch. 2011. Towards a User-Friendly Webservice Architecture for Statistical Machine Translation in the PANACEA project. The 15th Conference of the European Association for Machine Translation (EAMT'11): 63-70.

Varadi T, Krauwer S,Wittenburg P, Wynne M, Koskenniemi K. 2008. CLARIN: common language resources and technology infrastructure. The Sixth International Conference on Lan-guage Resources and Evaluation (LREC'08): 1244-1248.

Proposal for the International Standard Language Resource Number

Khalid Choukri, Jungyeul Park, Olivier Hamon, Victoria Arranz
ELRA/ELDA
55-57, rue Brillat-Savarin
75013 Paris FRANCE
http://www.elda.org

Abstract

In this paper, we propose a new identifier scheme for Language Resources to provide Language Resources with unique names using a standardised nomenclature. This will also ensure Language Resources to be identified, and consequently to be recognised as proper references in activities within Human Language Technologies as well as in documents and scientific papers.

1 Introduction

Every object in the world requires a kind of identification to be correctly recognised. Traditional printed materials like books, for example, have generally used the International Standard Book Number (ISBN), the Library of Congress Control Number (LCCN), the Digital Object Identifier (DOI) and several other numeric identifiers as a unique identification scheme. Book identifiers allow us to easily identify books in a unique way. Other domains make use of several other identifier schemes. For instance, it is not hard to come into contact with an International/European Article Number (EAN), which is a universal barcoding system for everyday products. Each of these schemes seems to have been the output of some specific need or circumstance within a domain.

In this paper, we review existing identifier schemes and conclude for the need to propose, specifically, the use of a new identifier scheme for language resources (LRs), namely, the International Standard Language Resources Number (ISLRN). It is meant to provide LRs with unique identifiers using a standardised nomenclature. This will ensure that LRs are correctly identified, and consequently, recognised as proper references for their sharing usage in applications in R&D projects, products evaluation and benchmark as well as in documents and scientific papers. Moreover, it is also a major step in the networked and shared world of Human Language Technologies (HLT) has become: unique resources must be identified as they are and meta-catalogues need a common identification format to manage data correctly. Therefore, LRs should carry identical identification schemes independently of their representations, whatever their types and wherever their physical locations may be.

LRs imply corpora, dictionaries, and lexical and morphological resources in machine readable digital format. We also consider software tools for natural language processing and corpus-based computational linguistics as LRs if they can be stably packaged and deposited. They may include part-of-speech taggers, noun phrase chunkers, syntactic and semantic parsers, named entity recognisers, language modelling toolkits, corpus aligners, etc. Multimodal resources and systems also considered as LRs. Technology is in constant evolution and so are LR types, in their objective to help technological developments.

A citation has the purpose of acknowledging the relevance of the works of others. It attributes prior work to the original sources. It also allows the reader to provide a stable way of identifying proper references. However, the practice of using its proper identifier for LRs to cite and reference scientific data, along with individual resources as well as data sets, is less well developed (ISO-24619, 2011). LRs might be sometimes cited in a footnote even with several different names. For instance, the European Parliament Proceedings Parallel Corpus (Koehn, 2005) which is one of most cited LRs in the seventh International Conference on Language Resources and Evaluation (LREC2010),

Proceedings of Workshop on Language Resources, Technology and Services in the Sharing Paradigm, pages 75–83,
Chiang Mai, Thailand, November 12, 2011.

is cited by using several different names such as EUROPARL|EuroParl|Europarl (Parallel) (Corpus)[1]. In any case, a sad conclusion is that LRs remain in the background simply because the focus of the research is not on the resource per se (Calzolari et al., 2010).

The main goal for introducing the ISLRN for LRs is to get a unique way for naming a resource through the several LR distribution institutions. For many different reasons, a LR may be duplicated (on different catalogues/databases), renamed, modified, moved, or deleted. Thus, a permanent and unique identifier associated to a LR will always permit to retrieve it. Furthermore, having the ISLRN requires also the building of the ISLRN centres that would manage their attribution. This is a mandatory step that will also have to work out the permanent localisation of a LR. The European Language Resources Association (ELRA) already has a role to discover, classify, collect, validate and produce LRs since 1995. Otherwise, the Linguistic Data Consortium (LDC), Gengo-Shigen-Kyokai (GSK), or Bavarian Archive for Speech Signals (BAS) play a similar role in the USA, Japan and Germany, respectively. However, current situation shows that each institution bears different types of identifiers even for the identical LR.

The remaining of this paper is organised as follows: We start by introducing a list of current identifiers in other domains (Section 2) and we also explore the actual LR identifiers introduced by several distribution institutions, in particular ELRA and LDC (Section 3). Then we explain the purpose of the new identifier for LRs and its associated metadata (Section 4). We provide our proposal for the new LR identifier (Section 5) and also provide previous other proposals for LR identifiers (Section 6), and we draw conclusions (Section 7).

2 Current Identification Schemes in Other Domains

Since we are forging a new identifier for LRs, we investigate in this section current identification schemes such as the ISBN for books, the AN in bioinformatics, the DOI and other schemes.

[1]That is, the corpus is cited as from simply EuroParl to more completely Europarl Parallel Corpus.

2.1 International Standard Book Number

The International Standard Book Number (ISBN) is used as a unique numeric book identifier. The 10-digit ISBN format was developed by the International Organization for Standardization (ISO) in 1970. Since 1st January 2007, ISBNs have contained 13 digits (See Figure 1). They consist of the EAN[2] code as GS1 prefix[3], the group identifier for language-sharing country group, the publisher code, the item number for the book title and a checksum character. The result is the ISNB such as 978-0060995058 for Milan Kundera's The Joke (English edition, published in 1993). Note that other than the check digit, no part of the ISBN will have a fixed number of digits[4]. For example, the group identifier can be from a 1- to 5-digit number such as 0 or 1 for English-speaking countries, 85 for Brazil, 99921 for Qatar, etc. In sum, ISBNs carry its own semantics derived from publishing industry practices.

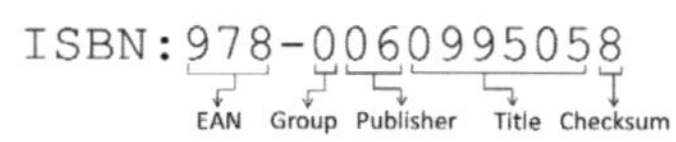

Figure 1: 13 digits ISBN.

2.2 Accession Number

An Accession Number (AN or AC) in bioinformatics is a unique identifier given to a Deoxyribonucleic acid (DNA) or protein sequence record to allow for tracking of different versions of that sequence record and the associated sequences over time in a single data repository. Researchers who wish to cite entries in their publications should always cite the first AN in the list (the primary AN) to ensure that readers can find the relevant data in a subsequent release. AN is used in several data resources such as the UniProt (SwissProt) Knowledgebase[5], GenBank[6], the EMBL Nucleotide Sequence Database[7], DNA Databank of Japan (DDBJ)[8], and Locus Reference

[2]EAN is for the International Article Number. Originally, it was the European Article Number.

[3]GS1 is an international association for the development and implementation of global standards such as the BarCodes identification system.

[4]http://www.isbn-international.org/en/manual.html

[5]http://www.uniprot.org

[6]http://www.ncbi.nlm.nih.gov/genbank

[7]http://www.ebi.ac.uk/embl

[8]http://www.ddbj.nig.ac.jp

Genomic[9], as identifier. While such sequence information repositories implement the concept of AN, it might have subtle variations. For instance, AN in the UniProt Knowledgebase consists of arbitrary 6 alphanumerical characters in the following format[10] (e.g. A1B123; P1B123; P12345):

1	2	3	4	5	6
[A-N,R-Z]	[0-9]	[A-Z]	[A-Z,0-9]	[A-Z,0-9]	[0-9]
[O,P,Q]	[0-9]	[A-Z,0-9]	[A-Z,0-9]	[A-Z,0-9]	[0-9]

Entries can have more than one accession number when two or more entries are merged, or when an existing entry is split into two or more entries. However, AN has different syntax through data repositories which cannot provide an identical identification schemes

2.3 Digital object identifier

A Digital Object Identifier (DOI) is a unique identifier for digital documents and other content objects[11]. It provides a system for persistent and identification (Paskin, 2006). For example, a DOI name doi:10.1000/182[12], where 10., 1000 and 182 represent the DOI registry, the registrant, and item ID, respectively, can embed a URL using http://dx.doi.org and it is also linked as http://dx.doi.org/10.1000/182 which makes a DOI name actionable. In sum the DOI system (i) assigns a number which can include any existing identifier of any entity, (ii) creates a description of the entity associated with metadata, (iii) makes the identifier actionable which allows a DOI name to link to current data, and (iv) allows any business model in a social infrastructure. As claimed, DOI's Identifier is a network actionable identifier which means that "click on it and do something". It is irrelevant to LRs because some LRs may not have the referable site.

2.4 Other identifiers

Biomedical scientific research papers already have a PubMed IDentifier (PMID) which is a unique number assigned to each PubMed record[13]. PubMed is a bibliographic database of life sciences and biomedical information. It includes bibliographic information for articles from academic journals. PMID consists of arbitrary 8 digits. For example, a PMID 20011301 is for "Surgical management of locally advanced and locally recurrent colon cancer" (Landmann and Weiser, 2005)[14].

The canonical representation of an Electronic Product Code (EPC) is a Uniform Resource Identifier (URI) which is generally used to identify a name or a resource on the Internet. The EPC URI is a string having the following form[15]:

urn:epc:id:scheme:*component1.component2...*

where scheme names an EPC scheme. The precise forms of following parts such as component1, component2 depend on which EPC scheme is used. An example of a specific EPC URI is the following:

urn:epc:id:sgtin:0614141.112345.400

Each EPC scheme provides a namespace of identifiers that can be used to identify physical objects of a particular type[16].

2.5 Summary

Several identifiers have been described in this section which may be potential LR identifiers. Current identifier schemes are summarised in Table 1 with their name, an example for their syntax, their target object, their characteristics and relevance for the LR identifier. Since most of them are developed for other entities such as books for ISBN, DNA for AN, etc., they do not offer encoding schemes for necessary features for LRs. Therefore, we do not consider them relevant as LR identifiers. Moreover, ISBN is conceived especially for books and closely related to copyright law which may be different and complicated in each country. We do not believe the DOI name to be an optimal descriptor of a LR identifier, neither because of its actionable characteristic. As we mentioned, some LRs may not have the referable site as for various reasons, notably confidential company matters. On the other hand, since the DOI uses the Handle System, it is not for free.

3 Actual LR Identifiers

Most applications in Natural Language Processing (NLP) mainly depend on the existence of sufficient LRs regardless of their nature (raw data or annotated corpora). Several institutions for LR

[9]http://www.lrg-sequence.org

[10]http://www.uniprot.org/manual/accession_numbers

[11]http://www.doi.org

[12]This is an actual DOI number for *The DOI Handbook*.

[13]http://www.ncbi.nlm.nih.gov/pubmed

[14]http://www.ncbi.nlm.nih.gov/pubmed/20011301

[15]*EPCglobal Tag Data Standard* Version 1.5. See http://www.epcglobalinc.org

[16]*ibid.*

Name	Example	Target	Characteristic
ISBN	ISBN:978-0060995058	Books	Closely related to copyright law
AN	A1B123, AB123456	DNA or protein sequence record	Different syntax through data repositories
DOI	doi:10.1000/182	Digital documents and other content objects	assigned by the copyeditor
PMID	PMID17170002	Bibliographic database	Life sciences and biomedical information
EPC	urn:epc:id:sgtin: 0614141.112345.400	Every physical object	Limited to physical object

Table 1: Current Identifiers.

distribution in the world, in particular ELRA and LDC, have been responsible for providing a large part of the considerable amount of LRs in the domain. An increasing number of LRs are made available in catalogues. Currently, ELRA proposes two types of catalogue for LRs, the ELRA Catalogue[17] and the Universal Catalogue [18]. Similarly, the LDC's Catalog also provides hundreds of corpora and other language data[19].

3.1 Identifiers at ELRA

The ELRA Catalogue offers a repository of LRs made available through ELRA. The catalogue contains over 1,000 LRs in more than 25 languages. Other LRs identified all over the world, but not available through ELRA, can be also viewed in the Universal Catalogue. LRs at ELRA consist of spoken resources, written resources, evaluation packages, and multimodal/multimedia resources. Written resources also contain terminological resources and monolingual and multilingual lexicons. The actual LR identifiers in the ELRA Catalogue contain ELRA as publisher code, a systematic pattern (B|S|E|W|M|T|L) and 4 digits. B stands for a bundle which can contain several LRs within and S|E|W|M|T|L stand for Speech, Evaluation, Written, Multilingual corpora, Terminology and Lexicon, respectively. For example, the bundle package B0008 contains two separate spoken corpora: the LC-STAR Spanish phonetic lexicon (S0035) and the LC-STAR Catalan phonetic lexicon (S0048)[20]. While the ELRA Catalogue does not contain language processing tools as LRs at present, the Universal Catalogue does. Since ELRA is a partner of the Open Language Archives Community (OLAC), its Catalogue can be viewed as an OLAC repository[21], Oxford Text Archive[22], etc. Note that most of them only contain arbitrary digits as identifiers. ELRA is also sharing the index of its Catalogue through META-SHARE[23], a network of repositories developed within the META-NET network of excellence[24].

3.2 Identifiers at LDC

LDC assigns LDC as publisher code with a year number followed by (S|T|V|L) and 2 digits. S|T|V|L stand for speech, text, voice, and lexical(-related) corpora, respectively. The LDC Catalog is classified by data type and data source, or release year. LRs in the LDC Catalog are first divided into major categories according to the type of data they contain, and then are further broken down into minor categories based on the source of the data. For example, lexicon is further divided into dictionaries lexicon, field recordings lexicon, microphone speech lexicon, newswire lexicon, telephone conversations lexicon, varied lexicon and web collection lexicon. LDC also classifies software tools as LRs, such as LDC2004L01 for *Klex: Finite-State Lexical Transducer for Korean* (Han, 2004).[25]

3.3 Identifiers at other institutions

Among other institutions that are responsible for providing LRs, we explore identifiers at NICT, GSK, and BAS. The National Institute of Information and Communications Technology (NICT), and Nagoya University, for the purpose of developing LRs efficiently, have been constructing a large scale metadata database named SHACHI[26] as their joint project by collecting detailed meta-

[17] http://catalog.elra.info

[18] http://universal.elra.info

[19] http://www.ldc.upenn.edu/Catalog

[20] http://catalog.elra.info/product_info.php?products_id=980

[21] http://www.language-archives.org

[22] http://ota.ahds.ac.uk

[23] http://www.meta-net.eu/meta-share

[24] http://www.meta-net.eu

[25] Note that LDC also introduces the ISBN for LRs unlikely ELRA. For example, (Han, 2004) can be identified with the ISBN 1-58563-283-x as well as LDC2004L01.

[26] http://www.shachi.org

data information on LRs in Western and Asian countries (Tohyama et al., 2008). Identified LRs from other distribution institutions are assigned 6 unique digits by following C|D|G|T|N which represent corpus, dictionary, lexicon, thesaurus-like lexicon, terminology-related resources, and others respectively, as their own identifiers. For example, C-001543 is for Translanguage English Database (TED) where they crawl from LDC's LDC2002S04. Gengo-Shigen-Kyokai (GSK) (literally: 'Language Resources Association') was established in June of 2003 to promote the distribution of LRs in Japan.[27] The Language Resources Catalogue at GSK provides dictionaries and corpora. These are identified with 4 digits for the year and a capital letter chronically. For example, there are GSK2010-A for *Annotated Corpus of Iwanami Japanese Dictionary Fifth Edition 2004* and GSK2010-B for *Konan Kodomo corpus*. The Bavarian Archive for Speech Signals (BAS) was founded as a public institution in January 1995 and is hosted by the University of Munich, presently at the Institut für Phonetik und Sprachverarbeitung (IPS). BAS is dedicated to make databases of spoken German accessible in a well-structured form to the speech science community as well as to speech engineering[28]. They provide a set of Speech Corpora and Multimodal Corpora with acronym-style identifiers such as RVG-J for Regional Variants of German J which contains recordings of read and spontaneous speech by adolescents age 13-20[29]. Chinese-LDC (Chinese Linguistic Data Consortium)[30] assigns CLDC as publisher code, followed by a category, a 4-digit year code and a 3-digit identifier, for example, CLDC-SPC-2006-008 for a telephone speech recognition corpus. HLT-Centrale (Centrale voor Taal- en Spraaktechnologie, 'Dutch HLT Agency')[31] uses an acronym-style identifier per corpus, for example, 27MWC for a 27 Million Words Dutch Newspaper Corpus.

Table 2 summaries the types of identifiers used by those different institutions. Table 3 shows the number of LRs per institution by May 2011. To conclude, no identical LR has yet been formally identified through several institutions which leads same resource bearing two different identifiers. One such example is the Translanguage English Database (TED), which is catalogued both as ELRA-S0031 and LDC2002S04, that is, in two different ways. Our objective is to converge them using a unique way, that is, by forging a new LR identifier.

Catalogue	Number of LRs
ELRA	1,100+
LDC	500+
NICT	2,500+
GSK	10+
BAS	150+
Chinese LDC	90+
HLT-Centrale	50+
Universal Catalogue	1,800+
LRE Map	2,800+
Total (including duplicates)	9,000+

Table 3: Number of LRs of each institution.

4 Purpose of the New LR Identifier

4.1 Motivation

Identification of existing LRs is an essential, but a difficult and fastidious task. One has to find all available sources, from industry to university, from commercial to research. ELRA has promoted the collection and the dissemination of existing resources through its Universal Catalogue or more recently, the Language Resources and Evaluation (LRE) Map[32]. Both tools help to acquire knowledge using participative work. Another trend concerns the sharing of LRs through catalogues (see for instance, META-SHARE), where users (i.e. researchers, commercial users) are able to look for a large panel of data and tools. However, those two movements have shown several drawbacks which the community needs to take into account. One of them is linked to the nature of the LRs in the Internet era. Indeed, LRs have been created but also moved, duplicated, modified, or deleted. The consequence is that a LR may exist under various shapes, starting by its name, but also its format or even its content. Therefore, the community needs a unique way to identify, access, discover and disseminate LRs.

For instance, "Journal Officiel de la Communauté Européenne" and "JOC" refer to the same LR (ELRA-W0017). On the other hand, "Corpus EMILLE/CIIL" (ELRA-W0037) and "Corpus

[27] http://www.gsk.or.jp

[28] http://www.phonetik.uni-muenchen.de/Bas

[29] http://www.phonetik.uni-muenchen.de/forschung/Bas/BasRVG-Jeng.html

[30] http://www.chineseldc.org

[31] http://www.inl.nl/en/producten

[32] http://www.resourcebook.eu

	ELRA	LDC	NICT	GSK	BAS	Chinese LDC	HLT-Centrale
Publisher	X	X		X		X	
Category	X	X	X			X	
Year		X		X		X	
Digit ID	X (4)	X (2)	X (6)			X (3)	
Letter ID				X			
Free ID					X		X
Software	X	X		X	X		X
Example	ELRA-S0035	LDC2004L01	G-00035	GSK2010-C	SC10	CLDC-SPC-2007-002	CORN

Table 2: Summary of identifier designs per institution.

EMILLE Lancaster" (ELRA-W0038) are two different corpora and not just a different nomenclature for a same resource. It is about time that we are helped to refer to the LRs that we are using formally and clearly, without any risk of confusion or ambiguity. Accordingly, our goal is to allow the classification within catalogues, even redundant catalogues. For instance, the NICT catalogue contains mostly LRs from other catalogues, or OLAC get the export of LRs from many sources and necessarily duplicate inputs. The new LR identifiers that we want to propose, strictly granted, should avoid duplication of LR identifiers in the destination catalogues.

Actually, this proposal does not address the single issue related to LR catalogues, that is a desired way to share LRs. Another application of the identification lies in the production of documentation such as scientific papers or technical reports. Without the unique identification for LRs, we would struggle in the formal identification of any cited LRs within a document. LRs may be referred to by the new LR identification number instead of current usages such as URLs or author-invented names. This also overcomes the problem of wrong, broken or incomplete URLs.

A potential third application handles the tools and software that may use one or several LRs. Using a unique LR identification number eventually guarantees the correct use of LRs along with resource content and version. It is crucial that LRs should be used for evaluations without any bias. Our goal is then to define permanent localisations using the unique identifier for each LR used for HLT.

4.2 Metadata

Metadata schemas have been in constant evolution throughout the years. The non-stopping technological development makes it a requirement that its classifying or cataloguing procedures remain dynamic and open to the new arrivals in the field. Furthermore, different LR users have different needs, which can be observed both in the way the schemas are structured (from rather flat to very hierarchical) and the content of their components/elements, etc. (from rather limited to large and rich proposals). As it can be expected, the needs coming from LR providers or LR consumers range considerably. Likewise when we take into consideration the repositories themselves, with issues such as links, updating of information, etc. All this is being taken into consideration within one of the latest schemas still under development (the META-MD proposed within META-NET).

In order to name just a few of those different metadata schemas that have seen the light, we can refer to the Open Language Archives Community (OLAC)[33], which is Dublin Core-compliant, but only includes a small number of elements trying to prioritise interoperability over very rich descriptions. As already mentioned earlier in this paper, both ELRA Catalogue and Universal Catalogue, as well as the LDC Catalog provide very populated catalogues of LRs. Their metadata, although different, follows a 2-level hierarchy, covering LR types.

When it comes to identifying LRs, most metadata schemas have used different terms to refer to the resource names. However, as it has been mentioned in earlier sections, these names are not always consistent across catalogues, publications or other citations. Having a unique identifier that prevails beyond versioning and location changes, and that is unambiguous through LR searching and retrieving has also become a key issue for metadata. It is in this regard that the current proposal lies, with the creation of an unique identifier that will be registered within the metadata schema and

[33] http://www.language-archives.org

that will contribute considerably towards the life and sustainability of each resource implementing it. For such purpose, the metadata schema will contain an unique identifier element within its resource information component, and such element will allocate the standard identification number that the resource will have been assigned. Figure 2 depicts the idea behind this ID mapping, to show its "unique label" nature.

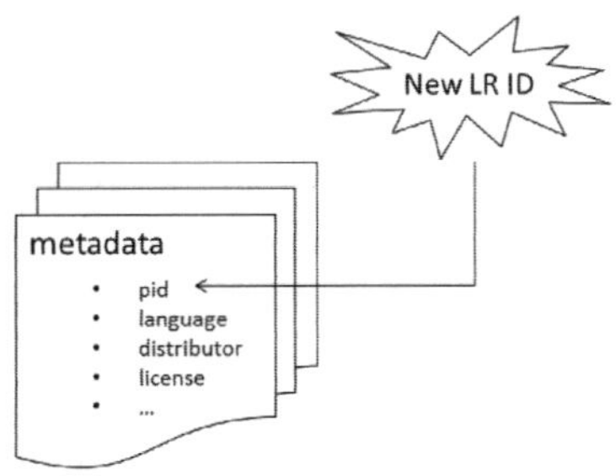

Figure 2: Mapping the new LR identifier to metadata as PID.

5 Proposal for the LR Identifier

In this section, a first formalisation of the International Standard Language Resources Number (ISLRN) is proposed. Then, several administrative characteristics that should be taken into account are defined.

5.1 Formal proposal for syntax

Such approach requires that an ontology in agreed upon within the community. Unfortunately, over the last couple of decades, no consensus emerged despite the number of proposals. It is easy to distinguish a large class of resources such as corpus versus lexicon, but within a corpus, we can imagine speech (signal and audio recordings) versus written texts. It is also difficult to build the commons over certain LRs such as a textual corpus consisting of transcribed audio data because one may always make a case that contradict such semantics. In this section, we review and criticise current practices for semantics of syntax introduced in current LR identification schemes.

- *Publisher* identifiers exist in ELRA, LDC, GSK and Chinese LDC classification. However, the ISLRN should not contain a publisher name, just as an institution name in general, because the distribution institutions are not usually a right holder of the LR and several institutions may distribute the same LR. An institution may also choose to distribute a LR anonymously.

- *Category* and *Type* identifiers are used by most of institutions. Even though it is important to keep an identification scheme symbolizing a categorisation, LRs can have very different categories and types as they evolve. Existing standards such as the BAMDES proposal (Parra et al., 2010) are also often limited, for instance it does not consider multimodal technologies. Moreover, the scope of LRs also leaves to LRs' provider and it make it more difficult to adopt proper categories or types.

- *Year* identifiers are used only by two institutions (LDC and GSK). Indeed, a resource may evolve over time and there may have a misunderstanding on the creation date, the delivery date or the last modification date.

- *Alphanumeric characters* identifiers are the most important, and are obviously used as identification schemes by all institutions, whatever they are digits or letters. Therefore, we should not avoid its introduction in the ISLRN. The size of the number should be decided according to the potential number of LRs (cf. Table 3).

One could suggest to add other semantics, but they are often limited to specific types of LRs. *Language* information, for instance, cannot apply to most of the multimodal technologies, and might not be easy when dealing with multilingual resources.

In sum, Publisher information do not appear in the LR identification scheme. As we mentioned before, wherever physical locations of LRs may be, a new LR identifier should be universal. A new LR identifier do not contain semantics about Category and Type, nor Year information. A LR identifier should delegate semantics of its syntax to metadata which can easily describe several semantics such as in DomainInfo, AnnotationInfo, etc., for example, in META-SHARE. Therefore, we decide to use 7-digit random numbers as the new LR identifier followed by 2-digit for version information and 1-digit for a checksum number. Having version information also allows us to describe LRs' granularity because information for resource bundles or resource collections can be encoded in Version information. The checksum number is encrypted from the preceding numeric identifier and version information. Our proposal is summarised in Figure 3.

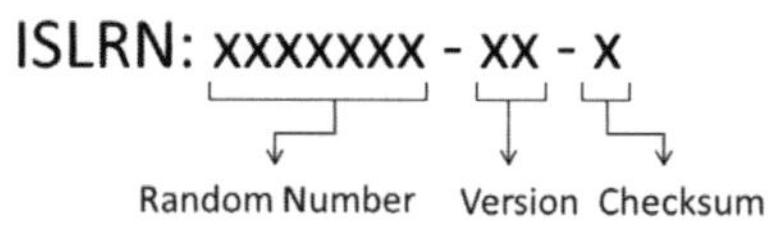

Figure 3: Proposal for the ISLRN syntax.

5.2 Administrative aspect

The definition of an ISLRN is certainly not the easier task, since administrative questions remain. First, the device to assign the ISLRN is crucial. ISLRN should be endorsed by major players and data centres, acting as an "umbrella" organisation. ISLRN attributions should be moderated, that is a small number of institutions should be granted the right to assign ISLRN. Prerequisite checking before assigning the ISLRN is also inevitable. LR Right holders or creators should provide minimum information to make their LRs be assigned ISLRN. Finally, we should pay attention to the legal issues regarding ISLRN and its usage. For instance, the ISBN is mandatory for printed, graphical and photographic documents subject ot a legal deposit. We may probably reflect the political importance of LRs as books are, meaning that the effort would be bigger than planned. However, the ISLRN should be assigned for free: no entry fee or no annual subscription: since the ISLRN will not be a legal deposit, the ISLRN is not an obligation, but rather an essential and best practice.

6 Other proposals for LR identifiers

FlaReNet (Fostering Language Resources Network)'s Blueprint of Actions and Infrastrucures would also "be a guideline for the LR community and National funding agencies, e.g. to prepare the ground for an EU directive concerning development of LRs at European scale"[34]. Currently, ISO already provides specifications both for the PID framework and its practice for referencing and citing LRs. The European Persistent Identifier Consortium also provides a service to name scientific data in a unique and timeless way.

[34] `http://www.flarenet.eu`

6.1 ISO's PISA

Actually, ISO already proposed *Language resource management - Persistent identification and sustainable access (PISA)* as the International Standard (ISO-24619, 2011). It specifies requirements for the persistent identifier (PID) framework and for using PIDs as references and citations of LRs in documents as well as in LRs themselves (ibid.). It provides general guidelines for attributing PIDs for LRs as a part of a resource, a resource itself and a resource collection. The PID framework supports encoding of the PID as a Uniform Resource Identifier (URI), allows multiple URIs to render identifiers actionable without requiring client modifications, should be used to associated with metadata, and finally provides adequate security to change the PID-URI mapping or the associated metadata. ISO's PISA suggests Handle System (HS) and Archival Resource Key (ARK) as persistent identifier system implementations.

6.2 EPIC

The European Persistent Identifier Consortium (EPIC) provides a new methods to reference the scientific data in order to name in a universal way, which are permanent and citeable references.[35] It is not only for LRs, but for general scientific data. The Persistent Identifier Service is based on the Handle System like a DOI and uses as a prefix the number `11858`; the ordinary handle has the form `11858/flag-institution-num1-num2-num3-checksum` where its semantics explain themselves. Only flag is not defined yet and remains for special purposes such as derived handles.

6.3 Summary

While ISO's PISA has not provide concrete syntax for PID, nor other standardised techniques yet, EPIC explicitly introduces HS as PID system. As we mentioned before, there are LRs which may not have the referable site and the persistent identifier system cannot be applied. Therefore, previous proposals are not relevant to our purpose.

7 Conclusion

In this paper, we propose the ISLRN to provide LRs with unique names. This allows LRs to be identified, and consequently to be recognised as proper references. Therefore, the ISLRN can be

[35] `http://www.pidconsortium.eu`

summarised as a unique identifier that allows to name and discover LRs. Actually, since we do not claim that the ISLRN is not a legal deposit, it is not an obligation. However, the ISLRN, when endorsed by major organisations involved in HLT, shall become an essential and best practice for LRs.

Acknowledgments

This work was partially supported by FlaReNet (ECP-2007-LANG-617001) and T4ME Net (META NET, FP7-ICP-4-249119),

References

Nicoletta Calzolari, Claudia Soria, Riccardo Del Gratta, Sara Goggi, Valeria Quochi, Irene Russo, Khalid Choukri, Joseph Mariani, and Stelios Piperidis. 2010. The lrec map of language resources and technologies. In *Proceedings of the Seventh conference on International Language Resources and Evaluation (LREC'10)*, Valletta, Malta, 19–21 May. European Language Resources Association (ELRA).

Na-Rae Han. 2004. *Klex: Finite-State Lexical Transducer for Korean*. Technical report, Linguistic Data Consortium, Philadelphia.

ISO-24619. 2011. *Language resource management – Persistent identification and sustainable access (PISA)*.

Philipp Koehn. 2005. Europarl: A Parallel Corpus for Statistical Machine Translation. In *Proceedings of MT Summit X*, Phuket, Thailand, 12–16 September.

Ron G. Landmann and Martin R. Weiser. 2005. Surgical Management of Locally Advanced and Locally Recurrent Colon Cancer. *Clinics in Colon and Rectal Surgery*, 18(3):182–189.

Carla Parra, Marta Villegas, and Nria Bel. 2010. The basic metadata description (bamdes) and theharvestingday.eu: Towards sustainability and visibility of lrt. In *Proceedings of workshop on Language Resources: From Storyboard to Sustainability and LR Lifecycle Management at LREC 2010*, pages 49–53, Valletta, Malta, May. European Language Resources Association (ELRA).

Norman Paskin. 2006. *The DOI Handbook*. International DOI Foundation, Inc., Oxford, United Kingdom.

Hitomi Tohyama, Shunsuke Kozawa, Kiyotaka Uchimoto, Shigeki Matsubara, and Hitoshi Isahara. 2008. Construction of an infrastructure for providing users with suitable language resources. In *Coling 2008: Companion volume: Posters*, pages 119–122, Manchester, UK, August. Coling 2008 Organizing Committee.

A Metadata Schema for the Description of Language Resources (LRs)

M. Gavrilidou, P. Labropoulou, S. Piperidis
ILSP / R.C. 'Athena'- Greece
{maria, penny, spip}
@ilsp.gr

M. Monachini, F. Frontini
CNR – ILC - Italy
{monica.monachini, francesca.
frontini}@ilc.cnr.it

G. Francopoulo
TAGMATICA - France
gil.francopoulo@tagmatica.com

V. Arranz, V. Mapelli
ELDA - France
{arranz, mapelli}@elda.org

Abstract

This paper presents the metadata schema for describing language resources (LRs) currently under development for the needs of META-SHARE, an open distributed facility for the exchange and sharing of LRs. An essential ingredient in its setup is the existence of formal and standardized LR descriptions, cornerstone of the interoperability layer of any such initiative. The description of LRs is granular and abstractive, combining the taxonomy of LRs with an inventory of a structured set of descriptive elements, of which only a minimal subset is obligatory; the schema additionally proposes recommended and optional elements. Moreover, the schema includes a set of relations catering for the appropriate inter-linking of resources. The current paper presents the main principles and features of the metadata schema, focusing on the description of text corpora and lexical / conceptual resources.

1 Credits

This paper has been written in the framework of the project T4ME, funded by DG INFSO of the European Commission through the 7th Framework Program, Grant agreement no.: 249119.

2 Introduction

The very diverse and heterogeneous landscape of huge amounts of digital and digitized resources collections (publications, datasets, multimedia files, processing tools, services and applications) has drastically transformed the requirements for their publication, archiving, discovery and long-term maintenance. Digital repositories provide the infrastructure for describing and documenting, storing, preserving, and making this information publicly available in an open, user-friendly and trusted way. Repositories represent an evolution of the digital libraries paradigm towards open access, advanced search capabilities and large-scale distributed architectures.

META-SHARE (www.meta-share.eu) is a sustainable network of repositories of ***language data, tools and related web services*** documented with high-quality ***metadata***, aggregated in central inventories allowing for uniform search and access to resources.

In the context of META-SHARE, the term ***metadata*** refers to descriptions of Language Resources, encompassing both data sets (textual, multimodal/multimedia and lexical data, grammars, language models etc.) and tools / technologies / services used for their processing.

3 Design principles for the metadata model

The metadata descriptions constitute the means by which LR users identify the resources they seek. Thus, the META-SHARE metadata model (Gavrilidou et al., 2010) forms an integral part of the search and retrieval mechanism, with a subset of its elements serving as the access points to the LRs catalogue. The model must therefore be as informative and flexible as possible, allowing for multi-faceted search and viewing of the catalogue, as well as dynamic re-structuring thereof, offering LR consumers the chance to easily and quickly spot the resources they are looking for among a large bulk of resources. Although META-SHARE aims at an informed community (HLT specialists), this is by no means interpreted as a permission to create a complex schema; user-friendliness of the search interface should be supported by a well motivated, easy-to-understand schema.

In this effort, we have built upon three main building blocks:

(a) study of *previous initiatives* (the most widespread in the LT area metadata models & LR catalogue descriptions[1]). The study has focused on the following issues: LR typologies, metadata elements currently in use and/or recommended, value types and obligatoriness thereof.

(b) *user requirements*, as collected through a survey conducted in the framework of the project (Federmann et al., 2011).

(c) *the recommendations of the e-IRG report of ESFRI* (e-IRG, 2009), in what concerns its purpose of usage, its aims and its features.

The basic design principles of the META-SHARE model are:

• semantic clarity: clear articulation of a term's meaning and its relations to other terms

• expressiveness: successful description of any type of resource

• flexibility: provision of complete descriptions of resources but also of minimal but informative descriptions

• customisability: adequate description of all types of resources (from the provider's perspective) and identification of the appropriate resource (user's perspective).

• interoperability (for exchange and harvesting purposes): mappings to at least the Dublin Core metadata & other widely used schemas and link of all elements to the ISOcat Data Categories

• user friendliness: provision of an editor to aid LR description

• extensibility: allow for future extensions, as regards both the model itself and the coverage of more resource types as they become available.

• harvestability: allow harvesting of the metadata (OAI-compatible).

4 The metadata model essentials

As a general framework, the mechanism we have decided to adopt is the *component*-based mechanism proposed by the ISO DCR model grouping together semantically coherent elements which form components and providing relations between them (Broeder et al., 2008). More specifically, ***elements*** are used to encode specific descriptive features of the LRs, while ***relations*** are used to link together resources that are included in the META-SHARE repository (e.g. original and derived, raw and annotated resources, a language resource and the tool that has been used to create it etc.), but also peripheral resources such as projects that created the LRs, standards used, related documentation etc.

The set of all the components and elements describing specific LR types and subtypes represent the ***profile*** of this type. Obviously, certain components include information common to all types of resources (e.g. identification, contact, licensing information etc.) and are, thus, used for all LRs, while others (e.g. components including information on the contents, annotation etc. of a resource) differ across types. The LR provider will be presented with proposed Profiles for each type, which can be used as templates or guidelines for the completion of the metadata description of the resource. Experience has proved that LR providers need guidelines and help in the process of metadata addition to their resources, and the Profiles are to be interpreted in this way and not as rigid structures to be adhered to.

In order to accommodate flexibility, the elements belong to two basic levels of description:

• an initial level providing the basic elements for the description of a resource (***minimal schema***), and

[1] The schemas taken into account include: Corpus Encoding Initiative (CES & XCES - www.xces.org/), Text Encoding Initiative (TEI - www.tei-c.org/index.xml), Open Language Archives Community (OLAC - www.language-archives.org/), ISLE Meta Data Initiative (IMDI - www.mpi.nl/IMDI/), European National Activities for Basic Language Resources (ENABLER - www.ilc.cnr.it/enabler-network/index.htm), Basic Metadata Description (BAMDES - www.theharvestingday.eu/docs/TheBAMDESIn2Pages-June2010.pdf), Dublin Core Metadata Initiative (DCMI - dublincore.org/), ELRA Catalogue (www.elra.info/Catalogue.html), ELRA Universal Catalogue (www.elra.info/Universal-Catalogue.html), LRE map (www.resourcebook.eu), LDC catalogue (www.ldc.upenn.edu/Catalog/), CLARIN metadata activities (www.clarin.eu) and the ISO 12620 – DCR (www.isocat.org/).

• a second level with a higher degree of granularity (***maximal schema***), providing more detailed information on each resource and covering all stages of LR production and use.

This has advantages for addition of metadata descriptions from scratch in two steps, first implementing the minimal schema, and subsequently, but not necessarily, the maximal schema. Harvesting is also served better by distinguishing between the two levels. Finally, LRs consumers can initially identify the resources best suited for their needs through the first level, and by accessing the second level, inspect the exact features of the resource.

The minimal schema contains those elements considered indispensable for LR description and identification. It takes into account the views expressed in the user survey concerning which features are considered sufficient to give a sound "identity" to a resource. It is considered as the "guarantee level" for interoperability as regards LR identification and metadata harvesting.

These two levels contain four classes of elements:

• the first level contains Mandatory (M) and Condition-dependent Mandatory (MC) elements (i.e. they have to be filled in when specific conditions are met), while

• the second level includes Recommended (R, i.e. LRs producers are advised to include information on these elements) and Optional (O) elements.

For each element, the appropriate field type has been chosen among the following options: free text, closed list of values, open list of values (recommended values are provided but users can add their own), numeric fields and special fields (e.g. urls, dates, phone numbers etc.). Special attention has been given to the choice of the field type, taking into consideration user requirements and metadata providers' practices; the intention has been to balance appropriately user-added with system-driven values in order to make the most of each approach. Consistency checking of user-added values will enhance the final results in the course of the META-SHARE operation.

Currently, the schema has been implemented as an XML schema (XSD), while implementation in RDF is also under consideration.[2]

[2] In the current version, all relations are represented in the form of elements.

To cater for semantic interoperability with other metadata schemas, all elements will be linked to existing ISOcat DCR data categories (ISO 12620, 2009) and, if they have no counterpart, they will be added to the DCR with appropriate definitions.

5 The META-SHARE ontology

META-SHARE takes a more global view on resources, which aims to provide users not only with a catalogue of LRs (data and tools) but also with information that can be used to enhance their exploitation. For instance, research papers that document the production of a resource as well as standards and best practice guidelines can play an informative role for LR users and an advisory role for prospective LR producers; similarly, information on the usage of a certain resource, as pointed out in the user interviews, is considered valuable for LR users wishing to find whether a certain resource is appropriate for their own application and the steps that they should take to get the best results.

Thus, the metadata model and its associated taxonomy should cover all types of resources (in the broad sense) to be included in META-SHARE.

In the proposed META-SHARE ontology, a distinction is made between LR per se and all other related resources/entities, such as:

• reference documents related to the resource (e.g. papers, reports, manuals etc.)

• persons and organizations involved in their creation and use (e.g. creators, funders, distributors etc.)

• related projects and activities (e.g. funding projects, activities of usage etc.)

• licenses (for the distribution of the LRs).

In the META-SHARE ontology, some of the entities will correspond to digital objects: for instance, all LRs descriptions will have a pointer to the resource itself, licenses and reference documents will point to document files (included in META-SHARE) etc. Entities such as persons and organizations, of course, can optionally be linked to external links (e.g. URL pointers for personal webpages). All these entities will be included in META-SHARE only so far as they are related to a LR.

The metadata model focuses on LRs per se (data and tools). For all other entities of the ontology, we take into account metadata schemas and relevant formats that have been devised specifically for them, e.g. CERIF for research entities (projects, actors etc.), BibTex for bibliographical references etc.

6 Proposed LR taxonomy

Central to the model is the LR taxonomy, which allows us to organize the resources in a more structured way, taking into consideration the specificities of each type.

The study of the existing LR taxonomies has revealed their diversity, which hampers the request for interoperability.[3]

The proposed LR taxonomy constitutes an integral part of the metadata model, whereby the types of LRs (attributes and values) belong to the element set. The *resourceType* is the basic element according to which the LR types and subsequently the specific profiles are defined and may take one of the following values:

- **corpus** (including written/text, oral/spoken, multimodal/multimedia corpora)
- **lexical / conceptual resource** (including terminological resources, word lists, semantic lexica, ontologies etc.)
- **language description** (including grammars, language models, typological databases, courseware etc.)
- **technology / tool / service** (including basic processing tools, applications, web services etc. required for processing data resources)
- **evaluation package** (for packages of datasets, tools and metrics used for evaluation purposes).

It should be noted here that, according to the practice of the HLT community, the term "language resource" is reserved for a collection/compilation of items (text, audio files etc.), mainly of considerable size or (in the case of tools) able to perform a well-defined task. Parts of LRs clearly identifiable can also be considered as LRs on their own: for instance, monolingual components of multilingual corpora can (and should) be regarded as monolingual corpora themselves. But the focus is on the set rather than the unit (e.g. single text / audio file, in the case of corpora, or word / entry, in the case of lexica).

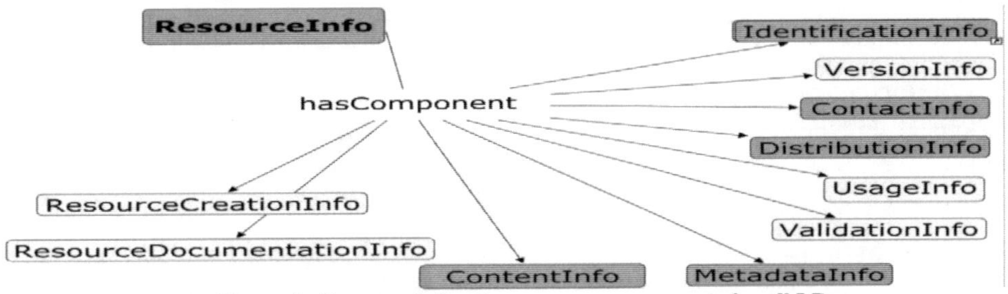

Figure 1 - ResourceInfo - the common components for all LRs

Further sub-classification is dependent upon sets of type-dependent features, which allow the viewing of the same resource along multiple dimensions. Thus, for instance *language* as an organizing feature can be used to bring together monolingual corpora / lexica and monolingual parts of multilingual corpora / lexica. Similarly, *domain*, *format*, *annotation* features etc. can be used as different dimensions according to which the catalogue of LRs can be accessed.

7 Contents of the model

The core of the model is the *ResourceInfo* component (Figure 1), which contains all the information relevant for the description of a LR. It subsumes components and elements that combine together to provide this description. A broad distinction can be made between the "administrative" components, which are common to all LRs, and the components that are idiosyncratic to a specific LR type (e.g. *CorpusInfo*, *LexicalConceptualResourceInfo* etc., as explained further below). For instance, elements needed for the description of video resources are only used for the specific *mediaType*.

The set of components that are common to all LRs are the following:

- the *IdentificationInfo* component includes all elements required to identify the resource, such as the resource full and short name, the persistent identifier (PID, to be as-

[3] For a more detailed discussion on the LR taxonomy discrepancies, cf. Gavrilidou et al. (2011).

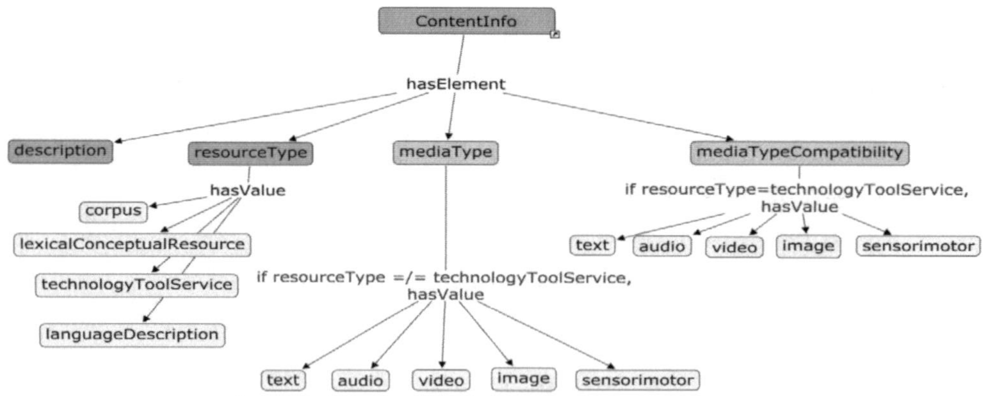

Figure 2 - The ContentInfo component and its elements

signed automatically by the system), identifiers attributed by the source organization or other entities (e.g. ELRA, LDC identifiers) etc.

- the *PersonInfo* component provides information about the person that can be contacted for further information or access to the resource
- all information relative to versioning and revisions of the resource is included in the *VersionInfo* component
- crucial is the information on the legal issues related to the availability of the resource, specified by the *DistributionInfo* component, which provides a description of the terms of availability of the resource and its attached *LicenseInfo* component, which gives a description of the licensing conditions under which the resource can be used; linking to the license documents themselves is also possible through the relevant relation.
- the *ValidationInfo* component provides at least an indication of the validation status of the resource (with Boolean values) and, if the resource has indeed been validated, further details on the validation mode, results etc.
- the *ResourceCreationInfo* and its dependent components group together information regarding the creation of a resource (creation dates, funding information such as funder(s), relevant project name etc.)
- the *UsageInfo* component aims at providing information on the intended use of a resource (i.e. the application(s) for which it was originally designed) and its actual use (i.e. applications for which it has already been used, projects in which it has been exploited, products and publications having resulted from its use etc.).
- the *MetadataInfo* is responsible for all information relative to the metadata record creation, such as the catalog from which the harvesting was made and the date of harvesting (in the case of harvested records) or the creation date and metadata creator (in case of records created from scratch using the metadata editor) etc.
- the *ResourceDocumentationInfo* provides information on publications and documents describing the resource; basic documents (e.g. manuals, tagset documents) can (and should be) included in the META-SHARE repository; the possibility to introduce links to published web documents and/or import bibliographic references in standard formats will be catered for
- finally, the *ContentInfo* component describes the essence of the resource, specifying the *resourceType* and the *mediaType* elements, which give rise to specific components, distinct for each LR type, as presented below.

A further set of four components enjoy a "special" status in the sense that they can be attached to various components, namely *PersonInfo*, *OrganizationInfo*, *CommunicationInfo* and *SizeInfo*. For instance, *PersonInfo* and *OrganizationInfo* can be used for all persons/organizations acting as resource creators, distributors etc. Similarly, *sizeInfo* can be used either for the size of a whole resource or, in combination with another component, to describe the size of parts of the resource (e.g. per domain, per language etc.).

The *ContentInfo* component (Figure 2) is meant to group together descriptive information as regards the contents of the resource. The elements included are:

- *description*: free text of the resource

• *resourceType* with the values corpus, lexical/conceptual resource, language description, technology/tool/service, evaluation package

• *mediaType* (used for data resources) & *mediaTypeCompatibility* (used for tools): the notion of medium constitutes an important descriptive and classificatory element for corpora but also for tools; it is preferred over the written/spoken/multimodal distinction, as it has clearer semantics and allows us to view resources as a set of modules, each of which can be described through a distinctive set of features. The following media type values are foreseen:

• text: used for resources with only written medium (and modules of spoken and multimodal corpora),

• audio (+ text): the audio feature set will be used for a whole resource or part of a resource that is recorded as an audio file; its transcripts will be described by the relevant Text feature set

• image (+ text): the Image feature set is used for photographs, drawings etc., while the Text set will be reserved for its captions

• video: moving image (+ text) (+ audio (+ text): used for multi-media corpora, with Video for the moving image part, Audio for the dialogues, and Text referring to the transcripts of the dialogues and/or subtitles

• sensorimotor: used for sensorimotor resources which contain data collected through the use of relevant equipment (gloves, helmets, body suits, laryngographs, etc.) and used to measure the activity of non-verbal modalities (such as gestures, facial expressions, body movements, gaze, articulatory activity, etc.) and their interaction with objects, be it common objects or control sequences of human-machine interaction (keyboard, mouse, touch screen).

A resource may consist of parts belonging to different types of media: for instance, a multimodal corpus includes a video part (moving image), an audio part (e.g. dialogues) and a text part (subtitles and/or transcription of the dialogues); a multimedia lexicon includes the text part, but also a video and/or an audio part; a sign language resource is also a good example for a resource with various media types. Similarly, tools can be applied to resources of particular types of medium: e.g. a tool can be used both for video and for audio files.

Each of the values of the *resourceType* and *mediaType* gives rise to a new component, respectively:

• *CorpusInfo*, *LexicalConceptualResourceInfo*, *LanguageDescriptionInfo*, *TechnologyToolServiceInfo* and *EvaluationPackageInfo* which include information specific to each LR type (e.g. subtypes of corpora and lexical/conceptual resources, tasks performed for tools etc.)

• *TextInfo*, *AudioInfo*, *VideoInfo*, *ImageInfo* and *SensorimotorInfo* which provide information depending on the media type of a resource; this information can be broadly described as belonging to one of the following categories (all represented in the form of components and elements):

• content: it mainly refers to languages covered in the resource and classificatory information (e.g. domains, geographic coverage, time coverage, setting, type of content etc.)

• format: file format, size, duration, character encoding etc.; obviously, this information is more media-type-driven (e.g. we have different file formats for text, audio and video files)

• creation: this is to be distinguished from the *ResourceCreationInfo* which is attached to the resource level; at the resource level, it is mainly used to give information on funding but also on anything that concerns the creation of the resource as a whole; at the media-type level, it refers to the creation of the specific files, e.g. the original source, the capture method (e.g. scanning and web crawling for texts, vs. recording methods for audio files)

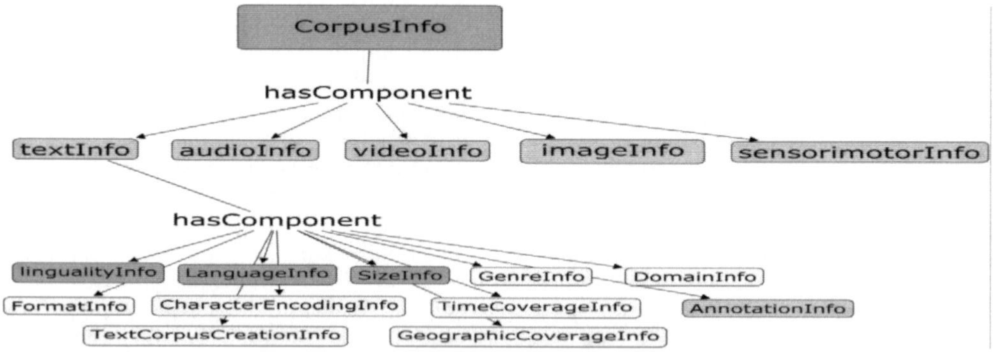

Figure 3 - Excerpt of the CorpusInfo component focusing on text corpora

• linguistic information encoding: the relevant components include information on the types, theoretic models, methods, tools etc. used for adding linguistic information to the resource, which takes the form of encoding for lexica and annotation for corpora and tools; it is both resource-type- and media-type-driven (e.g. morpho-syntactic tagging, parsing, semantic annotation is used for text files, while transcription, prosody annotation etc. for audio parts/corpora etc.).

The mandatory generic components and elements thereof for the description of a resource (for the **minimal schema**) are:

• *IdentificationInfo*, incl. name of the resource and persistent identifier

• *ContentInfo*: all elements (*description*, *resourceType* & *mediaType*) are mandatory

• *DistributionInfo*: *availability* must be filled in and depending on the type of availability, further elements are mandatory (e.g. license, distributor and distribution/access medium for all available resources, types of restrictions for resources available under restrictions etc.)

• *MetadataInfo*: depending on the way the metadata record has been created (harvesting vs. manual creation), a different set of elements must be filled in, some of which are automatically provided (e.g. *metadataCreationDate* vs. *harvestingDate*, *metadataCreator* vs. *source* etc.)

• *PersonInfo*: at least an *email* must be provided for the contact person.

Depending on the resource type, a further set of components are mandatory.

In the next sections, we provide a more detailed view of text corpora and lexical / conceptual resources as exemplary cases of the model.

8 Text corpora

Text corpora are marked as such by the element *resourceType=corpus* & *mediaType=text* and their description must include a *CorpusInfo* component and a *TextInfo* one (Figure 3). As aforementioned, here we include, alongside the traditional text corpora, also the textual parts of audio corpora (transcriptions) and video ones (e.g. subtitles).

Besides the generic components, the type dependent information for text corpora is represented in the following components:

• *LingualityInfo*: it provides information on the linguality type (mono-/bi-/multilingual corpora) and multilinguality type of text resources (parallel vs. comparable corpora)

• *LanguageInfo*: it comprises information on the language(s) of a resource and can be repeated for all languages of the resource; a *LanguageVarietyInfo* component is foreseen to supply further information if the resource includes data in regional language varieties, dialects, slang etc.

• *SizeInfo*: it provides information on the size of the whole resource but it can also be attached to every other component that needs a specification of size (e.g. size per language, per format etc.);

• *AnnotationInfo*: it groups information on the annotation of text corpora, such as specification of the types of annotation level (e.g. segmentation, alignment, structural annotation, lemmatization, semantic annotation etc.), annotation methods and tools etc.

The above four components are obligatory for all text corpora. A further set of components are recommended:

• *FormatInfo*: it gives information on the format (in the form of mime-type) of the corpus

• *CharacterEncodingInfo*: it includes information on character encoding of the resource

• *TextCorpusCreationInfo*: it is used to provide specific information on the creation of the text files, as aforementioned;

• finally, four components are used to give information on the classification of the corpus, namely: *TimeCoverageInfo* (for the time period of the texts), *GeographicCoverageInfo* (for the geographic region from which the texts are collected), *DomainInfo* (presenting the domains covered by the corpus) and *TextGenreInfo* (for the text genre / text type of the texts).

9 Lexical / Conceptual resources

The type dependent subschema for lexical / conceptual resources (LCRs) is activated if the *resourceType* element of the *ContentInfo* component has the value *lexicalConceptualResource* (Figure 4). If this condition is verified, the *LexicalConceptualResourceInfo* component becomes mandatory. In this component a first mandatory element is *lexicalConceptualResourceType*, where the provider is asked to define the type of LRC under description. There is still an open debate on what should be the values to be given in this part and as to which should be the labels thereof. An open list is currently proposed, its suggested values being: *wordList; computationalLexicon; ontology; wordnet; thesaurus; framenet; terminologicalResource; machineReadableDictionary*. Providers can choose to add other values if they consider these not appropriate.

Two optional components are foreseen:

• *LexicalConceptualResourceCreationInfo*, where information on the *originalSource*, a string field where the main sources (dictionaries, grammars, lexica, corpora,) for the creation of the LCR are listed; *creationMode*, with a closed list of values (automatic, semi-automatic, manual, mixed interactive); *creationModeDetails*, which allows to further specify the theoretical and practical principles that guided the creation of the resource; *creationTool*, a repeatable element where either a string, a url or a hyperlink can be entered, the latter enabling the provider to create a connection between the resource and the tool(s) used for its development.

• *LexicalConceptualResourceEncodingInfo* (which is recommended) groups all information regarding the contents of the LCR; it includes the following elements: the mandatory element *encodingLevel* with an open list of values (e.g. phonetics; phonology; semantics), the optional but more detailed *linguisticInformation* with a complex set of suggested values of a varying degree of granularity (e.g. partOfSpeech, syntax-SubcatFrame, semantics-relations, semantics-Relations-Synonyms, semantics-Relations-Antonyms etc.) and the optional *extratextualInformation* (with values images, videos, soundRecordings); this last element can be used for multimedia lexica; if a more detailed account is considered appropriate, the *AudioInfo*, *VideoInfo*, *ImageInfo* components can also be used.

The *TextInfo* and its subsumed components are also to be used for the description of LCRs; the only exceptions are the *TextGenre* and *Annotation* components, which are specific to text corpora.

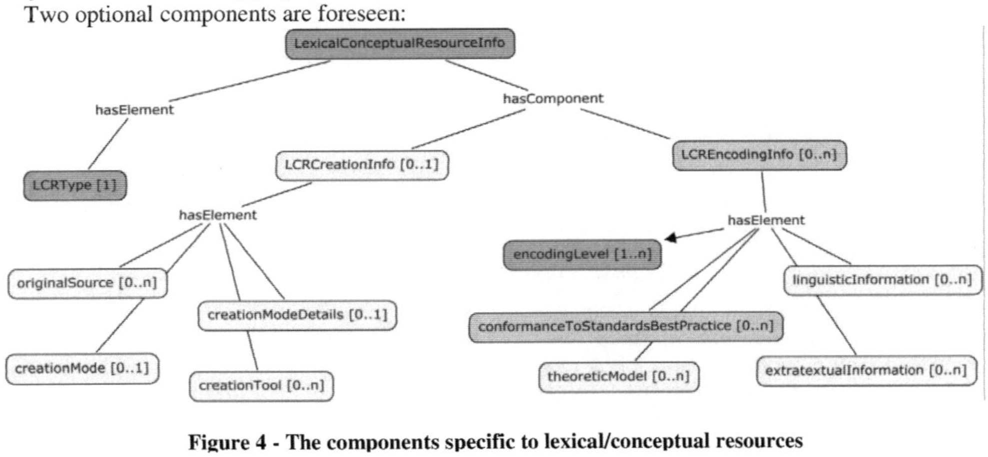

Figure 4 - The components specific to lexical/conceptual resources

10 Conclusions and future work

The current version contains, besides the general presentation of the model, the application of the model to text corpora & to LCRs as presented above. The next steps include:

- extension to other media and LR types: the application of the model to the remaining media types (*audio, video, image, sensorimotor*) and LR types (*languageDescription; technologyToolService; evaluationPackages*) is ongoing. In this process, the expressive power of the model is being tested and it is expected that new components and elements will arise.
- exemplary instantiations: a set of resources selected to represent all LR and media types is being described according to the model, in order to test its functionality; these resources with their descriptions will be uploaded in the prototype infrastructure for testing and exemplification purposes.
- discussion with experts group: this version of the model will be communicated to the metadata experts group that has been set up within WP7, with the purpose of getting feedback for its improvement.
- implementation of the schema for the description of LRs produced or collected by three collaborating projects, namely META-NET4U, CESAR and META-NORD.

References

Broeder, D., T. Declerck, E. Hinrichs, S. Piperidis, L. Romary, N. Calzolari and P. Wittenburg (2008). Foundation of a Component-based Flexible Registry for Language Resources and Technology. In Proceedings of the 6th International Conference of Language Resources and Evaluation (LREC 2008).

e-IRG (2009). eIRG Report on Data Mangement. http://www.e-irg.eu/images/stories/publ/task_force_reports/dmtfjointreport.pdf

Federmann, C., B. Georgantopoulos, R. del Gratta, B. Magnini, D. Mavroeidis, S. Piperidis, M. Speranza (2011). *META-NET Deliverable D7.1.1 – META-SHARE functional and technical specifications.*

Gavrilidou M., P. Labropoulou, E. Desipri, S. Piperidis (2010). Preliminary Proposal for a Metadata Schema for the Description of Language Resources (LRs) in Proceedings of the Workshop 'Language Resource and Language Technology Standards – state of the art, emerging needs, and future developments', LREC 2010, Malta 2010.

Gavrilidou, M., P. Labropoulou, S. Piperidis, M. Speranza, M. Monachini, V. Arranz, G. Francopoulo (2011). *META-NET Deliverable D7.2.1 - Specification of Metadata-Based Descriptions for Language Resources and Technologies*

ISO 12620 (2009). Terminology and other language and content resources -- Specification of data categories and management of a Data Category Registry for language resources. http://www.isocat.org

The Language Library: Many Layers, More Knowledge

Nicoletta Calzolari, Riccardo Del Gratta, Francesca Frontini, Irene Russo
Istituto di Linguistica Computazionale "A. Zampolli", Consiglio Nazionale delle Ricerche
Via Moruzzi 1 56126 Pisa, Italy
{name.surname}@ilc.cnr.it

Abstract

In this paper we outline the general concept of the Language Library, a new initiative that has the purpose of building a huge archive of structured colletion of linguistic information. The Language Library is conceived as a community built repository and as an environment that allows language specialists to share multidimensional and multi-level annotated/processed resources. The first steps towards its implementation are briefly sketched.

1 Introduction

In Natural Language Processing technologies even small amounts of annotated data can contribute to improve the performance of complex systems (Palmer and Xue, 2010). This evidence has led to the creation of many annotation schemes that encode our knowledge of syntactic, semantic and pragmatic features of every language.

Annotation is at the core of training and testing systems, i.e. at the core of NLP. Relations among phenomena at different linguistic levels are at the essence of language properties but we are currently over-simplifying annotation tasks, focusing mostly on one specific linguistic layer at a time, without (having the possibility of) paying attention to the relations among the different layers. At the same time our efforts are too much scattered and dispersed without much possibility of exploitation of others' achievements.

Today we have enough capability and resources for addressing the complexities hidden in multilayer interrelations. Moreover, we can exploit today's trend towards sharing for initiating a collective movement that works towards creating synergies and harmonisation among different annotation efforts that are now dispersed.

In this paper we present the Language Library, an initiative which is conceived as a facility for gathering and making available through simple functionalities all the linguistic knowledge the field is able to produce, putting in place new ways of collaboration within the LRT community.

The rationale behind the Language Library initiative is that accumulation of massive amounts of (high-quality) multi-dimensional data about language is the key to foster advancement in our knowledge about language and its mechanisms, in particular for finding previously unnoticed interrelations between linguistic levels. The Language Library must be community built, with the entire LRT community providing data about language resources and annotated/encoded language data and freely using them.

With the Language Library we thus want also to enable/promote a more global approach to language studies and start a movement aimed at – and providing the facilities to – collecting all possible annotations at all possible levels.

Given the state of the art of linguistic annotation, we can certainly hope to gather tens of different annotation layers and types on the same data; once this is obtained, it will allow for a better analysis and exploitation of language phenomena that we tend to disregard today. In particular, interesting interrelations are likely to become visible among levels that are not often considered together, thus leading to improved computability (e.g. a coreference annotation on top of simpler annotation layers would improve machine translation performance). Part of this multi-layer and multi-language annotation should be performed on parallel (or at least comparable) texts, so as to foster comparability of new achievements and equality among languages.

Even if the Language Library will contain all kinds of processed linguistic data, in this paper we concentrate on the frequent case of annotated data.

Proceedings of Workshop on Language Resources, Technology and Services in the Sharing Paradigm, pages 93–97,
Chiang Mai, Thailand, November 12, 2011.

2 Outline/General Concept

The Language Library is conceived as open and accessible repository where the language technology community can access and share corpora enriched with several layers of linguistic annotation. The Library is going to be:

- open, in that its content will be accessible to the community without restrictions;
- multilingual and multi-domain;
- multi-user and community oriented;
- multi-dimensional, containing multiple layers of annotation of the same text, possibly by multiple contributors;
- collaborative, in the sense of collaboration among experts, and also academics and NLP companies;
- reuse-oriented, promoting the reuse of annotated resources and annotation schemes;
- maintainable, endorsing the use of annotation standards;
- scalable, starting with a demo version with a limited number of texts and then progressively adding new features.

In order to reach this goal, a first population round of the Language Library will start around a core of parallel/comparable texts that will be annotated over and over again by several contributors submitting a paper for LREC2012. Hopefully the selected texts will be annotated with different tools and annotation schemes. The more this core grows, the more new contributors will be encouraged to participate by the possibility of building on existing layers of annotation to develop their own, which will be in turn added to the resource and become available to the NLP community. Notice that the Library should also be seen as a space where the theoretical and the applied linguistics communities could meet, in that the provided annotation can be both manually and automatically produced.

It is possible to envisage a scenario where an annotation layer (e.g. a human made annotation of coreferences on a portion of the texts from the Library) is first submitted by one author/researcher, used by another as a training set to tag a larger amount of the available texts, and then finally resubmitted enriched in size to be (at least partially) human checked again. By recursively doing so the Language Library could come to contain a great number of human checked sections, alongside increasingly accurate machine tagged ones.

In later stages the Library will grow both vertically by adding annotation layers and horizontally, by adding languages, domains, and by increasing the size of the corpora. At this point the possibility of comparing and cross-examining information from several annotation layers at a large scale will start to show its benefits both theoretically and in an NLP perspective.

In its mature stages the Library will consolidate by focusing on the enhancement of interoperability, by encouraging the use of common standards and schemes of annotation. It has to be underlined that the Language Library is conceived as a theory-neutral space which will allow for several annotation philosophies to coexist. The interoperability effort should not be seen as a superimposition of standards but rather as the promotion of a series of best practices that might help other contributors to better access and easily reuse the annotation layers provided.

In this sense encouraging the use of a representation format such as GrAF (Ide and Suderman, 2007) in a second stage might be helpful. On the one hand the stand-off approach of keeping each layer of annotation separated from the others and from the raw data seems particularly suitable for the Library; on the other hand GrAF enables a soft approach to interoperability, in that it can be used to uniformly represent formats that are both syntactically and semantically different and this could make it easier for the contributors to recognize compatible layers without forcing the adoption of a rigid standard. GraF converters from some known formats are currently under development and might be made available in the Language Library.

2.1 Building a community

As witnessed in the evolution of other collaborative resources, in order to attract the contribution of the community it is necessary to bring the Language Library to a level where the burden and the relative cost of sharing the resources is paid back by the possibility of accessing the resources released/produced by other researchers. In order to facilitate this the project will be built around existing frameworks of language resource sharing and around their existing communities.

A number of ongoing initiatives (FLaReNet, META-SHARE and CLARIN among others) have already attracted around themselves a growing LRT community that requires consolidation of its foundations and steady increase of its major assets, minimising dispersion of efforts and enabling synergies based on common knowledge and collaborative initiatives.

The Language Library initiative will build upon the large experience gathered and the best practices and tools developed in these projects, both in terms of documentation and of collection and storage of the resources. While these initiatives have concentrated so far on language resources and tools, with the Language Library - started as a FLaReNet[1] initiative - focus will shift mostly on linguistic knowledge.

Most specifically the Language Library will be strictly connected with the following initiatives:

- The LRE Map (Calzolari et al., 2010), started at LREC 2010, collecting metadata about Language Resource and Technology;
- META-SHARE (Piperidis et al., 2011), an open platform providing an open, distributed, secure, and interoperable infrastructure for the Language Technology domain.

Both these initiatives rest on the assumption that availability is not enough: resources must be visible and easily retrievable. The Language Library will be made visible through META-SHARE, where a complete set of Metadata is already available for language resources and it can be immediately applied to describe and catalog the first nucleus of the Language Library.

2.2 Comparison with other initiatives

Recently other initiatives that share some points of similarity with the Language Library here described have been launched, proving the fact that the community is currently oriented towards similar goals.

The Manually Annotated Sub-Corpus (MASC)[2] of the American National Corpus (ANC)[3] is an open and downloadable corpus that that shares with the Language Library the idea of collecting as many annotation layers for a single text collection as possible. However, it is not conceived as a multilingual project and is more strictly limited to one corpus.

The Human Language Project (Abney and Bird, 2010) on the other hand is a multilingual project, that aims to build a Universal Corpus of the world's languages. In this case the immediate goal is to reach horizontal completeness (document as many languages as possible, with a special attention to endangered ones) and the project is specifically geared towards the Machine Translation community.

The Language Commons[4] finally is an online archive for the collection of written and spoken corpora in the open domain. The Language Library idea bears similarities to this experience, but it will dramatically shift the focus on the vertical dimension, in that it focuses also on gathering as many annotation levels for the same texts as possible.

3 First Experiment

After the success of the LRE Map[5] introduced for LREC 2010 and now used in many conferences as a normal step in the submission procedure (EMNLP and COLING among others), LREC 2012 will be the occasion to launch the LREC Language Library, that will constitute the first building block of the Language Library.

Because of the huge amount of data about resources provided for the LRE Map, we believe that times are ripe for the promotion of such collaborative enterprise of the LREC Community that will constitute a first step towards the creation of this very broad, community-built, open resource infrastructure.

Together with ELRA we will prepare as a first step an LREC Repository, part of the META-SHARE network, hosting a number of raw data on all modalities (speech, text, images, etc.) in as many languages as possible. When submitting a paper, authors will be invited to process selected texts, in the appropriate language(s), in one or more of the possible dimensions that their submission addresses (e.g. POS-tag the data, extract/annotate named entities, annotate temporal information, disambiguate word senses, transcribe audio, etc.) and put the processed data back in the

[1] www.flarenet.eu

[2] www.americannationalcorpus.org/MASC/Home.html (Ide et al., 2010)

[3] http://americannationalcorpus.org/

[4] www.archive.org/details/LanguageCommons

[5] www.resourcebook.eu

LREC Repository.

The processed data will be made available to all the LREC participants before the conference, to be compared and analyzed, and at LREC some/an event around them will be organized.

This collaborative work on annotation/transcription/extraction/... over the same data and on a large number of processing dimensions will set the ground for the future Language Library, linked to the LRE Map for the description of the data, where everyone can deposit/create processed data of any sort all our "knowledge" about language.

3.1 A case study: Annotation Resources at LREC2010

With the aim to highlight the feasibility of the LREC Repository for the Language Library, we propose a brief analysis of the annotation guidelines/tools inserted by authors as resources in the LREC2010 Map during the submission process. This will enable us to make, at this preliminary stage, an educated guess on the number and variability (with respect to languages, modalities, uses) of annotated texts that will be part of the core of the Language Library.

Amongst over 1990 resources, 62 are listed as "Representation-Annotation Formalism/Guidelines" ("R-A F/G" in Tables 1 and 2) while 136 are described as Annotation Tool ("AT" in Tables 1 and 2). Not every submission that report on the usage of an annotation tool provided also description for an annotation formalism, therefore its possible that more annotation schemes have been used.

As expected, the vast majority of annotation tools (see Table 1) are listed/described as language independent (82/136), while among RepresentationAnnotation Formalism/Guidelines 10/62 have been developed for English, 20/62 are language independent and 12/62 have been applied in multilingual resources.

	R-A F/G	AT
Language independent	20/62	82/136
English	10/62	18/136
Multilingual	12/62	11/136

Table 1: Most frequent values with respect to the language

Concerning modality, very few formalisms have been proposed for modalities other than Written (6/62), but among annotation tools 25/136 resulted useful for Multimodal/Multimedia modality, 8/136 for Sign Language and 7/136 for Speech modality.

The range of resource uses (see Table 2) is quite wide, with a prevalence of Knowledge Discovery/Representation (8/62, 6/136), Information Extraction, Information Retrieval (7/62, 13/136), Machine Translation, Speech To Speech Translation (6/62, 8/136). For Annotation Tool, Discourse, Acquisition and Dialogue are the other most frequent uses.

	R-A F/G	AT
Knowledge Discovery/Representation	8/62	6/136
Information Extraction, Information Retrieval	7/62	13/136
Machine Translation, Speech to Speech Translation	6/62	8/136

Table 2: Most frequent with respect to the uses

This information relative to a small subsets of the resources described by LREC2010 authors shows how in the starting phase the Language Library will be easily enriched with texts annotated on the basis of guidelines elaborated by scholars for a wide range of uses. Even if the incidence of languages other than English and of modalities other than Written is not so high, the existence of guidelines/formalisms focusing on more than one language represents an interesting chance to enrich the Language Library with more annotated data.

Finally, 40/62 Representation-Annotation Formalism/Guidelines have been listed as Newly created-in progress or Newly created-finished, a figure that shows how the Language Library can foster the knowledge about brand new annotation formalisms.

3.2 Future developments

In the initial phases of the project the main challenge will be to motivate the large parts of the community to join in the enterprise; subsequently more steps will be taken in order to enhance interoperability and avoid the proliferation of various, slightly different but incompatible annotation schemes.

In order to improve this the platform should make annotation schemes and tools available to the users, in such a way as to encourage the sharing and use of already existing standards. Ideally the platform could at some stage enable the hosting of on-line annotation tools, thus becoming a virtual environment for the recruitment of annotating workforce in a crowd-sourcing modality.

Also the dimensions and the modality of annotated data will have to be taken into account: we hope that not just small written corpora will be annotated and that the efficient management of audio and video files will be allowed in the platform.

4 Conclusions

It has been recognized that Natural Language Processing is a data-intensive discipline, so the LR community must now be coherent and take concrete actions leading to the coordinated gathering – in a shared effort – of as many (annotated-encoded) language data as it is able to produce.

In doing this a positive inspiration can be drawn from the success of similar experiences in other disciplines, e.g. astronomy/astrophysics, where the scientific communities cooperate in accumulate huge amounts of observation data for better understanding the universe. The most significant model is the recent successful effort for the mapping of human genome. The Language Library could be considered as a sort of big Genome project for languages, where the community will collectively deposit/create increasingly rich and mutilayered linguistic resources, enabling a deeper understanding of the complex relations between different annotation layers.

Acknowledgments

We thank the META-NET project (FP7-ICT-4 249119: T4ME-NET) for supporting this work.
The Language Library started as an initiative within FLaReNet - Fostering Language Resources Network (Grant Agreement No. ECP-2007-LANG-617001).
The Language Library has been discussed, among others, with Khalid Choukri, Thierry Declerck, Olivier Hamon, Joseph Mariani, Stelios Piperidis.

References

Steven Abney and Steven Bird. 2010. The human language project: Building a universal corpus of the world's languages. In *Proceedings of the 48th Annual Meeting of the Association for Computational Linguistics*, pages 88–97, Uppsala, Sweden, July. Association for Computational Linguistics.

Nicoletta Calzolari, Claudia Soria, Riccardo Del Gratta, Sara Goggi, Valeria Quochi, Irene Russo, Khalid Choukri, Joseph Mariani, and Stelios Piperidis. 2010. The LREC Map of Language Resources and Technologies. In Nicoletta Calzolari, Khalid Choukri, Bente Maegaard, Joseph Mariani, Jan Odijk, Stelios Piperidis, Mike Rosner, and Daniel Tapias, editors, *Proceedings of the Seventh conference on International Language Resources and Evaluation (LREC'10)*, Valletta, Malta, May. European Language Resources Association (ELRA).

Nancy Ide and Keith Suderman. 2007. GrAF: A Graph-based Format for Linguistic Annotations. In *Linguistic Annotation Workshop, ACL 2007*, pages 1–8, Prague.

Nancy Ide, Christiane Fellbaum, Collin Baker, and Rebecca Passonneau. 2010. Masc: The manually annotated sub-corpus: A community resource for and by the people. In *Proceedings of the ACL 2010 Conference Short Papers*, pages 68–73. Association for Computational Linguistics.

Martha Palmer and Nianwen Xue. 2010. Linguistic annotation. In *The Handbook of Computational Linguistics and Natural Language Processing*, Blackwell Handbooks in Linguistics, pages 238–270. John Wiley & Sons.

Stelios Piperidis, Calzolari Nicoletta, and Maria Koutsombogera. 2011. META-SHARE: Design and Governance (Deliverable D6.2.1). Technical report, METANET, January. Dissemination Level: Restricted.

Sharing Resources in CLARIN-NL

Jan Odijk
Utrecht University
Trans 10, 3512 JK Utrecht,
The Netherlands
j.odijk@uu.nl

Arjan van Hessen
Twente and Utrecht Universities
Trans 10, 3512 JK Utrecht,
The Netherlands
A.J.vanhessen@uu.nl

Abstract

Sharing resources in a systematic way is essential for conducting high quality scientific research but it imposes requirements on the *documentation*, *visibility*, *referability*, *accessibility*, and *long term preservation* of these resources. Sharing resources only makes sense when others can actually use them, which imposes requirements of *interoperability* on resources. In this paper we describe how the CLARIN-NL project addresses these issues in order to maximize sharing of resources. We submit that the approach taken in CLARIN-NL is an exemplary approach that deserves adoption by other research communities, possibly slightly adapted to their own needs and requirements.

1 Introduction

Sharing resources in a systematic way is essential for conducting high quality research but imposes requirements on the *documentation*, *visibility*, *referability*, *accessibility*, and *long term preservation* of these resources. Sharing resources only makes sense when others can actually use them, which imposes requirements of *interoperability* on resources. We understand the notion *resources* here in a broad sense, including not only data, but also software, including applications and web services. In this paper we describe how the CLARIN-NL project addresses these issues in order to maximize sharing of resources. We submit that the approach taken in CLARIN-NL is an exemplary approach that deserves adoption by other research communities, possibly slightly adapted to their own needs and requirements.

This paper is organized as follows. We first briefly discuss the CLARIN-NL project (§2) and some of the subprojects and activities relevant to sharing resources it undertakes. Next we discuss each of the requirements for optimal sharing, and how they are worked on in the CLARIN-NL project: documentation (§3), visibility (§4), referability (§5), accessibility (§6), long term preservation (§7), and interoperability (§8). We end the paper with our conclusions (§9).

2 The CLARIN-NL Project

The CLARIN-NL project[1] (Odijk 2010) is a national project in the Netherlands that aims to design, construct, validate, and exploit a research infrastructure that is needed to provide a sustainable and persistent eScience working environment for researchers in the Humanities, and Linguistics in particular, who want to make use of language resources and technology for their research. The targeted users include researchers and developers of Human Language Technology (HLT), since they are largely part of the humanities in the Netherlands. The *use* of HLT will play an important role in the CLARIN infrastructure, but this infrastructure is not specifically dedicated to *research* into and *development* of HLT. This is one of the characteristics distinguishing the CLARIN infrastructure from e.g. META-SHARE (Piperidis 2010), the resource exchange facility being constructed in the context of the META-NET project.[2]

Since the targeted users are humanities researchers, the character of the resources differs widely, but their common denominator is that they have a language component. The data resources include dictionaries, text corpora, linguistic databases, audio and video containing speech, in a wide variety of languages, images of historical manuscripts, their transcriptions and annotations. The software resources include lan-

[1] www.clarin.nl/
[2] www.meta-net.eu/

Proceedings of Workshop on Language Resources, Technology and Services in the Sharing Paradigm, pages 98–106,
Chiang Mai, Thailand, November 12, 2011.

guage technology software for spelling normalization, morphological analysis, lemmatization, PoS-tagging, chunking, parsing, semantic annotation, named entity recognition, sentiment and opinion mining. On the speech side they include speech recognition software for transcribing speech or aligning speech with a transcript, diarisation software for isolating speech from non-speech sounds in an audio file (e.g. as part of an tool for annotating audio/video files created during linguistic field work). They also include a wide range of tools for manually annotating texts, audio and video.

The CLARIN-NL project is part of a Europe-wide enterprise to set up an infrastructure. This was initiated by the just finished CLARIN preparatory project (CLARIN-prep[3]) and is to be continued by a consortium of national projects united at the European level in the so-called CLARIN ERIC[4] expected to start early 2012. The Netherlands played an important role in CLARIN-prep, and the CLARIN ERIC is hosted by the Netherlands.

In the remainder of this section we describe the activities organized by CLARIN-NL that are relevant to the topic of sharing resources.[5]

2.1 Infrastructure implementation

CLARIN-NL will build the infrastructure through so-called CLARIN-Centres. Five organisations have expressed the ambition and the commitment to become such a CLARIN Centre, i.e. INL[6], MPI[7], MI[8], Huygens ING[9] and DANS[10]. They are all organizations that include making resources accessible in their mission. Candidate CLARIN Centres must meet several requirements before they will be recognized as actual CLARIN Centres. Several of these requirements will be described in this paper. A full list can be found in (Roorda et al. 2010).

The CLARIN Centres in the Netherlands work together in a number of projects to *implement the technical infrastructure*. This requires, inter alia, setting up authentication and authorizations systems, several registries, and various other infrastructure services. Especially relevant for sharing resources is the project to implement sophisticated *search facilities* in metadata and data to complement the browsing functionality for which a prototype (the Virtual Language Observatory, VLO[11]) was developed in CLARIN-prep.

2.2 Data curation projects

CLARIN-NL has set up a range of *data curation* projects, and will set up more in the course of 2011. The goal of a data curation project is to adapt an existing data set in such a way that it becomes properly documented, visible, uniquely referable and accessible via the CLARIN infrastructure. In addition, the format of the resource must be adapted to a standard supported in CLARIN, and the data categories used must be described in a data category registry. In short, these projects are aimed at making it optimally possible and useful to share the resource with other researchers.

In order to speed up the process of data curation and in order to include resources where the owner/researcher does not wish to submit a project proposal or the resource is too small to justify a data curation project, a Data Curation Service is being set up and targeted to start in September 2011.[12]

2.3 Demonstrator projects

CLARIN-NL has also set up a range of *demonstrator* projects. The goal of a demonstrator project is to create a documented web application starting from an existing tool or application that can be used as a demonstrator and function as a showcase of the functionality that CLARIN will offer. Though the main goal is to make a demonstrator, in practice it requires curating the tool or application, so that it becomes properly documented, visible, uniquely referable and accessible via the CLARIN infrastructure, and adapting it to work with CLARIN-supported standards both with regard to formats as well as with regard to the meaning of the data categories used.

In a collaborative project with Flanders the focus is even more on curating the tools and applications. In this project, existing language and speech technology tools for the Dutch language (shared between the Netherlands and Flanders), which were largely developed in the STEVIN programme[13], are turned into web services that

[3] www.clarin.eu
[4] ec.europa.eu/research/infrastructures/index_en.cfm?-pg=eric
[5] See www.clarin.nl/node/76 for a more detailed overview.
[6] Institute for Dutch Lexicology www.inl.nl
[7] Max Planck Institute for Psycholinguistics www.mpi.nl
[8] Meertens Institute www.meertens.knaw.nl/
[9] www.huygensinstituut.knaw.nl/
[10] Data Archiving and Networked Services www.dans.knaw.nl/

[11] www.clarin.eu/vlo/
[12] www.clarin.nl/node/147
[13] taalunieversum.org/taal/technologie/stevin/

can be used in a workflow system. This is only possible if the web services are properly documented, visible, uniquely referable and accessible via the CLARIN infrastructure, and if they operate on formats and work with data categories that are supported in CLARIN.

In short, these projects contribute directly to optimal sharing of tools and applications with other researchers in the CLARIN infrastructure.

2.4 Education and Training

Adapting resources so that they become documented, visible, uniquely referable and accessible, and comply with CLARIN-supported standards both on the formal and on the semantic level is a non-trivial task. The average humanities researcher does not have the knowledge and expertise to carry out such tasks completely independently. Therefore, education, training and support are needed. CLARIN-NL has organized various tutorials and workshops on relevant topics such as metadata and the CLARIN metadata infrastructure, and data categories and data category registries. It has set up a HelpDesk[14] to deal with technical questions on infrastructural matters, including a Frequently Asked Questions section, and appointed infrastructure specialists as second-line support.

3 Documentation

The first step in making a resource suited for sharing is to provide documentation of the resource. Even if a resource is not going to be shared, documenting it is required to guarantee that the resource can still be understood long after its development. So, documentation is a necessity for sharing but requires no or only limited additional effort.

Some parts of the documentation will have to consist of natural language text that is intended for human beings, for example a description of the design decisions in developing the resource. However, other parts of the documentation can be formalized. For example, certain properties of a resource can be systematically assigned to a fixed label (attribute), the possible values of each attribute can be characterized by a type, and in some cases the possible values of an attribute can even be restricted to a finite set or be constrained otherwise (e.g. by a template). In our view, all information of the documentation of a resource that can be formalized should be formalized, since a formalized representation encodes the information in the least ambiguous way (natural language is notorious for its ambiguity), and maximizes the potential for use of this information by software processes. Furthermore, this formalized documentation should be represented in a uniform manner. In CLARIN-NL, we have used and further extended the CLARIN Component-based Metadata Infrastructure (CMDI) originally developed in CLARIN-prep (§3.2).

3.1 Metadata

The term *metadata* is on the one hand very broad. Within a dataset usually a part can be characterized as the "primary data", and metadata then covers all data except the primary data, including annotations, formalized documentation, unformalized documentation, aggregate statistics on the resource, etc. That is such a broad notion, that it may hamper mutual understanding. On the other hand, the name *metadata (*lit. 'data about data'*)* suggests too narrow an interpretation, since we also need documentation (formalized and unformalized) for software. We will therefore try to avoid the term *metadata* here.

We assume that each dataset contains a set of "primary data" and a set of additional data with information on the primary data (which we will call *annotations*). Certain pieces of primary data and annotations form a natural unit (following in part from the nature of the data and/or the purposes of the data). We will call such a unit a *resource*. Multiple resources can be organized in composite resources recursively. A description of a resource is called a *resource description.* CMDI has mainly been developed for the formalized parts of resource descriptions. The term *resource description* is also more appropriate than the term *metadata* for resources that consist of software (e.g. applications, web services, command line tools, etc.)

3.2 CMDI

CMDI[15] is a flexible metadata infrastructure which enables the researcher to use a component-based approach to resource descriptions. Because it is component-based, it does not require a single rigid scheme, something that is not feasible given the wide variety of resources CLARIN-NL has to deal with. The meaning of the resource description elements and its values is encoded by linking the data categories used to

[14] trac.clarin.nl/trac

[15] www.clarin.eu/cmdi

a data category registry, which will be discussed in more detail in §8.2.

CMDI enables the researcher to make a resource description *profile* for a class of resources. Such a profile is composed of *components* recursively. This makes it possible to define small components that can be reused easily and provides the required flexibility for making resource descriptions while at the same time maximizing uniformity where this is possible. CMDI provides editors for components, profiles and resource descriptions, and a registry for storing new instances of such objects and finding existing ones for reuse.

CMDI has metadata elements that correspond to the Dublin Core[16] metadata elements also in use by OLAC[17] and is therefore fully compatible with Dublin Core but it allows for much more fine-grained metadata descriptions.

Providing flexibility entails the danger that different researchers will diverge in making resource descriptions even when there is no reason to do so, e.g. because they are working on resource descriptions independently. In order to prevent this and to offer maximum opportunities for reuse of profiles and components, CLARIN-NL started a project with a small team of specialists to make initial components and profiles for a wide variety of resources in the Netherlands. The researchers in the data curation and demonstrator projects, which started later, could therefore maximally reuse components and profiles created by this specialist team and optimally profit from the knowledge and expertise gained by this team. Unfortunately, such components and profiles were made only for data, not for software. So, a set of components and profiles that can be reused for describing software is urgently needed, as was clear from several data curation and demonstrator projects. A project to do exactly that is therefore planned for 2011.

Creating resource descriptions in accordance with CMDI for each relevant resource was a requirement for data curation and demonstrator projects. Therefore, an initial obstacle for sharing these resources in the CLARIN infrastructure has been overcome. The Data Curation Service will increase the number of resources with proper resource descriptions, and we already noticed that research projects unrelated to CLARIN-NL as well as several data providers are willing to provide CLARIN compatible resource descriptions for data they produce and/or make available.

4 Visibility

All resources and resource descriptions dealt with in a CLARIN-NL project must be stored on a server of a CLARIN-centre. CLARIN-centres are obliged to make the resource descriptions for these resources and for resources they have available from other sources available for harvesting (using a standardized protocol, OAI-PMH[18]). In the CLARIN infrastructure all resource descriptions are harvested regularly and made available via a central CLARIN portal. This ensures the *visibility* of the resources and the resource descriptions. Researchers only have to visit the CLARIN portal to find the resources they are looking for and are not dependent anymore of knowledge about resources via informal contacts, accidental encounters or effort-wasting search actions via the web or systematic visits of the catalogues of resource distribution centres.

The CLARIN portal will offer various opportunities for finding the resources one is interested in. This includes browsing facilities with faceted browsing, of which a first prototype developed in the CLARIN preparatory project is available (VLO, see above). It also includes facilities to search in the resource descriptions, not only with a Google-style string search but also with structured search that takes into account the resource description XML syntax and the semantics of the resource description elements and their values. It also includes search in the actual resources. However, the actual resources will be distributed over the various CLARIN-centres. Searching in the actual resources will therefore be carried out via *federated search*. Results of search queries can be collected and stored as a *Virtual Collection*, to which new, possibly more refined search queries can be applied.

Many CLARIN-supported standard formats for written resources consist of tagged text (e.g. XML). Searching in many (tagged) textual resources is generally not possible with computers in a reasonable amount of time. This problem will not disappear when computers are increasing in capacity every two years (as *Moore's Law*[19] appears to implicate), since (1) many problems are inherently intractable and solutions can only be approximated, and (2) the amount of data grows at least as fast and very likely orders of

[16] http://dublincore.org/
[17] http://www.language-archives.org/
[18] www.openarchives.org/OAI/openarchivesprotocol.html
[19] en.wikipedia.org/wiki/Moore's_law

magnitude faster. So even though Moore's Law may be true, it is also true and much more relevant that computers are slow[20] and getting slower every two years.

Fortunately, smart people have found smart ways to avoid the computer's slowness to a significant extent by a range of techniques. However, this requires storing the information contained in the tagged textual data in special formats in database systems (e.g. relational databases) and/or adding various indexes. In the central portal, the resource descriptions harvested from the various CLARIN centres will therefore also be stored in a way that makes fast searching and browsing possible. For the actual resources, federated search will issue search queries to local search engines for individual resources at the CLARIN-centres, where the local search will also take place on resources formatted and stored in a way that optimizes search.

In this way, visibility of the resources and their resource descriptions will be ensured.

5 Referability

There must be a simple way to refer to resources and resource descriptions. This is needed for humans (so that they know exactly which resource or resource description has been used in a particular research project), but also for machines. The search engines mentioned in the preceding section cannot work properly if they have no way of uniquely referring to resources and resource descriptions.

Natural Language One way of referring to a resource is by using a name or title for a resource in natural language (e.g. the title of a novel, article, etc.). This method is not suited for the purposes of CLARIN because it has all the disadvantages that natural language has as a means of communication. First, such names do not always refer to a unique resource (ambiguity). Names are often language-specific (e.g. *Corpus Gesproken Nederlands*), which leads to variants of the name in other languages (e.g. *Spoken Dutch Corpus*) (language-dependency). Furthermore, names and titles are typically long, which is inconvenient. But more importantly, names and titles are highly redundant. A little bit of redundancy is good for communication, but natural language has too much redundancy. This leads to shorter versions of the name (e.g. acronyms such as *CGN*), and to sloppiness with human users: typos (*Spken Dutch Cropus*) or changes in order (*Dutch Spoken Corpus*) are perhaps sometimes intelligible for humans but not (without special software) for computers.

URLs URLs are sometimes used to refer to resources and resource descriptions. URLs avoid most of the problems with natural language descriptions (though they tend to have too much redundancy) and have the additional advantage that they immediately specify where to find the resource. A big disadvantage of URLs, however, is that they are quite unstable and volatile (URLs are often changed or disappear completely).

PIDs What is needed is a means of referring that is not based on natural language, is a short as possible, has at most very little redundancy, and is stable. Persistent Identifiers (PIDs) have been proposed for this, accompanied by services to map from names/titles and/or URLs to PIDs and vice versa (resolution systems). PIDs are usually strings of digits and or letters. Familiar examples are ISBN numbers[21] for books and EAN numbers for products.[22]

A CLARIN-Centre must assign PIDs to the resources and resource descriptions it makes available. In CLARIN (and thus in CLARIN-NL) the preferred PID system is the Handle system[23], since it currently offers the most robust and best performing PID resolution system. Some centres, however, used the URN system[24] already before CLARIN started, and it is being investigated how this can be accommodated in the best way. Furthermore, there are also other PID systems[25] which may have to be accommodated.

The fact that CLARIN centres in the Netherlands assign a PID to each resource and resource description and offer the associated resolution services again take a way an obstacle for optimal and efficient sharing of resources.

6 Accessibility

The CLARIN infrastructure is a virtual web-based distributed infrastructure. The resources and resource descriptions are therefore accessible at virtually any time and from any place (with

[20] Where a computer is "slow" when the user has to wait an unacceptable amount of time for the computer's response. What is "unacceptable" may differ per application or circumstances.

[21] www.isbn-international.org/

[22] en.wikipedia.org/wiki/International_Article_Number_(EAN)

[23] /www.handle.net/

[24] www.w3.org/2001/tag/doc/URNsAndRegistries-50

[25] E.g. the DOI system: www.doi.org/

internet access[26]). Accessibility of the resources and resource descriptions for this aspect of access is therefore taken care of pretty well in CLARIN.

However, there are two other aspects of access: (2) intellectual property rights (IPR) and ethical issues, and (3) the attitude of researchers towards sharing resources.

IPR CLARIN-NL promotes maximal open access of resources. It has issued a declaration on this matter[27] and had discussions about it at various occasions.[28] Important research organizations such as the *Royal Netherlands Academy of Arts and Sciences* (KNAW) and the Dutch foundation for Scientific Research (NWO) also stimulate or even require open access to results of scientific research, esp. data and tools.[29]

CLARIN-NL realizes that there are many legacy data with legacy IPR arrangements that also need to be accommodated in the CLARIN infrastructure. This may involve special licenses, in some cases even license fees, restrictions on the usage of resources, limited periods of inaccessibility of the resource, etc. In all resources, ethical issues (e.g. privacy concerns) may play a role as well, restricting the usage of certain (parts of) resources. Problems of this nature have actually been encountered in the data curation projects. In one case it has led to a clear separation of the resources (and resource descriptions) that are freely accessible on the hand, and the resources and resource descriptions for which additional licenses are required on the other. In a second case, the participants in the resource have been approached again to clear these matters (successfully). CLARIN-NL is working on plans to implement policies and functionality to properly handle IPR and ethical restrictions. For some centres, these could be extensions of existing systems (e.g. DANS has the EASY system[30] and soon its successor EASY II[31]).

Mindset A third aspect related to accessibility is the mindset of researchers. Many researchers in the humanities are hesitant or even unwilling to share their resources with others.[32] There is therefore a big task for CLARIN-NL to discuss these matters, listen carefully what arguments are adduced against sharing resources, counter these arguments where appropriate and promote maximal open access, e.g. by illustrating the great potential offered by sharing resources. In some cases, arguments against sharing must be accommodated (because they are reasonable objections), and CLARIN-NL has done so already in its declaration. CLARIN-NL also supports researchers (logistically, organizationally, financially and by means of training and education) to enable them to share their resources.

In short, CLARIN-NL has developed a range of policies and facilities to maximize *accessibility* of resources and resource descriptions for a range of aspects of this term, thus directly contributing to optimal sharing of resources.

7 Long term preservation

Resources should be shared not only with contemporary researchers, but also with future generation researchers. This makes it necessary to carry out *long term preservation* of resources. In CLARIN-NL, each CLARIN centre is required to provide a solution for the long term preservation of the resources they maintain. Usually the centres in the Netherlands do not carry out this long term preservation themselves but make use of centres dedicated to it. For example, MI outsources this to DANS, and the MPI outsources it to the organization within the Max Planck Gesellschaft dealing with long term preservation.

The requirement for long term preservation of resources imposed on the CLARIN centres thus makes it possible to preserve the resources and share them with future generation researchers.

8 Interoperability

Resources can be used by other researchers only if they are interoperable. Interoperability is thus a necessary condition for resource sharing to be useful.

[26] This might be an obstacle for certain researchers, e.g. descriptive linguists doing field research in remote locations with no internet access. Functionality that enables one to work off-line and replicate off-line data and tools with the on-line CLARIN infrastructure are therefore desirable, and some applications in CLARIN already have this functionality.

[27] www.clarin.nl/system/files/Call%20Open%20-Data%20English%20101018.pdf

[28] For example at the *Open and Persistent Access Panel Discussion* at SDH/NEERI 2011, Vienna, see ztwweb.trans.univie.ac.at/sdh2010/

[29] See www.knaw.nl/Pages/DEF/29/838.bGFuZz1F-Tkc.html for the KNAW and www.nwo.nl/nwohome.-nsf/pages/NWOP_89BBXM_Eng for NWO

[30] https://easy.dans.knaw.nl/dms

[31]

[32] Though I understand from representatives from other disciplines that the Humanities are not unique in this respect.

Interoperability of resources is the ability of resources to seamlessly work together. The need for interoperability of resources is more stringent in CLARIN than in other domains, since the targeted users, humanities researchers, usually do not have the technical skills to make ad-hoc conversions and adaptations to make resources work together. But of course, even for HLT researchers and developers, full interoperability will save a lot of (often duplicated) effort for ad-hoc readjustment of resources to make them interoperable.

Full interoperability is only possible if the resources meet the requirements (1) of formal or *syntactic interoperability* and (2) of meaning or *semantic interoperability*. Projects in CLARIN-NL must attempt to meet these requirements, and report when problems for achieving this arise. In this way we learn about the limitations of various proposed standards and can make proposals to deal with them and make suggestions for improved standards and best practices. We will discuss syntactic and semantic interoperability in more detail in the next subsections,

8.1 Syntactic Interoperability

Syntactic interoperability in CLARIN is the requirement that the formats of data are selected from a limited set of (de facto) standards or best practices supported by CLARIN, and that software tools and applications take input and yield output in these formats. A list of the formats currently supported is provided by CLARIN. [33] Though currently this list is in a fixed document, it is evident that experience is teaching us that the list is incomplete and needs constant refinement and updating.

Applying the recommended standards and best practices is not easy. In many projects we have found that many standards are not fully applicable to existing data and need adaptations. For example, the DUELME database of Dutch multiword expressions (Grégoire 2010a) which was represented in an idiosyncratic format was converted to an XML format in accordance with the Lexical Markup Framework (LMF). [34] But the new representation requires properties that are not covered by LMF and should be considered as candidate extensions to LMF (Grégoire 2010b). Many resources are stored in relational databases or Excel files. No format supported by CLARIN can accommodate such data. The CSV format is mentioned but not explicitly recommended. An XML format implementing (a set of) CSV files using XML markup may have to be developed here. Such a format will also be able to provide facilities for semantic interoperability of such resources not offered by the CSV format.

Nevertheless, the only way to make any progress towards syntactic interoperability is by trying out the supported formats with existing data, learning about their opportunities and limitations, making concrete proposals to deal with these limitations and constructive proposals for extensions and/or adaptations of the standardized format. And this is exactly what CLARIN-NL is doing in a wide variety of projects and for a wide variety of data, including lexical databases, text corpora with various levels of annotations, audio and video data with their annotations, typological and other linguistic databases, and for a variety of tools and applications, *inter alia* data-specific search engines, part-of-speech taggers, lemmatizers, parsers, speech technology tools for recognition, alignment and diarisation, and many others.

Resource descriptions play a crucial role in ensuring syntactic interoperability. The resource description of a data resource should specify, in quite some detail, the format of the resource, and the resource description of a software resource should specify, in quite some detail, which format(s) it accepts as input and which one(s) it yields as output. Such specifications will prevent a non-technical user from applying software to data it is not suited for or warn the users for the limited validity of the results (e.g. textual resources with the wrong character encoding; a desktop speech recognizer applied to telephone speech, etc.)

By actively trying out the recommended standards and best practices for syntactic interoperability CLARIN-NL contributes directly to enabling sharing of resources and it makes the problems that arise with this explicit so that evidence-based recommendations can be made for extensions and adaptations.

8.2 Semantic Interoperability

Semantic interoperability of resources requires explicit semantics of elements in their contents (in the case of data) or interface (in the case of software). In CLARIN, the semantics of elements of resources is limited to the semantics of data categories (DCs). The basic idea is that the semantics of DCs is captured as follows: a privi-

[33] www.clarin.eu/system/files/Standards%20for%20LRT-v6.pdf
[34] www.lexicalmarkupframework.org/

leged data category registry (DCR) is set up containing (inter alia) DCs, unique persistent identifiers for DCs (PIDs), their semantics, a definition, examples and lexicalizations in various languages. The semantics of each data category (DC) used in a specific resource must be specified by mapping this resource-specific DC to a DC from the privileged DCR. This enables every researcher to use resource-specific DCs but at the same time guarantees that different DCs from different resources can be interpreted in the same way, via the DC of the privileged DCR, which acts as a pivot.

In CLARIN, ISOCAT[35] is used as one of the privileged DCRs.[36] In each CLARIN-NL project, all resource-specific data categories must be mapped to ISOCAT DCs, or, when no DC with the right interpretation exists, a new DC must be added to ISOCAT. ISOCAT can incorporate results of independent initiatives for defining DCs, and it actually incorporates a subset of the GOLD ontology[37] for linguistic description.

An example may illustrate how this could be useful. A search engine searching for occurrences of strings that are annotated for the ISOCAT DC *Part of Speech*[38] with as value the ISOCAT DC *noun*[39] will also find occurrences of data with resource-specific DCs *Substantiv*, *Nom* or *ZN,* if these resource-specific DCs have been mapped onto the ISOCAT DC *Noun.*

Achieving semantic interoperability is not easy, and even with the ISOCAT data category registry many problems arise once one really starts doing this. It would require a separate paper to discuss this in more detail, but such problems have been noted, have been discussed in workshops,[40] and for most problems solutions have been proposed in these workshops, including the set-up of a different registry to register relations between DCs, called RELCAT (Windhouwer 2011), and the proposed solutions are currently being tested.

However, one can only encounter such problems, and make progress in solving them, when one actually systematically attempts to achieve semantic interoperability for real resources. That is exactly what is being done in CLARIN-NL, and by doing so, CLARIN-NL contributes to optimizing the use of shared resources.

9 Conclusions

In this paper we have described how the CLARIN-NL project addresses crucial issues for maximizing the sharing of resources. We have described how CLARIN-NL addresses *documentation*, *visibility*, *referability, accessibility*, and *long term preservation* of the resources, as well as syntactic and semantic *interoperability*. None of adopted solutions is without problems, but it is only by systematically working on them that any progress can be made on these topics. And that is exactly what is being done in CLARIN-NL. We submit that the approach taken in CLARIN-NL is an exemplary approach that deserves adoption by other research communities, possibly slightly adapted to their own needs and requirements.

Acknowledgments

This work was funded by the NWO CLARIN-NL project. (www.clarin.nl).

References

Nicole Grégoire. 2010a. DuELME: A Dutch Electronic Lexicon of Multiword Expressions. *Journal of Language Resources and Evaluation* 44(1/2), 23-40. DOI 10.1007/s10579-009-9094-z

Nicole Grégoire. 2010b. En Garde Project. The redesign of a Dutch Electronic Lexicon of Multiword Expressions. Presentation held at the workshop *Lexicon Tools en Standards*, August 4, 2010, Max Planck Institute, Nijmegen. [pdf]

Jan Odijk. 2010. The CLARIN-NL Project. *Proceedings of LREC 2010*: 48-53. [pdf]

Dirk Roorda *et al.* 2009. CLARIN Centres. CLARIN Document. [pdf].

Stelios Piperidis. 2010. META-SHARE. Presentation held at the LREC 2010 Workshop on Language Technology issues for International Cooperation, Malta, 22 May 2010. [pdf]

Menzo Windhouwer. ISOcat. Presentation at the *Standards Workshop* (NEERI 09), Helsinki, Finland, September 30, 2009. [pdf]

[35] www.isocat.org/

[36] CLARIN supports multiple preferred DCRs if they are complementary. For example, CLARIN supports the use of ISO639 language codes contained in a different DCR (www.sil.org/iso639-3/codes.asp). In CLARIN-NL a project (CLAVAS) has started up to create a common interface to multiple DCRs.

[37] http://linguistics-ontology.org/

[38] More precisely, the ISOCAT DC with PID www.isocat.org/datcat/DC-396

[39] More precisely, the ISOCAT DC with PID www.isocat.org/datcat/DC-1333

[40] For example in the CLARIN Relation Registry Workshop, 8 Jan 2010 (www.isocat.org/2010-RR/) and in the CLARIN-NL ISOCAT Workshop, 21 Sep 2010 (www.isocat.org/2010-ISOcat-status/), both at MPI, Nijmegen.

Menzo Windhouwer. 2011. RELCAT and Friends. Presentation held at the CLARIN-NL ISOCAT Workshop, Utrecht, 5 May 2011. [pdf]

META-NORD: Towards Sharing of Language Resources in Nordic and Baltic Countries

Inguna Skadiņa
Tilde
Riga, Latvia
inguna.skadina@tilde.lv

Andrejs Vasiļjevs
Tilde
Riga, Latvia
andrejs@tilde.lv

Lars Borin
University of Gothenburg
Gothenburg, Sweden
lars.borin@svenska.gu.se

Koenraad De Smedt
University of Bergen
Bergen, Norway
desmedt@uib.no

Krister Lindén
University of Helsinki
Helsinki, Finland
krister.linden@helsinki.fi

Eiríkur Rögnvaldsson
University of Iceland
Reykjavik, Iceland
eirikur@hi.is

Abstract

This paper introduces the META-NORD project which develops Nordic and Baltic part of the European open language resource infrastructure. META-NORD works on assembling, linking across languages, and making widely available the basic language resources used by developers, professionals and researchers to build specific products and applications. The goals of the project, overall approach and specific action lines on wordnets, terminology resources and treebanks are described. Moreover, results achieved in first five months of the project, i.e. language whitepapers, metadata specification and IPR management, are presented.

1 Introduction

In the last decade linguistic resources have grown rapidly for all EU languages, including lesser-resourced languages. However they are located in different places, have been developed using different standards (if any) and in many cases are not well documented.

High fragmentation and a lack of unified access to language resources are the key obstacles to European innovation potential in language technology (LT) development and research.

To address these issues the European Commission has dedicated specific activities in its FP7 R&D and ICT-PSP programmes[1]. The overall objective is to ease and speed up the provision of online services centred around computer-based translation and cross-lingual information access and delivery. The focus is on assembling, linking across languages, and making widely available the basic language resources used by developers, professionals and researchers to build specific products and applications.

Several projects have been started to facilitate creation of a comprehensive infrastructure enabling and supporting large-scale multi- and cross-lingual services and applications. These projects closely cooperate and form the common META-NET network[2]. One of its main activities is creation of META-SHARE – a sustainable network of online repositories for language data, tools and related web services.

At the core of the META-NET is the T4ME project which is funded under FP7 programme. The Central and Southeast part of META-NET is covered by the CESAR project, United Kingdom and Southern European countries are represented by the METANET4U project, while the META-NORD project aims to establish an open linguis-

[1] http://ec.europa.eu/information_society/activities/ict_psp/documents/ict_psp_wp2010_final.pdf
[2] http://www.meta-net.eu/

Proceedings of Workshop on Language Resources, Technology and Services in the Sharing Paradigm, pages 107–114, Chiang Mai, Thailand, November 12, 2011.

tic infrastructure in the Baltic and Nordic countries.

This paper describes the key objectives and activities of the META-NORD project, presents its first results and discusses cooperation with other similar projects, e.g. CLARIN (Váradi et al., 2008).

It is an integral part of the META-NET and other related initiatives like CLARIN to create a pan-European open linguistic resource exchange platform.

2 The META-NORD Project

The META-NORD project focuses on 8 European languages – Danish, Estonian, Finnish, Icelandic, Latvian, Lithuanian, Norwegian and Swedish, – each with less than 10 million speakers. The project partners are University of Copenhagen, University of Tartu, University of Bergen, University of Helsinki, University of Iceland, Institute of Lithuanian Language, University of Gothenburg, and Tilde (coordinator).

META-NORD contributes to the pan-European digital resource exchange facility by mapping and describing the national language technology landscape, identifying and collecting resources in the Baltic and Nordic countries and by documenting, processing, linking and upgrading them to agreed standards and guidelines. A particular focus of META-NORD is targeted to three horizontal action lines: treebanks, wordnets and terminology resources.

In addition important collaboration with other EU partners is established within the Initial Training Network in the Marie Curie Actions CLARA[3]. The CLARA project aims to train a new generation of researchers who will be able to cooperate across national boundaries on the establishment of a common language resources infrastructure and its exploitation.

3 Language Whitepapers

The META-NORD consortium has prepared reports of the language service and language technology industry for all the languages targeted by the project: Danish, Estonian, Finnish, Icelandic, Latvian, Lithuanian, Norwegian (Nynorsk and Bokmål) and Swedish.

The reports are written as a series of separate publications for each language, but they are closely coordinated in structure. The reports contain information on general facts of the language (number of speakers, official status, dialects, etc.), particularities of the language, recent developments in the language and language technology support, core application areas of language and speech technology, and the situation in the language with respect to these areas.

For each language, an analysis of the language community has been conducted and the role of the language in the respective country/language community is described. The language technology research community and the language service and language technology industry are identified. The importance of language technology products and services in the language community are assessed. Legal provisions related to language resources and tools, which may differ from country to country, are outlined.

The reports also present a detailed table with ratings of language technology tools and resources for each language compiled on the basis of the same framework that is used in the whole META-NET network. Experts were asked to rate the existing tools and resources with respect to seven criteria: quantity, availability, quality, coverage, maturity, sustainability, and adaptability. Results are summarized in Figure 3 and Figure 4 for tools and Figure 2 and Figure 5 for resources.

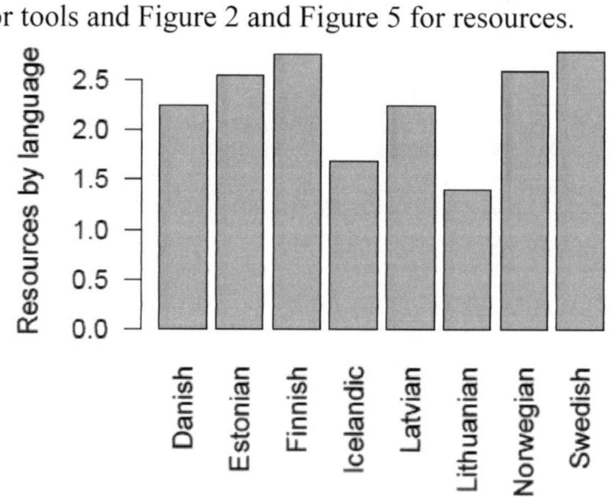

Figure 1. Average scores for resources.

The results indicate that only with respect to the most basic tools and resources such as tokenizers, PoS taggers, morphological analyzers/generators, syntactic parsers, reference corpora, and lexicons/terminologies, the status is reasonably positive for all the META-NORD languages. Furthermore, all the languages seem to have some tools for information extraction, machine translation and speech recognition and synthesis, as well as resources such as parallel corpora, speech corpora, and grammar, although these tools and resources are rather simple and

[3] http://clara.uib.no/

have limited functionality for some of the languages.

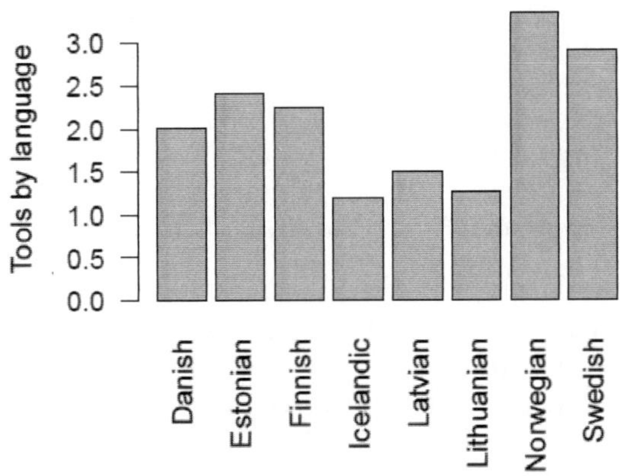

Figure 2. Average scores for tools.

When it comes to more advanced fields such as sentence and text semantics, information retrieval, language generation, and multimodal data, it appears that one or more of the languages lack tools and resources for these fields.

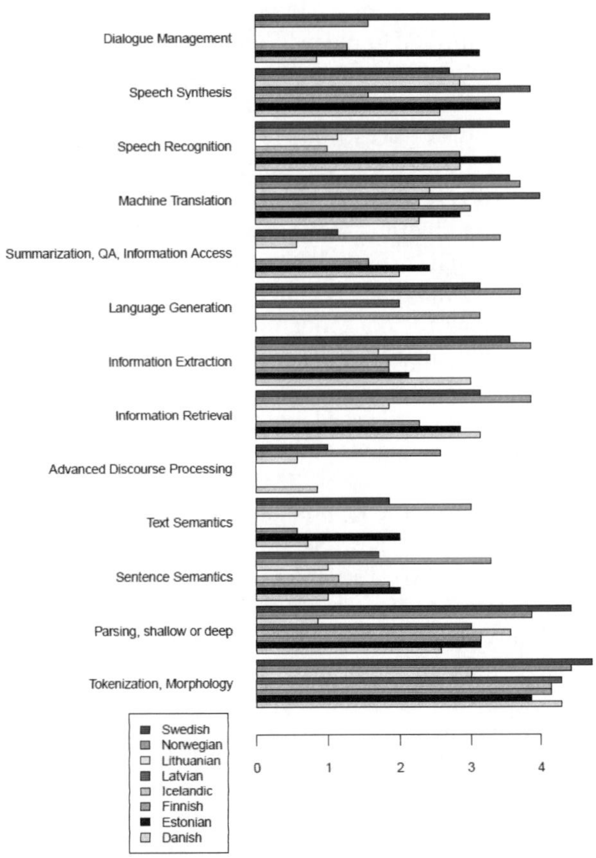

Figure 3. Evaluation results for tools.

For the most advanced tools and resources such as discourse processing, dialogue management, semantics and discourse corpora, and ontological resources, most of the languages either have nothing of the kind or their tools and resources have a quite limited scope.

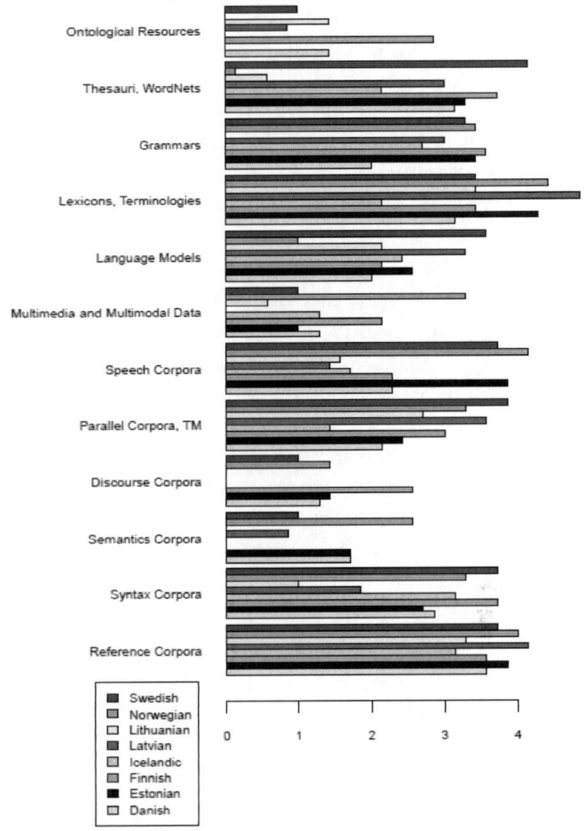

Figure 4. Evaluation results for resources.

The figures for all the languages taken together indicate that quantity and availability may be a greater concern than quality; this need is the very *raison d'être* of the META-NORD project.

4 Horizontal Action on Multilingual Wordnets

Wordnets organized according to the model of the original Princeton WordNet for English (Fellbaum 1998) have emerged as one of the basic standard lexical resources in our field. They encode fundamental semantic relations among words. In many cases these relations have counterparts in relations among concepts in formal ontologies, so that a straightforward mapping from the one to the other can be established.

According to the BLARK (Basic Language Resource Kit) scheme (Krauwer, 1998), wordnets along with treebanks are central resources when building language enabled applications. The BLARK lists Computer Assisted Language Learning (CALL), speech input, speech output, dialogue systems, document production, information access and translation applications as dependent of wordnets. The semantic proximity metrics among words and concepts defined by a wordnet are very useful in such applications because in addition to identical words, the occurrence of words with similar (more general or more specific) meanings contribute to measuring of the similarity of content or context or recognizing the meaning.

Different translations of the same master wordnet, such as the Princeton WordNet, can be linked with each other resulting in a multilingual thesaurus and also a dictionary which is useful e.g. in aligning multilingual parallel documents and other translation oriented tasks. With such linked resources, cross- and multilingual IR applying semantically-based query expansion becomes feasible. Another possible application for these resources is Machine Translation (MT). The hierarchical structure of wordnets ensures that a translation can be found (going up or down in the hierarchy) even if a precise equivalent is not present between the specific languages.

During the last decades, wordnets have been developed for several languages in the Nordic and Baltic countries including Finnish, Danish, Estonian, Icelandic and Swedish. Of these wordnets, Estonian WordNet is the oldest one since it was built as part of the EuroWordNet project in the 1990s (Vossen, 1999). In contrast, most of the other wordnets have been recently initiated, e.g. the Danish wordnet has been under development since 2005 (cf. Pedersen et al., 2009).

The builders of these wordnets have applied different compilation strategies: where the Danish, Icelandic and Swedish wordnets are being developed via monolingual dictionaries and corpora and subsequently linked to Princeton WordNet, the Finnish wordnet has applied the translation method by translating Princeton WordNet into Finnish for later adjustment.

From the above mentioned different time perspectives and compilation, there is a need for upgrade of several wordnet resources to agreed standards, which constitutes a prelimary task of this META-NORD action.

A prerequisite for multilingual use of the resources is that the monolingually based resources are enhanced with regards to either synsets and/or more links to Princeton WordNet. From these links, which will primarily constitute the so-called "core synsets" extracted at Princeton University, pilot cross-lingual resources will be derived and further adjusted and validated.

Partial validation of the resources will be performed by means of comparison with bilingual dictionaries for the given languages (where they exist). An additional aim of the multilingual task is to investigate the possibility of making the relevant wordnets accessible through a uniform web interface.

5 Horizontal Action on Multilingual Terminology

Among specific activities of the META-NORD project will be consolidation of distributed multilingual terminology resources across languages and domains, and upgrading terminology resources to agreed standards and protocols.

META-NORD will extend an open linguistic infrastructure with multilingual terminology resources. The META-NORD partners Tilde, Institute of Lithuanian Language, University of Tartu and University of Copenhagen have already established a solid terminology consolidation platform EuroTermBank (Vasiljevs et al., 2008). This platform provides a single access point to more than 2 million terms in 27 languages.

EuroTermBank platform will be integrated into an open linguistic infrastructure by adapting it to relevant data access and sharing specifications. META-NORD is approaching holders of terminology resources in Nordic countries with the aim of facilitating sharing of their data collections through cross-linking and federation of distributed terminology systems.

Mechanisms for consolidated multilingual representation of monolingual and bilingual terminology entries will be elaborated. Sharing of terminology data is based on the TBX (TermBase eXchange) standard recently adapted as ISO 30042. It is an open XML-based standard format for terminological data, created by the now dissolved Localization Industry Standard Association (LISA) to facilitate interchange among termbases. This standard is very suitable for industry needs as TBX files can be imported into and exported from most software packages that include a terminological database.

6 Horizontal Action on Treebanking

Treebanks are among the most highly valued language resources. Applications include development and evaluation of text classification, word sense disambiguation, multilingual text alignment, indexation and information retrieval, parsing and MT systems.

The objective of META-NORD is to make treebanks for relevant languages accessible through a uniform web interface and state-of-the-art search tool. In cooperation with the INESS project in Bergen, an advanced server-based solution will be provided for parsing and disambiguation, for uploading of existing treebanks, indexing, management, and exploration. The treebanking tools will run on dedicated systems and provide fast turnaround. Existing treebanks available in the consortium will be integrated into this platform.

A second objective is to link treebanks across languages using parallel multilingual treebanking based on existing language and corpora.

Parallel treebanks can be used for translation studies, for bilingual dictionary construction, for identifying and characterizing structural correspondences, for multilingual training and evaluation of parsers, and for the development and test of MT systems.

Linguistically motivated interactive linking with XPAR technology will initially be performed for LFG-based parsebanks which support f-structure linking. Danish, Norwegian and English will be used in the first pilot, based on the multilingual Sofie-corpus. In the second phase, linking will be extended to dependency treebanks, e.g the Finnish treebank, using technology from FIN-CLARIN. Combining these technologies, a pilot parallel treebank is planned for Norwegian, Danish, Finnish and English.

A particular goal is to extend the Estonian TreeBank and improve its quality/format/querying interface. The rule based parsing system for Estonian can be used for building Estonian Treebank.

The FinnTreeBank can be used for training parsers and taggers for Finnish. In the META-NORD project the goal is to extend the Finnish treebank with a parser and sample quality testing to a Finnish ParseBank for the Europarl corpus in order to create a multilingual treebank so that it will be applicable to training e.g. MT systems. In particular, the efforts will be coordinated with the Norwegian and Danish treebank projects.

The Icelandic treebank consist of approximately one million words (cf. Rögnvaldsson et al., 2011). The main emphasis is on Modern Icelandic but the treebank will also contain texts from earlier stages of the language. Thus, it is meant to be used both for language technology and for syntactic research. This is a Penn-style treebank but it should be possible to convert it to other formats so that it can be linked to other treebanks via the Norwegian treebanking infrastructure.

7 Management of Intellectual Property Rights

IPR issues are becoming increasingly important in our field as standardization initiatives advance in the areas of data formats and content structure, making IPR the remaining obstacle to wide-scale reuse of resources.

Promoting the use of open data and following the Creative Commons and Open Data Commons principles, META-NORD will apply the most appropriate license schemes out of the set of templates provided by META-NET. Model licenses will be checked by the consortium with respect to regulations and practices at national level, taking account of possibly different regimes due to ownership, type, or pre-existing arrangements with the owners of the original content from which the resource was derived. Resources resulting from the project will be cleared i.e. made compliant with the legal principles and provisions established by META-NET, as completed/amended by the consortium and accepted by the respective right holders.

7.1 Open content and open source licenses

The most widely used **Open content license** system is Creative Commons, CC. The CC licenses do not require that the user be part of any predefined group. The CC-licenses give the user the right to modify, to copy, to present, and to distribute the resource. META-NORD recommends using of CC-licenses for open content resources when the above definition of usage applies.

The **Open source licenses** are specifically designed for software and tools. The only widely translated license is EUPL (European Union Public License) but it is not yet widely used. The most popular license for software programs has lately been the GNU General Public License (GNU GPL or GPL). It provides anybody a right to use, copy, modify and distribute the software and the source code. If the program is distributed further, or if it is part of a derivative, it has to be licensed with the same license without any additional restrictions. LGPL (Lesser General Public License) differs from the GPL licenses in that where GPL lets the software be combined only with other open source programs, LGPL allows combining the software with proprietary software as well, as long as the open software is distributed with its source. Only an Apache license or similar will also allow distribution of the open software in closed form. Other open source licenses are MsPL and BSD.

7.2 META-SHARE licenses

META-SHARE licenses are based on the CC-licenses discussed above. The only difference is that they are restricted to users within the META-SHARE community. The resource can be distributed via an organisation that is a Member of META-SHARE. All the same restrictions apply.

META-SHARE licenses are applicable to resources where the copyright holder wants the potential users to belong to a predefined group. The distribution is not worldwide but restricted to the META-SHARE community. This can be essential for some copyright holders. The number of potential users is smaller than with CC-licenses. The licenses cover IPR issues in connection with collective works, databases and works of shared authorship.

7.3 CLARIN model agreement templates

CLARIN agreement templates are designed for tools and resources distributed within the research community but the Deposition & License agreement allows commercial use within the scope of the legislation by default when it is not explicitly ruled out (Oksanen et al., 2010). Without modification, the CLARIN agreement templates do not allow a right for sub-licensing and they apply within the CLARIN community. The agreements presume that the copyright holder either retains the right to grant usage rights or delegates this task to the repository or some other body but the process can also be more automatic.

The CLARIN agreements are templates. The agreements can be modified to meet the requirements of the copyright holder. This option is not available with the CC-licenses or the META-SHARE licenses as they are fixed licenses.

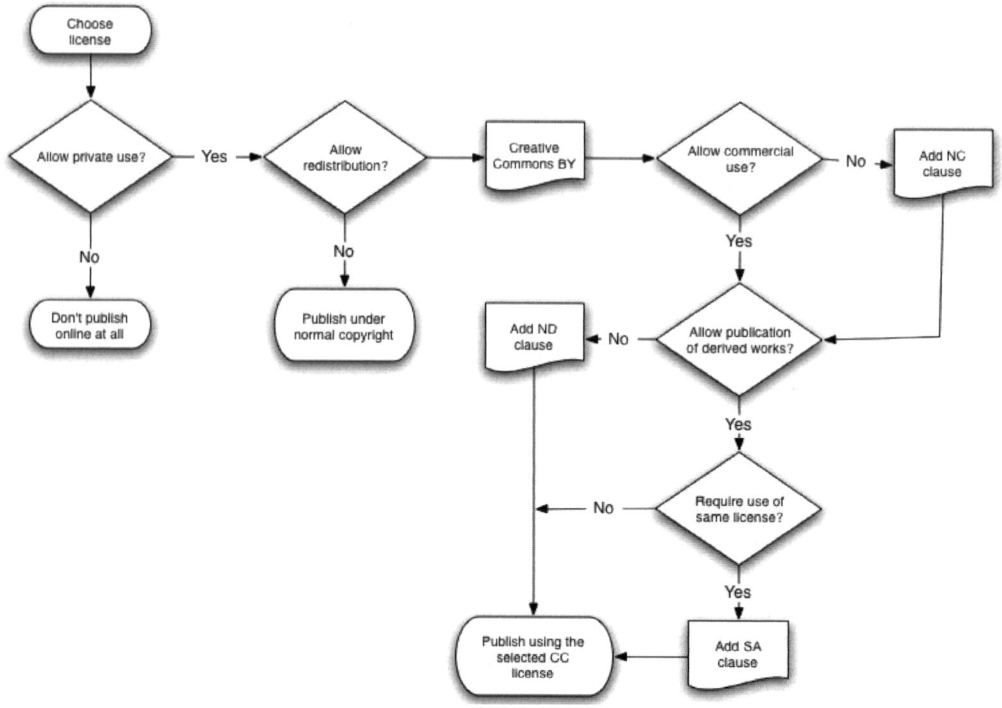

Figure 5. Selection of the appropriate open content license.

The CLARIN model agreements can be modified and are thus applicable to all kinds of purposes. It is, however, advisable to use the existing CC, META-SHARE or CLARIN licenses, if applicable, and modify the CLARIN licenses only for any remaining purpose.

The CLARIN Deliverable D7S-2.1[4] includes two agreements, a deposition agreement and an upgrade agreement. In addition to this, the appendices include other relevant agreements, such as terms of service (between the user and the repository), privacy policy issues (for making sure that the details on the user are protected), an application form for use of restricted data from the repository, data user agreement (between the user and the repository) and the data processor

[4] http://www-sk.let.uu.nl/u/D7S-2.1.pdf

agreement (between the content provider and the service provider).

8 Metadata and Content Standards

An important aim of META-NORD is to upgrade and harmonize national language resources and tools in order to make them interoperable, within languages and across languages, with respect to their data formats and as far as possible also as regards their content.

Since resources and to some extent tools normally will remain in one location – one of a number of META-NORD centers – the preferred way of accessing and utilizing resources and tools will be through *metadata* and *APIs*, allowing the assembly of on-the-fly toolchains made up of standardized component language technology tools, processing distributed – and in many cases interlinked – language resources in standardized formats.

8.1 Metadata standards

META-NORD is working on standardized top-level resource descriptions (metadata) for all relevant types of resources, based on a recommended set of metadata descriptors for documenting resources provided by META-NET through META-SHARE. It will produce such descriptions for each and every resource contributed to the shared pool. Metadata sets include mandatory as well as optional elements, together with sets of recommended values whenever possible and appropriate. According to the META-SHARE model[5], metadata must include at least a specified minimum of information in each of the following categories: *identification* (including a persistent identifier); *resource type*; *licensing/distribution*; *validation*; *metadata provenance*; *funding*; *contact information*. The model then allows for extensive further elaboration of each information category, so that metadata records for resources and tools can be arbitrarily informative.

The inspiration for the META-SHARE metadata model comes largely from the CLARIN Metadata Initiative (renamed to *Component Metadata Initiative* (CMDI[6])), which can be seen as building on top of earlier relevant initiatives – e.g., DC and OLAC – and which now aims to become an ISO standard. The data categories, e.g., ISOcat, are the main concern of standardization, not the metadata schema per se.

In most cases, the resources and tools to be made available in META-NORD do not come equipped with the required metadata information, let alone encoded as formal metadata. The main exceptions are corpora in TEI or XCES format which often have header elements containing at least some of this information, which can be automatically extracted. Some partners are already publishing structured metadata records for at least some of their resources, e.g., the Language Bank of Finland is publishing OLAC – and the obligatory DC – through OAI-PMH for a number of corpora already. In case existing resources are described using popular metadata sets – OLAC being a case in point – the consortium will upgrade them using converters, mappers and other tools provided by the META-NET, or in some cases developed by the META-NORD.

8.2 Content standards

We can foresee that users will want access to the META-NORD language resources in at least the following three ways:

(1) *In toto*, i.e., the resource can be downloaded. This requires that the resource is in a standardized, well-documented format, or it won't be very useful to our target groups. It also requires that all IPR issues have been cleared and licensing terms stated (see section 7 above).
(2) Online browsing either in a standard web browser or through a dedicated tool. Here, standardized metadata must provide sufficient information for a user to find the URL providing the application. However, the base resource may be in a proprietary format (although any export facility should provide a standardized format).
(3) In the form of a web service or other API. Here, standardized metadata are needed. Further, any data returned by a web service should be in a standard format.

Consequently, metadata and resource formats in META-NORD should support at least these three resource usage scenarios.

META-NORD greatly benefits from the work conducted in CLARIN for best practices and guidelines with respect to formats for language resources, language tools and metadata.

From information provided by partners, it is clear that the META-NORD resources and tools come in many formats. Some resources are in

[5] http://www.meta-net.eu/public_documents/t4me/META-NET-D7.2.1-Final.pdf
[6] http://www.clarin.eu/cmdi

RDB formats (SQL, Access), some in proprietary formats, etc. For interoperability, such resources should probably be converted into other formats. Data format conversion is generally not a problem, and should be implemented in many cases, since partners may have invested heavily in such formats and in such cases we should simply consider a solution whereby conversion is made on demand into an interoperable export format. The only problem with this solution is that it will add complexity, since any change made to the original format must be accompanied by the corresponding change in the conversion utility.

A point of greater concern is that, according to the provided information, many of the resources and tools lack an explicit and formal content model. This issue will need to be addressed in META-NORD.

META-NORD will put considerable effort into making content models of resources and tools as interoperable as possible. This can imply adopting more strictly structured formats, such as LMF rather than proprietary XML or SQL for lexical resources. Regardless of this, it will almost certainly imply a mapping to a set of standardized data categories, such as that of ISOcat. This can mean a considerable amount of work and careful consideration is needed in order not to waste effort. On the other hand, the rewards of the interoperability achieved in this way are potentially great.

For new resources and tools or for those where conversion of the base resource is desirable, the following formats are recommended:

- corpora: TEI or (X)CES format (standoff annotation in ISO formats will be allowed);
- lexical resources: LMF or Princeton WordNet format;
- terminology resources: TBX;
- tools: at least as web services (if possible), described using WSDL.

9 Conclusions

Language whitepapers prepared by the META-NORD project show that the Nordic and Baltic countries still have a long way to go to implement the vision of making the area a leading region in language technology. META-NORD project lays the ground for a fruitful cooperation in identifying, enhancing and sharing of language tools and resources created in the Nordic and Baltic countries, which will considerably strengthen the field in a near future.

Acknowledgements

The META-NORD project has received funding from the European Commission through the ICT PSP Programme, grant agreement no 270899.

References

Fellbaum, C. (ed). 1998. *WordNet – An Electronic Lexical Database*. The MIT Press, Cambridge, Massachusetts, London, England.

Krauwer, S. 1998. *ELSNET and ELRA: A common past and a common future*. The ELRA Newsletter, Vol. 3, n. 2, Paris.

Oksanen V., Linden K., Westerlund H. 2010. Laundry Symbols and License Management – Practical Considerations for the Distribution of LRs based on experiences from CLARIN. In the Proceedings of LREC 2010.

Pedersen, B.S, S. Nimb, J. Asmussen, N. Sørensen, L. Trap-Jensen, H. Lorentzen. 2009. *DanNet – the challenge of compiling a WordNet for Danish by reusing a monolingual dictionary*. Language Resources and Evaluation, Computational Linguistics Series. Volume 43, Issue 3:269-299.

Rögnvaldsson, E., A. K. Ingason and E. F. Sigurðsson. 2011. Coping with Variation in the Icelandic Diachronic Treebank. In Johannessen, J. B. (ed.): *Language Variation Infrastructure. Papers on selected projects*, pp. 97-111. Oslo Studies in Language 3.2. University of Oslo, Oslo.

Vossen, P. (ed). 1999. *EuroWordNet, A Multilingual Database with Lexical Semantic Networks*. Kluwer Academic Publishers, The Netherlands.

Váradi T., Krauwer S., Wittenburg P., Wynne M., Koskenniemi K. 2008. *CLARIN: common language resources and technology infrastructure*. Proceedings of the Sixth International Language Resources and Evaluation Conference.

Vasiljevs, A., Rirdance, S., Liedskalnins, A., 2008. *EuroTermBank: Towards Greater Interoperability of Dispersed Multilingual Terminology Data*. Proceedings of the First International Conference on Global Interoperability for Language Resources ICGL 2008. Hong Kong, 2008, pp.213-220.

Author Index

Association for Computational Linguistics
209 N. Eighth Street
Stroudsburg, Pennsylvania 18360

CURRAN ASSOCIATES INC.
proceedings.com

ISBN 978-1-62276-454-9
9 781622 764549

6th Workshop on Cognitive Aspects of Computational Language Learning (CogACLL 2015)

Held at EMNLP 2015

Lisbon, Portugal
18 September 2015